CAMPAIGN ADVERTISING AND
AMERICAN DEMOCRACY

Campaign Advertising

and

American Democracy

MICHAEL M. FRANZ, PAUL B. FREEDMAN,
KENNETH M. GOLDSTEIN, AND
TRAVIS N. RIDOUT

TEMPLE UNIVERSITY PRESS
Philadelphia

TEMPLE UNIVERSITY PRESS
1601 North Broad Street
Philadelphia PA 19122
www.temple.edu/tempress

∞

The paper used in this publication meets the requirements
of the American National Standard for Information Sciences—
Permanence of Paper for Printed Library Materials, ANSI Z39.48-1992

Library of Congress Cataloging-in-Publication Data

Campaign advertising and American democracy / Michael M. Franz ... [et al.].
p. cm.
Includes bibliographical references and index.
ISBN 13: 978-1-59213-455-7   ISBN 10: 1-59213-455-6 (cloth : alk. paper)
ISBN 13: 978-1-59213-456-4   ISBN 10: 1-59213-456-4 (pbk. : alk. paper)
1. Political campaigns–United States.   2. Advertising, Political–United States.
I. Franz, Michael M., 1976–
JK2281.C27 2007
324.7'30973—dc22   2007022655

2   4   6   8   9   7   5   3   1

For Laura, Sarah, Amanda, and Carolyn

CONTENTS

LIST OF FIGURES AND TABLES

Figures

Tables

PREFACE

This book does not represent our first take on the effect of televised political advertising. Over the past seven years we have gathered, analyzed, and tested the effects of political advertising in a range of years and over a range of election contests. Some of the analyses that we present here have been published in previous journal articles. This book ties together our theoretical expectations, empirical findings, and normative judgments about the effect of political advertising, in general, and negative advertising, in particular, in modern election campaigns in the United States.

This work draws heavily on University of Wisconsin Advertising Project data on the content and targeting of television advertisements. We were able to release aggregate totals on advertising activity in real time during the course of the 2000 and 2004 campaigns and have then been able to provide the full data set to colleagues for scholarly work. We had a tremendous amount of fun working with scores of students at the University of Wisconsin to process and release these data. Joel Rivlin, who is currently finishing his graduate studies in political science at the University of Wisconsin, deserves particular thanks for overseeing the huge data processing and real time release of data during the 2004 elections. Members of the University of Wisconsin's political science department administrative staff, Debbie Bakke, Tammi Simpson, and Diane Morauske, helped keep the project running behind the scenes and managed the many logistical hurdles of a large research project with great skill and cheer. We thank them and the many students who worked tirelessly on the project.

This work would not have been possible without the support, advice, criticism, and assistance of many colleagues at our various home institutions including Steven Finkel, Charles Franklin, Pat Kenney, Kim Kahn, and Dhavan Shah.

Dhavan also deserves particular thanks for allowing us to utilize the DDB-Needham political surveys that he coordinated in 2000 and 2004.

The University of Wisconsin Advertising Project, our previous work, and this book would not have been possible without the generous support of the Pew Charitable Trusts. We owe a particular debt of thanks to Sean Treglia, who was our program officer at the Trusts. We are incredibly grateful for his advice and support.

Additionally, we are very thankful to Evan Tracey, Harley Ellenberger, and the good folks at Campaign Media Analysis Group. Harley has gone above and beyond in working with the "geeky" data requests of scholars. Evan, the chief operating office of CMAG, gave data to a scraggly graduate student in 1996, and we have very much enjoyed working with him for the last ten years. Not only have we learned from his data, but we have learned much from his experience and insight about the use of political advertising and greatly value his friendship.

On opposite sides of the political fence, we also appreciate the support and insight of Robin Roberts and William Feltus of National Media Incorporated and of Steve Rabinowitz from Rabinowitz media. All three, along with the scores of reporters and practitioners we have spoken to over the years, have had a profound impact on our thinking about political advertising. Steve's friendship and tireless efforts getting the results of our studies into the public arena is also greatly appreciated.

Finally, a warm thanks to Alex Holzman and his staff at Temple University Press for guiding this project with great competence and good cheer.

As the standard disclaimer goes, even with all these thanks, we are, of course, responsible for all analyses and interpretations that appear here. We very much hope that colleagues and students continue to make use of data from the Wisconsin Advertising Project in future years.

CHAPTER ONE

Campaign Advertising

The Whipping Boy of American Politics

AMERICAN-STYLE DEMOCRACY may or may not ultimately take root in Iraq, but Pulitzer Prize–winning cartoonist Mike Luckovich has a point in any case, and it's an important one: For most people, the idea of exporting to an emerging democracy the kind of campaign ads Americans have come to know—and supposedly loathe—is a joke (see cartoon on page 2). The notion that American-style campaign advertising might find a place in a democratic Iraq is simply laughable. Campaign advertising, according to conventional wisdom, is a corrupted form of democratic discourse—something we would be better off without, and something which we need to be on guard against.

In the election of 2004, when all was said and aired, more than three million political spots for candidates up and down the ballot had been broadcast in the nation's 210 media markets.[1] More than $800 million was spent on television advertising in the race for the White House alone, more than in any presidential campaign in history (Seelye 2004). In all, the presidential candidates and their party and interest group allies broadcast more than one million ads in the 2004 election, well more than twice the number aired four years earlier.

What kind of impact did this campaign advertising have when it came to what citizens thought and knew and how they acted during the course of an election campaign? What difference did the disparate patterns of advertising in 2000 and 2004 make? Did people know more or less about the candidates and their positions as a result of how many ads—or which types of ads—they saw? Did they feel more or less connected to the campaign and the political system in general? And were they more or less likely to vote on Election Day as a result of what they saw?

Our objective in this book is to provide answers to these types of questions, making sense of campaign advertising using data from the 2000 and 2004

By permission of Mike Luckovich and Creators Syndicate, Inc.

elections, and, in the process, evaluating campaign advertising in the larger context of democratic citizenship. To be clear, this book is not about how campaign advertising influences voters' opinions of candidates or the outcomes of elections. It's about how campaign advertising affects citizens' grasp of the alternatives in a campaign, their evaluation of the electoral process, and their inclination to participate in it.

Damned Spot!

Nobody, it seems, has a kind word to say about the thirty-second spot. Television advertising is a favorite whipping boy of American politics. Campaign ads, according to their many critics, are misleading, manipulative, and mean-spirited. The typical campaign ad—nasty, brutish, and short—is thought to produce citizens who are alienated, poorly informed, and disengaged from the political process. "Campaign ads dumb down the terms of political debate and reduce nuanced policy positions to buzzwords and slogans," complains a recent critic (Macek 2004). Particular scorn is reserved for negative or "attack" ads, which are thought to debase politics, degrade democratic citizenship, and turn off potential voters.[2]

Many of these suspicions are enshrined in the Bipartisan Campaign Reform Act (BCRA), the most recent effort to reform the federal campaign finance system. The legislation, signed into law in 2002 and upheld in 2003 by the Supreme Court, requires candidates for federal office to "stand by their ads," stating explicitly that they approve the ad's message (just as Luckovich's Sheik Abu does). Yet no such disclaimer is required for other campaign communications such as print ads or political mail.[3]

BCRA's other main provisions were also driven by concerns about television advertising. The law bans parties from raising soft money (contributions not restricted by source or amount) and prohibits interest groups funded by corporate or union money from airing any television ad mentioning a candidate for federal office within sixty days of a general election (and thirty days of a primary) unless the spot is paid for with regulated "hard money." BCRA says nothing about the content of direct mail or newspaper advertisements.

So there would seem to be something wrong, something suspect, something inherently troubling about TV political advertising, which Madison Avenue pioneer David Ogilvy once called "the most deceptive, misleading, unfair and untruthful of all advertising" (Zhao and Chaffee 1995, 42). Richard Lau and Gerald Pomper argue,

> In the pre-television era, the mass media were thought to have minimal political effects, largely reinforcing attitudes and commitments, but television has apparently changed all that. When skillfully used, television's multiple modes of communication and powerful ability to orient attention can invite strong, unthinking negative responses in low involvement viewers (2004, 2).

Consider the following proclamation from an editorial in a small newspaper in Maine:

> Those who defend negative campaigning do so on the basis that an opponent's public record, positions and behavior are legitimate objects of critical evaluation during an election campaign. And so they are. The trouble is that in a 30-second ad there is little room for anything resembling honest discussion. What viewers usually get are out-of-context distortions and worst-possible-light references to an opponent's record, more often than not raising pointed questions about the motives and integrity of the person under attack. . . . If a sustained diet of attack ads merely convinces voters that all politicians are crooks, liars, incompetents and cheats, who really does win in the end? The losers are left with reputations in tatters and the survivors inherit an institutional position that they have spent an entire campaign thrashing. The truth is it doesn't work. The truth is that we all lose.[4]

Finally, consider the following editorial cartoons for additional evidence of the extent to which such negative perceptions of campaign advertising are embedded in the political culture and popular discourse. No campaign ad writer would contemplate accusing a political opponent of kicking a cat, but that is precisely the kind of thing that cartoonists believe, and the conventional wisdom suggests, a campaign ad writer might do (if only to stay in practice).

We hold a different view, and our argument in this book is a simple one: When it comes to campaign advertising, the conventional wisdom is wrong. We see no convincing theoretical reason why television advertising should be expected to have such a deleterious effect on American democracy. Far from being the bane of democratic citizenship, there are good reasons to believe that political ads may actually educate, engage, and mobilize American citizens. To be sure, we do not expect these effects to be massive; as decades of research on political communication have demonstrated, the impact of campaign messages of any type is likely to be relatively marginal. Nevertheless, at a time when citizens are assailed for being politically uninformed and electorally disconnected, campaign ads may serve an essential democratic function, one that should be recognized by political scientists and the general public alike.

Our "priors" on this topic and the arguments we make are similar to those John Geer (2006) has made in his excellent and comprehensive examination of negativity in presidential advertising over

Source: from top to bottom:

ⓒ Jimmy Margulies, The New Jersey Record, and politicalcartoons.com

ⓒ Mike Keefe, The Denver Post, and politicalcartoons.com

ⓒ Larry Wright, The Detroit News, and politicalcartoons.com

ⓒ John Darkow, Columbia Daily Tribune, and politicalcartoons.com the past four decades. Geer's book focuses on the content of ads and on negativity in presidential elections. Here, we employ data that enable us to take a more comprehensive look at the use and targeting of ads in all sorts of contests, and that allow us to develop measures of ad exposure to test the effect of advertising on voter turnout, voter knowledge, and a range of other political behaviors.

We begin our examination by taking a more detailed look at what the critics of political advertising have in mind when they take aim at the most widely used tool of campaign communication in American politics today.

The Case against Campaign Advertising

Three strands of criticism in particular are leveled at campaign advertising. First, as suggested by the editorial cartoons and enshrined in the BCRA provisions, television advertising is seen as a debased form of campaign discourse that should be distinguished from loftier forms of communication, such as stump speeches, debates, convention addresses, and in-person appearances. This distrust of television advertising often seems to reflect an older, more general distrust of the mass media as a forum for political communication. Indeed, one can detect the vestiges of an old and menacing "hypodermic" model of media influence, in which mass communication was thought to have potentially huge persuasive effects, getting "under the skin" in a variety of direct, indirect, and even subliminal ways.

This model—rooted in fears about the role of the media in the rise of fascism during World War II and the spread of communism in its aftermath—was largely undermined by subsequent scholarship that demonstrated minimal media impact on people's political attitudes and behavior (Berelson et al. 1954; Lazarsfeld et al. 1948). Nevertheless, the torrent of criticism of campaign advertising bespeaks a lingering suspicion that, left unchecked, these nefarious and misleading political messages will infect, confuse, and corrupt the American public.

To be sure, there clearly are features that set television ads apart from other forms of campaign communication. First, when a candidate is on the stump or at the podium, there are few questions about who is doing the speaking, and this fact may provide some degree of a constraint on the kinds of claims candidates make. "I'm not questioning Governor Bush's heart," Al Gore was quick to point out during an October 2000 stump speech, "I'm questioning his priorities."[5] Television ads, in contrast, are produced and paid for by a variety of players; it's not always clear whose message is being presented, as an ad produced by a candidate can be almost indistinguishable from one made by a political party or interest group. As a result, the gloves may be more likely to come off on television than on the stump.

Another important difference between campaign ads and other campaign activity is that citizens must actively seek out exposure to other sorts of campaign communications. Even media coverage of candidate speeches is something that citizens must make an effort to encounter. By contrast, television advertising comes to them. Citizens see campaign ads when they are watching television—often television that has little to do with the candidates and campaigns.

As a result of these differences, whatever one thinks of the BCRA "stand by your ad" provisions, they do reflect an important point: Television advertising is indeed a distinct form of political communication, and what makes television advertising distinct has implications—both good and bad—for democratic citizenship.

These concerns are closely related to a second strand of criticism: that there has been a change in the nature of campaigns in recent years, and that campaigns and campaign ads have grown increasingly negative. Such claims have become a predictable staple of campaign reporting for more than two decades.

Writing about the 1980 presidential contest between Ronald Reagan and Jimmy Carter, for example, chief *New York Times* political reporter Adam Clymer quoted Lois Haines of Goshen, Ohio: "People are being turned off by dirty politics, our country did not start out that way." And second-grade teacher Patricia Williams complained that "there's an awful lot of mudslinging" (Clymer 1980).

Eight years later, in an article about the 1988 contest between George Herbert Walker Bush and Michael Dukakis, Paul Taylor and David Broder bemoaned "the most negative—and among the most effective—presidential campaigns waged in the television era" (Taylor and Broder 1988). In 1992, writing about the race between Bill Clinton and incumbent President George H. W. Bush, chief *New York Times* political writer Richard Berke grumbled, "the view from America's living rooms is not a pretty one" and "the campaigns are leaving unmistakably depressing images" (Berke 1992). And, in 2006, current chief *New York Times* political writer Adam Nagourney kept up the tradition with an article titled "New Campaign Ads Have a Theme: Don't Be Nice" (Sept 27, 2006).

Is television advertising really to blame for the sorry state of campaign discourse? "Anybody who blames television for the practice of opponent-bashing betrays an innocence of the history of American politicking," notes television critic Walter Goodman. "Candidates have in fact become noticeably more polite in the last 150 years" (Goodman 1989). There is a long and proud tradition of campaign mudslinging in American elections. As the *Washington Post's* Dana Milbank observes

Implicit in the media coverage is an assumption that we've turned our backs on some golden era of high-minded campaigning. But when, precisely, was that age? Was it before Thomas Jefferson's opponents called him 'a mean-spirited low-lived fellow, the son of a half-breed Indian squaw'? Or was it after the pols called Abe Lincoln (who engaged in many nasty attacks during the 1858 Lincoln-Douglas Senate campaign debates) 'the original gorilla' and mocked his 'hideous apelike form'? (Milbank 2000)

Exactly. Negativity in American political campaigns is nothing new. Election campaigns have always been hard-hitting, muddy affairs. "Nobody ever said democracy is supposed to be a tea party," election analyst Richard Scammon once quipped. "It's rough, it's bawdy, it's brawling, it's crude, and it's almost always been that way" (Taylor 1988). Indeed, candidates and their supporters historically were just as vituperative, just as misleading, and just as mean-spirited in speeches, pamphlets, and broadsides as their modern counterparts have been in their television spots (Jamieson 1996).

In the election of 1828, for example, Andrew Jackson "was accused of multiple murders, of extreme personal violence, and of having lived in sin with his wife Rachel." Jackson's opponent, John Quincy Adams, "was attacked for his legalistic attitudes and reportedly for having procured young American virgins for the Russian Czar as the primary achievement of his diplomatic career. Adams's critics mockingly referred to him as 'His Excellency,' while Jackson came under attack as an ill-mannered, barely civilized backwoods killer of Indians."[6] In the absence of television advertising, Jackson's and Adams's supporters were forced to make their case through "election materials such as campaign buttons, slogans, posters, tokens, flasks, snuff boxes, medallions, thread boxes, match boxes, mugs, and fabric images."[7]

In the introduction to their book on negative campaigns in Senate elections, Lau and Pomper cite the work of Noble Cunningham (1972) on the presidential election of 1800, during which John Adams was denounced as "head of the monarchical party in the United States intent on excluding from office honest Americans, who braved the perils of a long and bloody war." Thomas Jefferson, on the other hand, was attacked as someone who would "trample those morals that guard the chastity of our wives and daughters from seduction and violence." Lord Bryce characterized American elections as a "tempest of invective and calumny ... thick with charges, recriminations, till the voters know not what to believe" (Lau and Pomper 2004, 1). Still, if campaigns in general are not necessarily more negative than they once were, there is evidence that campaign advertising in particular has grown more so in recent decades. Geer (2006), for example, calculates that in 1960, fewer than 10 percent of "appeals" made by candidates in their ads were negative, rising to 30 percent four years later and peaking at 45 percent in 1996 before settling back to 39.5 percent in 2000. Using different measurement approaches (and slightly different pools of presidential campaign ads), William Benoit (1999), Kathleen Hall Jamieson et al. (2000), and Darrell West (2001) all document similar trends. If hard-hitting campaigns are nothing new, the propensity of political actors to deploy such weaponry on television does seem to have increased in recent years. The key question is: with what effect?

This brings us to the third strand of criticism when it comes to advertising, and the one we challenge in this book: that political advertising has a causal and corrosive effect on American citizens and on American democracy. As we saw above, scholars and pundits alike have assailed the thirty-second spot in recent years, taking campaign advertising to task for producing a disengaged, ill-informed, and alienated electorate that is ill-equipped and disinclined to shoulder the responsibilities of democracy. Implicit—and frequently explicit—in most critiques is the claim that advertising is the culprit for declining voter turnout and increasing political ignorance. Election campaigns are in sorry shape, citizens are worse, and there is a causal connection between the two. As David Broder bemoaned in the aftermath of the 2000 election, "These ads are killing our democracy" (2002).

As we noted above, concerns about political advertising in general and negative advertising in particular led to the 2002 BCRA requirement that every campaign ad in federal elections include a full-screen view or "clearly identifiable photographic image" of the candidate with the candidate's voice claiming responsibility for the content of the ad. This "stand by your ad" provision had long been advocated by reformers on the assumption that candidates would be less likely to engage in negative attacks if they were required to appear in and take responsibility for the content of an ad. The BCRA provision was added by Representative (and political scientist) David Price (D-NC), who modeled the requirement on a similar regulation in North Carolina law. Price explained in a press release, "The American people are sick of the relentlessly negative tone of campaigns, particularly in presidential races. 'Stand By Your Ad' isn't just about restoring civility to campaigns. It's also about restoring people's faith in our political process" (Price press release, Jan 21, 2003).[8] As a result of these changes, many predicted that campaign advertising, deprived of the oxygen of unlimited party and interest group soft money, would decline in importance. By 2004, the argument went, people were sick and tired of thirty-second spots; Stand By Your Ad meant that the scourge of negative advertising would disappear from the nation's airwaves. More generally, broadcast ads would give way to the narrowcasting of the Internet and the micro-targeting of in-person, mail, and telephone contacts. Wall Street analysts even went so far as to suggest that those companies who owned local TV stations would see their profits decline because of the steep drop in political advertising revenues. In short, according to the experts, the era of big television advertising was over.

But reports of the death of television advertising have been greatly exaggerated. Television advertising was alive and well in 2004. It started early, it was strategically targeted, and it was as negative as ever. Most of all, there was lots of it. And 2008 promises much more of the same.

By the time the 2008 presidential nominees have been selected (earlier this season than ever before), the airwaves will have been saturated with campaign advertising that first started almost a year earlier. In fact, the first presidential election ad of the 2008 cycle—a primary ad for Republican candidate Duncan Hunter—was broadcast in Iowa in January 2007 (followed closely by ads for Republican Mitt Romney of Massachusetts). By Election Day, hundreds of millions of dollars and hundreds of thousands of ads will have flooded targeted media markets in competitive states. Should we be concerned?

Hand-wringing over the state of American democracy—and confidence about particular causes and cures—is certainly a longstanding tradition, and hand-wringing over political advertising clearly is in vogue. The claims and concerns of the media and some policy makers are clear. But, as we show in the next chapter, past scholarly research provides a mixed bag of fodder for advertising's critics and ammunition for its defenders. Ultimately, the debate over political advertising—both among scholars and among pundits—is plagued by a paucity of empirical evidence and an inadequate theoretical understanding of how advertising actually influences what citizens know and how they act politically. It is these gaps that we seek to fill.

Plan of the Book

If the central theme of this book is that campaign ads can have beneficial—if often unintended and unexpected—effects, a second theme is that the study of advertising and media effects more generally poses interesting and important methodological challenges, and that answering the most enduring and most important questions often involves searching for new methods and new data.

Our aim in this study is to provide a more comprehensive, theoretically rich, and methodologically rigorous account of the role of campaign advertising in American democracy than has been possible before, one that takes seriously past research on election campaigns, vote choice, media effects, and public opinion, but one that moves beyond prior work with new data and new methods. To do so, we combine traditional survey research with a comprehensive source of ad tracking data. These data, collected and coded by the Wisconsin Advertising Project, show which ads appeared in a given election campaign, how often these spots were broadcast, and where they were aired.

These data allow us to investigate the political impact of exposure to campaign advertising with far greater precision than has been possible to date. Ultimately, they enable us to identify the ways that campaign ads—despite their reputation as the no-good outlaws of American electoral politics—actually serve to enhance democratic citizenship.

In Chapter Two, we put televised political advertising into theoretical perspective and outline a framework for understanding how advertising in general and negative advertising in particular influences what citizens know and how they act. We use this framework to address a series of important questions and to review previous research, much of which has been inconclusive or has reached inconsistent conclusions. We develop a series of hypotheses about advertising effects, addressing questions such as whether citizens learn from ads, whether ad exposure increases campaign engagement, and whether and how campaign ads affect political efficacy, trust in government, and voter turnout. In answering these questions, we are guided by the assumption that ads may have both direct and indirect effects on attitudes and behaviors, and that there may be important heterogeneity when it comes to who is most affected by campaign ads.

Perhaps the primary reason for the inconclusive state of the scholarly literature on campaign advertising is a lack of adequate data, along with disagreements about methodological approaches to the study of advertising effects. In Chapter Three, we review and critique previous methods of studying campaign advertising, and we introduce our own approach to the measurement of advertising exposure. We use these data to derive important lessons about political campaigns and how and where advertising is targeted. We focus on the importance of competition and geographic targeting for determining the volume and mix of ads that citizens encounter.

In Chapter Four, we introduce data from the Wisconsin Advertising Project. Since 2000, the Wisconsin Advertising Project has gathered, processed, coded, and made available to the scholarly community tracking data originally collected by TNS Media Intelligence/Campaign Media Analysis Group (CMAG). These tracking data represent the most comprehensive and systematic collection of political advertisements ever assembled for a given election. Finally, we describe how advertising tracking data can be processed, coded, and merged with various sorts of survey and election data to create reliable individual-level measures of relative exposure to advertising.

In Chapter Five, we employ our data on the content and targeting of political advertising as a "dependent variable" and seek to explain the factors that influence campaigns' use of advertising. In this chapter, we generate some important lessons about the use of advertising that guide our analysis and, we hope, will guide the analysis of others testing the effects of advertising empirically.

In Chapters Six, Seven, and Eight, we look at a series of ancillary or spillover effects of advertising on the attitudes and behavior of American citizens. These effects are not necessarily those intended by campaign strategists, but they are no less important from the perspective of American democracy. We look closely at the impact of aggregate ad exposure on political participation and citizen engagement, exploring what effects ads have when it comes to campaign interest, political knowledge, and voter turnout; and we investigate whether these effects are the same for everyone or if they vary systematically.

In Chapter Nine, we turn our attention to the role of negative or "attack" advertising, asking whether these ads in particular have the kinds of negative effects on democracy that critics have suggested. We conclude in Chapter Ten with observations about the role of campaign advertising in American democracy, the nature of the ad war in 2004, and the future of campaign advertising in American elections.

CHAPTER TWO

Campaign Ads as Information Supplements

A Spillover Theory of Advertising Effects

T HIS BOOK IS ABOUT HOW campaign advertising affects citizens' grasp of the alternatives in a campaign, their evaluation of the process, and their inclination to participate in it. It is not about the effects of advertising on voters' opinions about the candidates or the outcome of elections; we largely sidestep questions of candidate evaluation and vote choice, asking instead how campaign ads affect what voters know about the candidates, how interested and engaged they are in the election process, and whether or not they actually participate. Although these questions are vitally important for American democracy, they are of little interest to candidates and campaign decision-makers who share a single, simple objective: winning elections. In this sense the effects we are concerned with are really unintended byproducts of efforts to influence election outcomes. As such, we label them spillover effects, but recognize that they are direct effects and of primary importance.

How then does campaign advertising affect American democracy? Our argument is relatively simple: Given the gap between the dictates of democratic theory and the realities of democratic citizenship, and given the content and packaging of most campaign commercials, campaign ads serve as vital information supplements; they enable people, in the absence of necessary information or sufficient motivation, to make reasonable electoral decisions. In a democratic sense, campaign ads can help sustain the body politic, keeping it healthier than it might otherwise become. But just as the biological body cannot survive on multivitamins alone, citizenship requires more than thirty-second supplements. In order for democracy to flourish, citizens need a more balanced diet of information, opinion, and discussion. Our argument is not that campaign ads are all citizens need, or that advertising itself can cure the challenges that face our democracy—far from it. Rather, we claim that thirty-second spots do little harm and some real good when it comes to political nutrition. To take seriously the project of restoring and revitalizing American democracy requires a careful and accurate assessment of campaign ads, and an appreciation of their actual effects on citizens.

The Disquieting Gulf

Central to most notions of representative democracy is the simple idea that citizens ought to participate in the process of choosing leaders and expressing opinions on matters of policy. Engaged, attentive, and informed citizens, it is widely held, should be able to select representatives and make other meaningful political choices consistent with their preferences and interests. Key to this exercise of informed democratic decision-making is the assumption that there will be sufficient, relevant data available in the political environment, and that citizens will be able and inclined to draw on this information in making their choices.

Democratic reality, of course, falls far short of this ideal, and the project of saving democracy from the shortcomings of the American citizen has been an ongoing challenge for political science. How is it that a disengaged, ill-equipped, and poorly informed citizenry has managed to maintain a democracy? Specifically, how can people with little interest in and even less knowledge about politics arrive at more or less reasoned political judgments? We suggest that over the last several decades the informational needs of the American citizen have been subsidized by an important but overlooked source: the thirty-second television campaign advertisement. Rather than causing injury, could political ads actually have served to strengthen democratic citizenship?

Political science has long wrestled with the disquieting gulf between the ideals of democratic citizenship and the reality of the American citizen. In a classic, oft-cited formulation, Berelson, Lazarsfeld, and McPhee explained that "The democratic citizen is expected to be interested . . . and to be well informed about political affairs. He is supposed to know what the issues are, what their history is, what the relevant facts are, what alternatives are proposed, what the party stands for, what the likely consequences are. By such standards the voter falls short" (1954, 308).

As Bartels (1986) noted, the "intellectual pedigree" of this vague "democratic ideal" is rarely articulated by empirically oriented political scientists. It is also the case that there is more to liberal democracy than informed, participatory citizens. Equality, justice, tolerance, and institutional accountability are democratic values of comparable importance. Put simply, democracy requires more than information and participation. Empirically oriented scholars tend to pay less attention to these values, however, in part because they are more difficult to operationalize and measure at the individual level. Nevertheless, in the half century since Berelson and his associates delivered their dismal verdict on the

American citizen, the focus has been on how much people know and do in the realm of politics, and here the weight of the supporting evidence has been definitive: When it comes to politics and political information, most Americans are severely malnourished. They are inattentive to most things political; they care little, know less, and participate in politics only when absolutely necessary (and often not even then). Their political views are peripatetic, hastily assembled, unconstrained by ideology, and unencumbered by data (Campbell et al. 1960; Converse 1964; Kinder 1983; Bartels 1986; Delli Carpini and Keeter 1996; Zaller 1992). Americans, in short, fail to meet the dictates of even the most charitable versions of democratic theory.

Still, in spite of this anemic citizenry, American democracy has managed to endure: Leaders are chosen and held accountable, public policy is made, and popular preferences, such as they are, are often translated successfully into political outcomes. How is it that democracy can survive—some might claim thrive—when citizens are so disengaged, so preoccupied with interests and anxieties distant from the world of politics?

Scholars have provided a number of answers, struggling to save the American citizen from the harsh judgment of political science and, simultaneously, to save democracy from the American citizen. Some have turned to the "miracle of aggregation," through which "errors" in preferences and vote choices cancel each other out when the analyses and choice mechanisms shift from the individual to the aggregate level (Condorcet 1785; Converse 1990; Page and Shapiro 1992). Through the babble of noisy opinions, according to this logic, a clear, rational signal emerges, guided in part by the steady hand of a small cadre of educated and informed citizens. Although there is evidence to support this view, Bartels points out that it is predicated on the largely untenable assumption that individual "errors" are, in fact, random. To the extent that errors are correlated—that citizens' opinions are subject to systematic bias and distortion—Condorcet's logic and the miracle of aggregation break down (Bartels 1996, 200; see also Althaus 1998).

Others have focused on the role of elites in shaping mass opinion and effecting reasonably democratic decision-making. Zaller, for example, imagined a world in which citizens "simply select from the menu of elite-supplied opinions" and rarely, if ever, think for themselves (1992, 314). In such a world, democratic outcomes are possible, provided two conditions hold: First, there must exist a rough balance in the competing messages available; second, people must be able to align themselves with a subcommunity of experts who share their general values. As Zaller argued in his parable of Purple Land, "it is possible at least to imagine conditions in which the dependence of mass opinion on the information and analysis carried in elite discourse is great, and yet in which elite domination of public opinion . . . is unlikely to occur" (1992, 314). Expert opinion, in other words, can save democracy without destroying democratic citizenship.

A third approach recognizes that information is costly to acquire and that citizens therefore have an incentive to remain, at least to some extent, ignorant (Downs 1957). These costs are dictated in part by the cognitive resources needed to assemble and make sense of politically relevant information and, in part, by the availability of such information in the first place. Given the nature of media coverage of politics, even a voracious consumer of the news might find it difficult to fulfill democratic theory's recommended daily allowance of political nutrition.

In the face of this paucity of political information, people employ a variety of heuristics and information shortcuts. These enable them to approximate rational decision-making on the basis of a limited—in some cases vanishingly small—supply of actual information. Heuristics, as described by Sniderman, Brody, and Tetlock, "are judgmental shortcuts, efficient ways to organize and simplify political choices, efficient in the double sense of requiring relatively little information to execute, yet yielding dependable answers even to complex problems of choice" (1991, 19).

Such shortcuts allow individuals to compensate for a lack of information by making decisions on the basis of a candidate's party, ideology, position on a particular issue, demographic characteristics or standing in the polls, or the endorsements of individuals or organizations (Lau and Redlawsk 2001; Lupia 1994). In addition to such cognitive shortcuts, citizens also rely on more affective cues—notably what Sniderman and his colleagues called the likeability heuristic, according to which people make informational inferences on the basis of what groups they like and dislike (Brady and Sniderman 1985; Sniderman, Brody, and Tetlock 1991). Affect, in this sense, can serve a heuristic function, enabling cognitive-miserly citizens to make reasoned judgments with a limited store of information (Chaiken 1980; Popkin 1991; Tversky and Kahneman 1974).

By employing a mix of affective and cognitive shortcuts, "people can be knowledgeable in their reasoning about political choices without necessarily possessing a large body of knowledge about politics" (Sniderman, Brody, and Tetlock 1991, 19). Heuristic processing therefore enables even poorly informed citizens to make more or less rational judgments with a limited store of information, a fact long recognized by social psychologists and other social scientists (Chaiken 1980; Fiske and Taylor 1991; Popkin 1991; Tversky and Kahneman 1974; Kahneman, Slovic, and Tversky 1982). As a result, everyday people are able to engage in political life with some degree of rationality and efficiency.

We believe that heuristic processing—particularly the use of the likeability heuristic—is especially important for understanding the role played by campaign advertising. However, it is important to recognize that each approach to bridging the gap between democratic aspirations and empirical realities is predicated upon the availability of at least some politically relevant information from which citizens can draw. Whether one puts faith in miracles of aggregation, looks to the discourse of competing elites, or falls back on cognitive shortcuts, someone, somewhere, must be in possession of some supply of information. These are, after all, efforts to account for democratic decision-making in the face of limited, but not nonexistent, information. In the context of an election campaign, each approach requires at least some information about the candidates, parties, or issues to be available to at least some segment of the citizenry. Where does such information come from? What is the source of the raw informational ingredients that make democracy possible?

Campaign Ads as Informational Multivitamins

One common answer to the problem of the disquieting gulf is that elites can provide relevant information through election campaigns. Campaigns ideally are seen as capturing the attention of citizens, activating their political predispositions, and, at least potentially, shedding some light on the political choice at hand (Alvarez 1997; Coleman and Manna 2000; Finkel 1993; Gelman and King 1993; Popkin 1991; Simon 2002). Candidates and parties help subsidize the costs of information, and their interest group allies do their part as well, distributing voting guides, candidate scorecards, and primers designed to make a given set of electoral choices more comprehensible. Organizations such as the National Rifle Association, the Sierra Club, and NARAL Pro-Choice America all attempt to subsidize the costs of acquiring politically relevant information in an easily digestible form. As we have suggested, one of the most important tools for doing so is the thirty-second television spot.

Campaign ads constitute candidates' efforts to speak to voters directly, in their own words, on their own terms. For thirty seconds, a candidate has complete control over his or her message. Candidates can say exactly what they want, illustrating their claims with words, images, and music of their choosing. Such control over their own message and image is essential in a media environment in which election coverage tends to focus on the horse race and strategic analysis rather than on issue positions and policy implications (Patterson 1994; Capella and Jamieson 1997; Farnsworth and Lichter 2003), in which stories are framed episodically rather than thematically (Iyengar 1991), and in which the average length of network news candidate sound bites has declined from a full forty-two seconds in 1968 to less than eight seconds by 2000 (Adatto 1990; Farnsworth and Lichter 2003). News coverage of elections, as Patterson put it more than a decade ago, "has become a barrier between the candidates and the voters rather than a bridge connecting them" (1994, 25).

Against this media backdrop, candidates struggle to get their message out to voters in ways that are unimpeded—unmediated—by the analysis, interpretation, and criticism of a cynical and competitive news media. Campaign advertising offers a solution. One of the central claims of this book is that a spillover effect of candidates' efforts to communicate with voters (and ultimately to win elections) is a more informed, more engaged citizenry. Campaign advertisements, we argue, represent important informational supplements, enhancing the otherwise impoverished political diet of the American citizen.

This spillover theory takes as its starting point the fact that campaign ads tend to be rich in informational content. Moreover, advertising conveys information in an efficient, easily digestible way. Like product advertising, political commercials are carefully tested and skillfully produced. Text, images, and music work to complement and reinforce each other. And an ad's basic message—its bottom line—is usually simple to identify (it is often the first and the last line of the ad). Most political advertising, in fact, reduces to a single, simple message: one of proximity. Regardless of the type of race, the sponsor, the tone of the ad, and no matter what words or images or music the spot features, the ultimate message is that the favored candidate is, in some substantive way, closer to the viewer than his or her opponent. There are several dimensions to this proximity message: The candidate may be closer on issue positions, in terms of ideology, or closer to the viewer's values. Candidates usually portray themselves as honest, trustworthy, religious, hardworking protectors and providers for their families: closer to how the voters see themselves—or would like to see themselves—than their less-virtuous opponents. Campaign advertising also portrays candidates as closer geographically ("She's not a *real* New Yorker"), in terms of occupation ("He understands the needs of farmers because he is one"), or in terms of class ("I can't afford a lot of fancy television ads like my opponent, so I'll have to talk fast!").

When a candidate's objective is to communicate a message of proximity, a good deal of information is included in the process. Citizen learning is thus an important byproduct of candidates' efforts to maximize support. Ultimately, if the political diet of most Americans is lacking in crucial information, campaign ads may represent the multivitamins of American politics.

Equally important, this informational content is contained in an easy-to-swallow emotional coating. Campaign ads are rarely presented in dispassionate, emotionally neutral terms. Rather, ads tend to be emotionally rich; they provoke diverse responses including fear, pride, and sympathy, either directly, through the script of the ad, or indirectly, through the use of images and music. As Brader has recently argued, "campaign ads use symbolic images and evocative music to trigger an emotional response in viewers. By appealing to different emotions, ads can influence the participation and choices of viewers in distinct ways" (2006, 13). Brader demonstrated experimentally that cueing enthusiasm, fear, or other emotions can influence subjects' interest in the campaign, intention to vote, and information recall. As Graber (2004) noted, emotional appeals are both more likely to be noticed and more likely to be recalled than other sorts of messages. Indeed, by making emotional connections, ad exposure can facilitate use of the likeability heuristic described earlier (Sniderman, Brody, and Tetlock 1991).

For the most part, however, research on the emotional and attitudinal effects of media have focused on free media. Mutz and Reeves (2005), for example, found that exposure to uncivil appeals in mock televised policy debates lowered assessments of trust in government and Congress. They called this the "New Videomalaise," referring to a popular hypothesis about the effects of television (see Robinson 1975; and, more recently, Putnam 2000), but one without significant supporting evidence. Indeed, it appears the conventional wisdom happily has extended the videomalaise hypothesis into the world of paid media.

As for the idea that campaign ads can help inform citizens, prior work provides some measure of support for these proposed effects. Most famously, Patterson and McClure found campaign advertising during the 1972 presidential election to be rife with issue content, leading them to conclude that "presidential advertising contributes to an informed electorate" (1976, 117). Indeed, according to Patterson and McClure, television advertising led to a greater degree of issue learning than did television news (at least among the voters of Onondaga County, NY).

Similarly, Brians and Wattenberg (1996) used survey data to compare the relative impact of self-reported ad exposure, newspaper reading, and television news viewing on knowledge of the 1992 presidential candidates. They found that all three media produced information gains, but that self-reported ad exposure was the strongest predictor of political learning of the three. And in the final month of the campaign, exposure to political advertising was the only significant predictor of issue recall. Interestingly, these findings held when Brians and Wattenberg examined only exposure to negative political advertising, leading them to suggest that concerns about negative advertising are without warrant: "The fact that much of viewers' knowledge comes from negative advertising should serve to reassure critical observers who fear that political attacks harm the American viewing and voting public" (1996, 187).

Zhao and Chaffee (1995) provided additional, albeit more limited, support for the conclusions of Brians and Wattenberg. Zhao and Chaffee examined surveys taken in six different electoral contests. Advertising had a discernible positive impact on learning in three, and in one advertising had a greater effect on knowledge than did television news viewing (that occurred in the high-profile and racially charged 1990 North Carolina Senate race, which pitted Senator Jesse Helms against Democratic challenger Harvey Gantt).

Others have argued that the effects of advertising on knowledge are conditional: that is, exposure to advertising is more likely to have an impact in certain situations and on certain voters. For instance, advertising may be more effective at conveying information to less interested and less informed individuals than other media. Just, Crigler, and Wallach concluded that ads do a better job of informing electorates than debates do because debates can be confusing for many voters. By contrast, "ads, which tend to present a single viewpoint, reduce confusion and aid learning for all kinds of viewers" (1990, 131).[1]

Additionally, the experimental work of Hitchon and Chang (1995) suggested that issues mentioned in ads sponsored by women are more easily recalled by viewers than issues mentioned in ads sponsored by men, and that recall is better for neutral ads and positive ads than for negative ads. Knowledge of candidates' positions is also heightened when the ad is sponsored by a candidate as opposed to being sponsored by an interest group (Pfau et al. 2002). Finally, people tend to recall more information about an advertisement when it is sponsored by a preferred candidate than when it is not (Faber and Storey 1984).

Most of the prior work on the informational impact of campaign advertising has necessarily relied on relatively indirect measures of exposure to campaign advertising. Inferring exposure to ads outside of the laboratory (where such inference is unnecessary) has been a tenuous project at best. In some cases scholars have relied on contextual measures of campaign spending or advertising activity. More commonly, studies have used survey measures of self-reported ad exposure to demonstrate that advertising can boost knowledge and increase campaign interest (e.g., Zhao and Chaffee 1995). There are, however, important methodological problems with using self-reported exposure to campaign advertising; concerns about endogeneity when relying on self-reports are especially pronounced in models of political learning (Ansolabehere, Iyengar, and Simon 1999). We take up these questions in greater depth in Chapter 3.

The Impact of Negative Advertising

The most vehement criticism of campaign advertising is reserved for negative ads, commonly referred to as "attack advertising" (the phrase invokes fangs and perhaps foaming at the mouth). Attack ads almost universally are condemned for being corrosive of American democracy. They are unpleasant, impolite, and on the rise. Most important, they are thought to demobilize the American electorate.

The demobilization hypothesis has had its clearest expression in the work of Ansolabehere, Iyengar, Simon, and Valentino (1994) and Ansolabehere and Iyengar (1995). Drawing on a series of carefully conducted experiments, these authors argued that exposure to negative advertising can reduce voter turnout rates by as much as 5 percent (and more than twice that among political independents). They supported this claim with an analysis of aggregate turnout in Senate elections, where they found a similar decline. Clearly, this was an important finding that, if true, served as a warning that the ubiquitous thirty-second commercial posed a threat to American democracy.[2]

Ansolabehere and Iyengar identified a relatively straightforward causal path: Exposure to negative attacks causes viewers to become disgusted, alienated, and disengaged, leading ultimately to a decline in political efficacy—the sense that their vote matters, that their voice can be heard, that politics is something worth participating in. Accordingly, they are less likely to turn out on Election Day. Call it the Timothy Leary Effect: Viewers tune in, get turned off, and drop out from political life.

There are, however, good reasons to question the demobilization hypothesis. As Lau and Pomper (2004) found in their comprehensive review of the literature on negative campaigning, the empirical case for demobilization effects is weak at best. Many studies, including Lau and Pomper's own thorough analysis of a decade of Senate elections, show that the conditions under which negative campaigns may show any demobilizing effects at all are extremely narrow. More commonly, scholars have argued that, all else equal, negative advertising actually is more likely to stimulate voter participation than to demobilize.[3] As Geer recently argued, "negativity can advance and improve the prospects for democracy" (2006, 10).

A good deal of past research on the topic of negative advertising generally supports the claim that it either increases or has no impact on voter turnout. Wattenberg and Brians (1999), for instance, examined the 1992 and 1996 National Election Studies and found that negative advertising had a mobilizing effect in 1992 but no impact on turnout in 1996. Finkel and Geer (1998) also found a conditional impact of advertising tone on turnout. Only among political independents did tone affect potential voters' probability of voting: Independents exposed to a negative campaign were more likely to participate in an election. Similarly, Djupe and Peterson (2002) discovered a mobilizing effect of negative advertising in the 1998 U.S. Senate primaries, although Garramone et al. (1990) found no difference in the likelihood of turnout between subjects shown negative ads about a fictional candidate and those shown positive ads about a fictional candidate.

A different experiment found that election involvement (measured by a scale that tapped the degree to which subjects cared about an election and found it interesting, stimulating, and exciting) rose as the amount of negativity in an advertisement rose, prompting Pinkleton (1998) to suggest that increased involvement might lead to increased participation at the polls. Finally, Clinton and Lapinski's (2004) series of experiments in the 2000 presidential election revealed that negative advertising had no significant effect on turnout in either direction.

Prior work, therefore, provides a mixed account of the effects of negative advertising. Most research, however, coalesces around two broad sets of claims: first, that negative advertising demobilizes the electorate; second, that negative advertising has no demobilizing effect and may actually stimulate voter turnout. We obviously fall in the second camp. In previous work, we have argued that turnout rises as negativity increases (Freedman and Goldstein 1999; Goldstein and Freedman 2002). We maintain that, all else equal, negative campaign ads are more likely to stimulate and inform rather than to depress and obscure. These expectations rest on an important assumption about what kinds of ads provide the best shortcuts for voters looking for cues. There are several reasons to suspect that negative advertisements serve this function to a greater extent than positive spots. First, negative ads are more likely to be noticed, more likely to be recalled, and more likely to convey a sense of urgency, activating what Marcus, Neuman, and MacKuen (2000) call the "surveillance system."

Negative ads also play into the preference voters have for minimizing bad outcomes. Consistent with prospect theory, people are motivated more by the desire to evade costs than they are by the desire to capture benefits (Tversky and Kahneman 1974; Kahneman and Tversky 1984). People are, the argument goes, more or less hardwired to flee from danger. For risk-averse potential voters concerned about minimizing bad outcomes, negative information may provide a particularly useful and compelling signal: Citizens are motivated to avoid a corrupt, incompetent, or immoral politician more than they seek to elect a virtuous one. Prospect theory also helps to explain the finding that anxiety serves to heighten attention to the campaign, as voters, in essence, perk up their ears when they hear a negative message.

Finally, as we demonstrate in Chapter 9, negative ads actually contain more substantive information than positive ads (see also Geer 2006). As Jamieson, Waldman, and Sherr (2000) documented, negative ads are more likely to focus on candidates' policy positions than are positive spots. Moreover, negative ads also are more likely to use supporting sources than positive ads. Furthermore, negative ads are likely to be rich in anxiety-producing appeals—precisely the kind of emotional content that Marcus and MacKuen (1993) found heighten awareness and interest in the campaign. And, as Rahn argued, emotions themselves can play a heuristic function: "Affective (i.e., emotional) experiences affect political reasoning and facilitate low-information rationality" (2000, 130).

This contention is essentially the account put forward by Lau, who argued that, against a background of near-constant communication, negative information "may be perceptually more salient, more easily noticed, and therefore more readily processed" than positive information (1985, 121). Indeed, negative information may be especially likely to be both stored in and retrieved from memory (Kahn and Kenney 2000). Moreover, there is evidence that negative information is more heavily weighted when people make evaluative judgments (Ito et al. 1998). Put simply, when juxtaposed against the clamor of an election campaign—in addition to the white noise of modern mediated life—negative ads may simply stand out more effectively, as if to say, "Look! A fight!" And, as in grade school, when there's a fight, people show up.

It is also important to be very clear about exactly what a negative advertisement is and is not. As we note above, the phrase evokes images of dirty tricks, slurs, and venomous language. In other words, the term "negative advertising" has, well, negative connotations. Negative advertising, however, is really only a sort of advertising in which the focus is on criticizing the opponent's record rather than promoting one's own record. Critics certainly can point to mean-spirited ads in every election cycle. But, the overwhelming majority of negative advertisements deals with policy matters and eschews personal attacks or mudslinging. They are simply advertisements about the other candidate.

Questions and Hypotheses

With the foregoing discussion in mind, in the chapters that follow we take up a number of specific questions relating to the effects of campaign advertising:

1. Do citizens learn from ads?
2. Does ad exposure make people more likely to tune in and pay attention to the campaign, or does advertising turn voters off?
3. Does ad exposure make citizens more or less likely to vote?
4. What sorts of effects do campaign ads have on attitudes like efficacy and trust in government?
5. What kinds of ads have the most pronounced effects on citizen learning, political engagement, and voter turnout? *participation*
6. What kinds of citizens are most affected by exposure to advertising?

In answering these questions, we test a series of hypotheses about the impact of campaign advertising. We are guided by the assumption that ads may have both direct and indirect effects or intended and unintended effects on attitudes and behaviors, and that there may be important heterogeneity when it comes to who is most affected by campaign ads. The implicit null hypothesis, of course, is that ads do not matter at all, that exposure to campaign commercials has no effect on citizens' interest, information, or levels of participation. We have tried to build a case in this chapter that ads should indeed matter, but it's important to recognize that there is good reason to expect such effects to be small. Compared to "big-ticket" predictors such as education, strength of partisanship, or campaign and party mobilizing contacts, the impact of television ads on interest, information, and participation is likely to be quite small indeed. Small effects, however, can still be important ones. Moreover, even null findings would stand in sharp contrast to the arguments of campaign ad detractors. To show that ads do not have the corrosive effects on democracy that so many critics assume would be an important corrective. But our theory goes further, maintaining that ads are not simply an inert or irrelevant feature of the campaign landscape. Ads, we hypothesize, matter in positive ways, and to the extent that we are able to demonstrate positive effects—even modest ones—we will have gone beyond merely refuting the claims of those who hold the evils of ads to be self-evident.

Against this backdrop of positive-but-small expectations, we offer the following hypotheses. First, the *information hypothesis* holds that citizens exposed to campaign advertising actually will learn something about the candidates and their messages. In this sense, we argue that ads, acting as informational multivitamins, convey relevant and useful political information that is not lost on the viewer. Second, the *system support hypothesis* predicts that exposure to television ads will inspire higher levels of interest in the campaign, as well as raise levels of trust in elections and democracy. To that end, we expect little evidence that videomalaise—if it exists—is transmitted through campaign ads. Third, the *engagement hypothesis* suggests that, due in part to its information-enhancing function and in part to the emotional content of much campaign advertising, ad exposure will cause people to be more interested in a particular election, more cognitively and affectively involved with the campaigns, and ultimately more likely to participate by turning out on Election Day. Contrary to the demobilization school, then, we expect to find evidence that ads get people off the couch instead of compelling them to stay put. Fourth, we propose a *differential effects hypothesis*, suggesting that these effects will be greatest among those who need the information most: citizens who have lower levels of political information to begin with. This expectation is grounded in common sense: Those who know least obviously have the most to learn. Moreover, past research provides some support for the hypothesis.[4] However, it rubs against assumptions underlying existing models of media effects.

Theories of media effects usually differentiate among three components of the communications process: exposure, reception, and acceptance of new information (Hovland, Janis, and Kelley 1953; Price and Zaller 1993; Zaller 1992, 1996). Exposure involves the physical encounter with a media message, reception refers to the process of "taking in" or comprehending a message, and acceptance entails "yielding" to a message that has been received (leading to, under certain conditions, attitude change). Our focus is on reception. We are concerned primarily with whether information conveyed by advertising "gets through" to viewers rather than whether it has a persuasive impact (a question of acceptance). To the extent that advertising leads to increases in political information or campaign interest, we consider messages as having been received. Importantly, unlike most work conducted outside of the laboratory, we employ independent estimates of advertising exposure that allow us to untangle patterns of exposure from effects on reception. Thus, we ask what information people receive given our estimates of what messages—specifically, patterns of advertising—they have been exposed to.

It is most often assumed that reception of political messages rises with cognitive sophistication and political engagement. In part, this reflects the fact that exposure to political messages increases with sophistication, and exposure and reception are usually conflated in nonexperimental studies.[5] In the present study, however, we have independent estimates of exposure and need not rely on measures of reception to infer exposure.

In addition to differences in patterns of exposure, past work usually has assumed that less-informed citizens fail to receive messages they encounter because they lack the cognitive skills needed to make sense of new communications. Zaller's "reception axiom," for example, held that, "the greater a person's level of cognitive engagement with an issue, the more likely he or she is to be exposed to and comprehend—in a word, to receive—political messages concerning that issue" (1992, 42). More generally, the assumption in much of the literature is that as media messages are encountered, "the informationally rich get richer," while those with fewer informational resources get left behind (Price and Zaller 1993, 138).[6]

Our differential effects hypothesis, therefore, runs counter to Zaller's reception axiom and the expectation that informational gains are concentrated among those who already possess an appreciable store of political information. Given exposure to advertising (which, again, we measure separately), we hypothesize that the least sophisticated (as measured by levels of general political information) are the most likely to take in new information from political advertising (though those higher in sophistication may still gain some knowledge from advertising). The difference between our expectations and the work of Zaller (1992) reflects the nature of the information conveyed by political ads versus other sources of political information like newspapers or television news. The informational content of most political ads is relatively straightforward, requiring little in the way of cognitive processing, and usually is accompanied by simple emotional cues. Ads are, we argue, information subsidies akin to multivitamins: attractively (and expertly) packaged, simple to comprehend, easy to digest. The cognitive resources necessary to receive information from advertising are thus much less than might be assumed for other types of political messages.

Reception therefore is easier; those who have the most to learn, we hypothesize, experience the greatest gains. Furthermore, these multivitamins can be accessed while viewing a wide variety of shows. While much campaign advertising is aired on news programs, ads appear on a wide variety of other broadcasts as well. Compared to information conveyed by newspapers and television news, ads present more readily digestible information to which viewers can be exposed without purposively seeking it out.

As a corollary to the differential effects hypothesis, we also offer the *partisan hypothesis,* which proposes that political independents are more influenced by ad exposure than partisans. Although political independents are not obviously low in information, they are less disposed to be interested in politics than partisans, less likely to participate in elections than partisans, and more skeptical about the functioning of American democracy than partisans. Because political independents are more in need of the supplementary benefits that we believe advertising provides, we expect them, like those low in political knowledge, to be moved most by the emotional and informational appeals found in television advertising (Lau 1982; Lau and Pomper 2001).

Our final hypothesis, which we examine in Chapter 9, is the *negativity hypothesis,* which suggests—perhaps to the surprise of American voters allegedly fed up with the negativity they see on television—that negative advertising stimulates and informs those exposed to it. We show that negative ads—because they draw people's attention, are easier to remember, and raise the stakes—have a greater impact on citizens' attitudes and behaviors than positive ads. Specifically, we expect that exposure to negative advertising leads to greater gains in information, increased interest in the campaign, and, ultimately, a greater like-lihood of turning out to vote.

At the same time, the advertising data that we utilize give us a unique oppor-tunity to look specifically at the extent to which negative ads focus on the policy positions of candidates or their personal characteristics. Building upon Kahn and Kenney's (1999) discussion of "mudslinging" in campaigns, we extend the negativity hypothesis (call it the policy corollary) to suggest that negative ads con-taining policy content inform, raise campaign interest, and boost turnout rates. It is only those ads containing purely personal negative appeals that demobilize or confuse the electorate.

Summary

The thirty-second television spot represents the most important form of political campaign communication in contemporary American democracy. To be sure, the stump speech, the convention address, the candidate debate, the direct-mail flier, and various Internet strategies are all alive and well in American politics. But the fact remains that to communicate an effective political message in the twenty-first century—to reach out and touch a political constituency of any sort—means to create, target, and disseminate political television advertising. When candidates reach out to voters, when parties seek to expand their bases of support, or when interest groups work to promote or oppose a piece of legislation, one of their most important resources is their ability to create and distribute television ads. In short, television advertising is the primary means by which most modern political campaigns try to persuade potential voters and mobilize probable supporters. It is essential, therefore, to assemble an accurate picture of what effects these efforts have.

CHAPTER THREE

Measuring Exposure to Campaign Ads

THE DISPARATE CLAIMS about campaign advertising and its effects on American citizens, explored in the last chapter, reflect in part the myriad methodological approaches that have been brought to bear on the subject. The methodological pluralism represented in the literature is, by some measures, a good thing; however, at times it seems as though the field has been left with more questions than answers. Ultimately, the study of campaign advertising—and its impact on citizens—has been hampered by a dearth of good empirical data and an insufficient understanding of how advertising is crafted and deployed in political campaigns.

In a perfect world, scholars seeking to describe the nature of a political ad war and its effects would have precise information on exactly which ads were aired (and how many times) and exactly who saw them (and how many times). In this perfect world, scholars also would have detailed information on the demographics, attitudes, and political predispositions of those exposed to particular ads. Of course, in a perfect world, political strategists also would randomly deploy their advertising efforts, thereby allowing scholars to attribute any differences in advertising exposure purely to the advertising.

In the laboratory, perfect information and randomization are easy to come by; researchers know precisely what ads subjects have been exposed to. Sadly, in the real world, matters are a good bit more difficult. The absence of comprehensive data on the content, timing, volume, and targeting of political advertising has limited what scholars can report about the strategies employed by campaigns and the balance of advertising in particular contests. More important, the lack of comprehensive data has made it difficult for scholars to measure citizens' exposure to advertising and to study the effectiveness of these communications.

We begin this chapter with a detailed critique of several approaches to the study of political advertising. Some of these approaches focus on measuring the advertising environment of a particular campaign through the use of aggregate campaign spending data, archival collections of television commercials, and logs from the public files of television stations. Other approaches—experimentation, self-reports by survey respondents, and proxy measures of exposure—attempt to measure the effects of advertising. Each of these methods has advantages, but each also has weaknesses that make it difficult for scholars both to characterize the information environment and to infer how campaign messages influence the attitudes and behavior of citizens.

Campaign Spending

One common proxy for the campaign information environment is candidate spending. By measuring campaign expenditures, scholars have sought to make descriptive inferences about the relative volume and impact of candidate messages. For instance, some scholars have examined the relationship between expenditures and election outcomes (Green and Krasno 1990; Jacobson 1992; Gerber 1998); others have explored money's impact on voter knowledge and affect toward candidates (Coleman and Manna 2000; Coleman 2001). While candidate spending may be a reasonable "quick and dirty" proxy for the intensity of campaign communications, the measure can be far removed from the actual messages that voters receive and to which they respond. Indeed, researchers have recognized this mismatch, referring to a "black box" through which campaign money is translated into electoral outcomes. As Coleman and Manna acknowledged, "campaign money must work through campaign strategy, advertising content, advertising frequency, and other intermediaries" (2000, 759).

There are few places left in American where money can directly buy votes. Rather, money affords candidates the means by which to spread their messages or bring their supporters to the polls, two activities designed to increase the candidates' vote shares. The important point, as Ansolabehere and Gerber noted, is that "total campaign spending may not be a good measure of expenditures devoted to actual campaigning" (1994, 1107). Making use of Fritz and Morris's (1992) comprehensive analysis of Federal Election Commission spending reports, Ansolabehere and Gerber separated campaign expenditures into three types: "direct communications with voters," such as radio or television commercials; other campaign activities, such as polling, office expenses, or the hiring of a consultant; and spending unconnected to a candidate's own campaign, such as a donation of money to another candidate. Ansolabehere and Gerber find that House challengers devote, on average, only 58 percent of total expenditures to campaign communications. For House incumbents, the comparable figure is just 42 percent (1994, 1110).

More generally, there are three drawbacks to the use of aggregate spending data in tapping the information environment and testing for campaign effects. First, the use of aggregate spending assumes that every citizen in a particular constituency is exposed to the same volume of campaign messages. Such an assumption is just plain wrong. Political advertising is not evenly distributed across the United States—or even across a given state (Goldstein and Freedman 2002). There is substantial variation across media markets in the volume of candidates' advertising. These differences are particularly striking in presidential campaigns, in which some television markets receive no advertising at all while others receive thousands of paid spots.

Similarly, the amount of advertising a campaign dollar will buy varies geographically. For example, in their experimental work with a random nationwide sample of potential voters, Clinton and Lapinski (2004) used the log of Democratic spending in a state as a measure of state campaign intensity. Even if we assume perfectly symmetrical spending by the Republicans and no variance in spending patterns by outside groups, an unweighted dollar figure still contains significant measurement error. Quite simply, $100,000 will purchase much more television advertising—as well as just about everything else—in Cheyenne, Wyoming, or Traverse City, Michigan, than it will in Los Angeles or New York City. Spending measures, then, are not comparable across media markets.

One possible way to address this problem is to weight spending by a program's gross ratings points, or GRPs. GRPs are a measure of the size of the audience for a television program. One ratings point, on average, is equal to 1 percent of the television household audience in a particular media market. GRPs are helpful in determining the audience for a particular political commercial. For example, if an ad were aired eighty times, each with an average ten-point rating, that ad would achieve a total of 800 GRPs. This is the equivalent of all television households viewing the spot eight times or half of all television households viewing the spot sixteen times. Although weighting by GRPs may address the problem of comparing differently sized markets, such ratings information is not readily available, and few scholars have taken the time to make such corrections.

A final drawback of using aggregate campaign expenditures as a measure of campaign advertising exposure is that such figures ignore the spending of noncandidate actors, including parties and interest groups. This has become an increasingly important limitation because "soft money" expenditures have skyrocketed over the past few years; even after the passage of the Bipartisan Campaign Reform Act (BCRA), interest group advertising continues to comprise a large share of political advertising, in part, through the efforts of "527" organizations. (See Chapter 5 for a more detailed description of interest groups that fall under the 527 label.) The bottom line is that researchers who make use of candidate spending measures as reported to the Federal Election Commission (FEC) may be fundamentally understating the extent of campaign spending in a race. Moreover, the error in the measure is likely systematic, not random, because both party and interest group spending is generally targeted at a small number of very competitive races (Herrnson 2001).

Archival Data

A second common approach to measuring the content of campaign messages makes use of archived political advertisements. For example, Finkel and Geer (1998), who estimated the effect of campaign tone on voter turnout, utilized a detailed content analysis of presidential advertisements obtained from the political commercial archives at the University of Oklahoma, as did Geer in his more recent work on negative ads (2006). Kahn and Kenney (1999) took this same approach in their study of negative advertising in U.S. Senate elections, while Kaid and Johnston (1991) used the Oklahoma archive to assess the negativity of presidential campaign advertising over time. If the goal is to describe the characteristics of the advertisements that a campaign produces, this approach is a good one. (Moreover, for historical analyses, this may be the only approach available.) But if one's purpose is to study the effects of advertising exposure— as Finkel and Geer and Kenney and Kahn sought to do—or even to describe the information environment, then this measure is of limited use. Specifically, even if archives have a complete collection of advertisements produced in a particular election—an assumption challenged by Jamieson, Waldman, and Sherr (2000, 7)—archival collections contain no information on how many times each ad was actually broadcast. By default, then, an advertisement that was aired one hundred times receives the same weight in analyses as an advertisement that was aired one thousand times. Indeed, some spots held by archives may never have been broadcast at all. Prior (2001) addressed this problem in one market by showing that substantive conclusions may depend on whether one examines advertisements aired or advertisements made. For instance, he found that Republican presidential advertising in Columbus, Ohio, in 1996 appeared much less negative when one examined each ad produced (essentially, weighting each equally) than when one examined the frequency with which each was aired.

Beyond questions of broadcast frequency, ad archives generally lack state- and market-level data on the geographical distribution of airings, necessitating the assumption that all voters in a given year were exposed to the same volume and mix of advertisements. As argued above with respect to campaign spending, this simply is not the case. Archival data do allow researchers to describe the content of advertisements produced, but they leave them unable to speak about the actual distribution of advertisements on the air or the effects of viewing these advertisements in a campaign context.

Ad Buys

Alternatively, some scholars have collected advertising data directly from television stations, examining station logs (legal documents used by stations and buyers for auditing purposes), billing invoices, or advertising purchase contracts. The advantage of this approach is that one can get a good sense of the volume and timing of ads aired in a given market during a campaign. Magleby (2001) is one of the few scholars who have measured advertising exposure by obtaining documents from television stations. To do so, he collaborated with researchers from across the country, each of which monitored advertising in a different competitive race by visiting local television stations.

This approach, however, has several drawbacks. Although station logs detail when an ad actually aired on a television station, our experiences have shown that they are not always made available to researchers. Billing invoices for candidates, which accurately report what was aired and the price paid for each ad, also frequently are omitted from a television station's public files. Moreover, because many interest group ads (and, before BCRA, party ads as well) were technically not counted as "electioneering," some stations omit billing invoices and contracts issued to political parties and interest groups.

Purchase contracts (or "buy sheets"), a third type of document, are agreements between buyers and stations to air ads. All stations must retain and make these documents available in their public files. The problem is that all advertisements listed on a purchase contract are not necessarily broadcast, nor broadcast in the time period indicated on the contract. Television stations often preempt a commercial's broadcast, a practice that especially is common close to the day of the election when candidates may engage in a price war for scarce commercial time.[1] And so while the ideal situation would be one in which a station keeps detailed invoices and logs for all candidate, party, and interest group activity, this is rarely the case.

Another major problem with collecting television station records is that the task is time-consuming and logistically difficult. While stations must make information on political buys available to the public, they will not provide information over the phone or post it on the Internet. Researchers must visit four or more individual stations in each market. If one is interested in a single campaign (and hence at most a handful of media markets), this approach may be tractable, but any analysis of multiple campaigns would require intensive data collection; such efforts—given more than 200 media markets in the United States—would be nearly impossible for a presidential campaign or for the universe of congressional campaigns. This limits the ability to generalize claims drawn from an analysis of a handful of television stations. In addition, television stations provide the researcher no information about the content of ads, making it impossible to say anything about the tone of the campaign or the issues mentioned.[2]

Experimental Manipulation

The three methods discussed above have been used both to describe the volume or content of political advertising in a campaign and sometimes, in turn, to estimate the effects of exposure to this advertising. Other methods bypass direct measures of the campaign information environment in their attempts to gauge the individual-level effects of advertising exposure.

Campaign advertising research has made sporadic but significant use of experimental design (Ansolabehere, Iyengar, Simon, and Valentino 1994; Ansolabehere and Iyengar 1995; Brader 2006; Clinton and Lapinski 2004; Garramone et al. 1990; Kahn and Geer 1994; Noggle and Kaid 2000; Valentino, Hutchins, and White 2002). The allure of experimentation is obvious: By enabling researchers to control which subjects are assigned to which treatments, the nature of the stimuli to which subjects are exposed, and the conditions under which such exposure takes place, experiments afford an unparalleled degree of internal validity. Moreover, by manipulating specific components of a stimulus, experimental researchers can achieve a high degree of specificity in the causal inferences they make. As Kinder and Palfrey argued in calling for more experimentation in political science, experiments offer an "unrivaled capacity . . . to provide decisive tests of causal propositions," and constitute "a tool of unexcelled power and precision" (1993, 11). In a series of elegantly crafted experiments, Ansolabehere and Iyengar (1995) manipulated very specific elements of fictional campaign advertisements to suggest that it is the negative tone and not some other feature of the ads (or, more broadly, of candidates or races) that leads to reduced voter turnout. In one experiment, subjects saw one of two ads, either a positive ad sponsored by a candidate or a negative ad attacking that candidate's opponent. The authors found that subjects exposed to the positive ad were more likely to express an intention to vote, had more confidence in the electoral process, and had higher levels of political efficacy.

As is well known, however, the clear advantages of experimentation are offset by obvious pitfalls. There is a direct tradeoff between internal validity, made possible by the rigorous control of the laboratory, and external validity, the ability to move outside the lab and beyond a particular experimental context in making inferences. Put simply, how a particular group of subjects responds to a particular set of stimuli is not in and of itself useful; experimental findings are useful only to the extent that they allow us to make inferences about processes that occur in the real world. For many questions—including some asked in the social sciences— the fit between what goes on in the laboratory and the analogous process in the real world may be close enough to draw meaningful inferences. When it comes to measuring the impact of campaign ad exposure, however, external validity may be so compromised that researchers must proceed with caution in drawing inferences on the basis of experimental findings. Specifically, there are concerns about the nature of the treatment, the setting in which the treatment is administered, and the measurement of the outcome variables of interest.

When it comes to the realism of the treatment, there are a number of issues. First, researchers must take care that the stimuli—the manipulated ads themselves—successfully mimic the kinds of spots that candidates and their allies are actually producing and broadcasting. This, of course, is easy enough to accomplish with modern digital editing techniques. Actual ads can be spliced and diced in convincing ways without doing too much damage to realism. This is done well in many studies. Second, in the real world ads are embedded in television shows—most often news broadcasts—and therefore experiments should not test spots in isolation. Once again, better studies are careful to present ads in the context of actual programming. A third issue, however, concerns the number, the intensity, and the pacing of the spots to which subjects are exposed. In the real world, people are exposed to a given spot dozens, even hundreds of times over the course of an increasingly long campaign period. In the lab, however, it is unusual to find subjects exposed to a spot more than a few times during an experiment. Thus, experiments must make inferences about overall exposure effects on the basis of spots seen only a handful of times (at best).

An additional concern emerges from the setting in which ad exposure typically takes place. The most common circumstance for encountering a political advertisement is in one's own living room, usually some time after dinner but before prime time. People see ads while they are sitting on couches or in favorite chairs, talking on the phone, chasing children or dogs or both, finishing a meal, or reading a magazine. In short, they encounter campaign spots while going about their own lives in their own homes. This is obviously a far cry from the relatively sterile, decidedly artificial environments in which even the best laboratory experiments are conducted. To be sure, researchers may take pains to alleviate such artificiality, providing couches, reading material, and doughnuts or other snacks in an effort to make the viewing experience as normal as possible. Moreover, with the advent of WebTV and other new technologies, researchers have the ability to deliver advertising and other stimuli to subjects in their natural environments. This is a potentially significant step forward, although scholars only recently have begun to take advantage of these opportunities. Of course, even such advances as these do nothing to address the issues just raised about the nature of the treatment itself.

In addition to concerns about the delivery of the experimental treatment, i.e., the independent variable, experimental approaches also raise questions about the validity of the outcome, or dependent variable. Particularly when researchers are interested in the effects of ad exposure on political behaviors such as voter turnout (or, for that matter, actual vote choice), it is difficult to find studies that go beyond hypothetical and prospective reports such as intended turnout. Obviously, there is reason to be concerned about subjects' ability to evaluate accurately and to report fairly the probability of future (especially hypothetical) behavior, and these concerns are exacerbated when such behavior is clearly subject to social desirability biases.

Using the Knowledge Network (KN) sample and technology, Clinton and Lapinski (2004) attempted to remedy some of these common pitfalls of experiments while retaining the power of randomized treatments to determine causality. The KN method, which involves a panel of randomly recruited respondents, enables researchers to expose a representative sample of potential voters (not just college students or those responding to an ad) to different sorts of political advertising in the comfort of their own homes. After showing actual political ads from the 2000 presidential campaign to a large sample of subjects, Clinton and Lapinksi found no evidence to support either the mobilization or demobilization hypothesis. This was the case both right after the treatment (seeing one, two, or no ads) when subjects were asked a vote intention question and when respondents were contacted again after the election and asked about their actual voting behavior. While the KN methodology should be lauded for enabling researchers to experiment with large random samples from the general population, it is hard to imagine that one or two commercials (no matter how good, bad, negative, positive, or emotional) would meaningfully influence one's voting behavior in a presidential race given the intense national news coverage such campaigns are given, not to mention tens of thousands of ads being aired in targeted markets.

Given these fundamental impediments to external validity, researchers engaged in the study of campaign advertising must find ways to move outside the laboratory. Indeed, this was the impulse behind Ansolabehere and Iyengar's blending of experimental and nonexperimental approaches. But leaving the laboratory involves real challenges, and, ultimately, many of the most common approaches suffer from their own fundamental limitations.

Individual-Level Recall

One method of measuring advertising exposure outside of the experimental laboratory asks survey respondents if they recall having viewed a political advertisement, and, if so, what the advertisement was about (Wattenberg and Brians 1999; Brians and Wattenberg 1996). The advantage of this approach is that it creatively measures the campaign environment by looking at a presumed effect of advertising exposure—the ability to recall the advertisement. Thus it is something of a "bottom-up" rather than a "top-down" measure. Although the approach has the potential for greater external validity than experimental studies, the internal validity of the recall measure is questionable, making it difficult to establish the causal chain connecting advertising exposure and behavior.

First, there is evidence that, in general, people's ability to recall a range of politically relevant information is poor (Niemi, Katz, and Newman 1980). This appears to hold true in the context of campaign advertising as well. Ansolabehere, Iyengar, and Simon (1999), for example, showed experimental subjects a series of ads and then, thirty minutes later, asked them to list the ads they had just seen. Over half of the subjects failed to recall the political ads they had been shown. Moreover, as adherents of on-line models of information processing would argue, even though a viewer may not recall an ad, it still may have had an effect on his or her evaluation of the featured candidate (Lodge, McGraw, and Stroh 1989).

Second, and more seriously, there is potential endogeneity between ad recall and political behavior (Ansolabehere, Iyengar, and Simon 1999). For example, while seeing campaign advertisements may influence one's probability of voting, one's propensity to vote may influence how much attention one pays to campaign messages (and, importantly, to which messages one attends). Similarly, as research on selective recall has shown (see Graber 2002), partisan predispositions and candidate preferences may affect differential recall of candidates' ads, as people may be more likely to recall ads on behalf of their preferred candidate (and more likely to recall them in more favorable terms) than ads aired on behalf of the opponent.

In addressing the problems of endogencity in recall measures, Ansolabehere, Iyengar, and Simon proposed a two-stage estimation procedure in an effort to control for "actual" exposure. Specifically, they built an instrument—purged of correlation with turnout—using three variables: the total number of GRPs aired in a state (assuming respondents not only were likely to be exposed to more ads but to a greater proportion of negative ads in a heavily targeted state), the date of interview (assuming that respondents interviewed closer to Election Day would have been exposed to a greater proportion of negative ads), and the day of the week (assuming that viewing patterns varied by day of week; 1999, 902). Although the authors are motivated by an important concern, if one examines the constituent parts of the measure, there are strong reasons to suspect that it is not a valid measure of exposure to negative advertising (see Goldstein and Freedman 2002).

First, there are few empirical or theoretical reasons to believe that aggregated GRP totals for a state over the course of the entire campaign are a good measure of individual-level exposure to negative advertising in a particular media market at a particular point during the campaign. Political advertising is bought at the market level, and it is often the case that markets in the same state are targeted at dramatically different levels. Second, there are problems in the way that Ansolabehere, Iyengar, and Simon uses GRPs, which are a proportional measure (as noted above, each ratings point represents 1 percent of the television sets in a market) that cannot be summed and averaged. Moreover, the GRP totals used by Ansolabehere, Iyengar, and Simon only measured campaign activity after Labor Day and thus did not include the significant amount of campaigning that went on in the spring and over the summer. A final problem with the instrument created by Ansolabehere's team is that it assumed that every voter in a particular media market was exposed to the same number of commercials. As we have already noted, this obviously is not the case.[3]

Other Proxy Measures

Because self-reported exposure to news media can be unreliable, Zaller (1992) and Price and Zaller (1993) argued that message reception (being exposed to a message and accepting it) could be best tapped by an individual's level of political awareness, as measured by a political information scale constructed from a set of factual questions about current events and leaders. In other words, they gave up on measuring exposure and used political knowledge questions to measure reception.

This measurement strategy may make sense when applied to messages from news media or to a total campaign environment, but it is less useful when applied to the specific case of political spot advertising. To measure the effect of television advertising, it is necessary to utilize a variable that measures exposure to and reception of television advertising. Knowing who Vladimir Putin and William Rehnquist are, for example, may have little relation to whether one watches television programs during which many campaign commercials typically air. Although it is possible that viewers may pick up such information while watching local news programs (during which many political ads are broadcast), advertising appears during many types of shows, including those unlikely to convey political information (game shows and afternoon talk shows, for example). Furthermore, even local news has a large and not necessarily sophisticated audience. Political

TABLE 3.1   Summary of Advantages and Disadvantages of Approaches to Measuring Advertising Exposure

Approach	Advantages	Disadvantages
Campaign spending	Easily available measure	Taps more than advertising Assumes equal exposure across individuals Costs not comparable across markets Ignores "soft" money
Archival data	Ad content available	Assumes each ad aired equal number of times No market-level data
Ad buys	One knows when and where spots aired	Purchase contracts don't necessarily reflect what aired Invoices and logs are not always available No information on ad content Collection is time consuming
Individual-level recall	"Real-world" measure	People forget much of what they see Endogeneity between recall and behavior
"Awareness" proxy	Demonstrated valid measure	Works better for political news than advertising
Experiments	High internal validity	Do not examine real behavior Low external validity

knowledge is a tenuous proxy for campaign ad exposure and overestimates the prior sophistication that likely is needed to receive a political ad.

Summary

Our goal here has not been simply to "go negative" on previous advertising research. Each of the six approaches that we have reviewed has contributed a great deal to what we know about campaign advertising, and each approach has guided us in our own thinking on the subject. Moreover, it is encouraging to see scholars using such a wide variety of approaches. As is apparent, though, each of the six approaches we have reviewed has decided advantages as well as disadvantages when it comes to describing the ad environment in a given election—and especially when it comes to estimating individual-level ad exposure in the real world. Ultimately, none of these methods is adequate to the task of making valid inferences about the impact of campaign advertising. That is one of the reasons why we wrote this book.

Table 3.1 summarizes our arguments about the advantages and disadvantages of existing approaches to measuring political advertising and its effects. In the following chapter, we introduce a relatively new source of information about television advertising: the Wisconsin Advertising Project tracking data. We describe the potential these data hold for studying the impact of advertising, and we demonstrate how to employ them to create a relative measure of individual-level ad exposure.

CHAPTER FOUR

Tracking the Volume and Content of Political Advertising

S INCE 2000, THE WISCONSIN Advertising Project has gathered, processed, coded, and made available to the scholarly community tracking data originally collected by TNS Media Intelligence/Campaign Media Analysis Group (CMAG).[1] This commercial firm specializes in providing detailed, real-time tracking information to corporate and political clients. Such information is employed by candidates and corporations seeking market-level information on where their opponents are advertising and what they are saying. It also enables candidates and corporations to verify that the ads they paid for indeed have been broadcast by a television station at the time promised.

These tracking data represent the most comprehensive and systematic collection on the content and targeting of political advertisements ever assembled for a given election. The data include two types of information. First, frequency information tells when and where ads aired with precise details on the date, time, market, station, and television show. Figure 4.1 illustrates the raw targeting information (in this case, a series of ads by the Bush campaign aired in March 2004).

Second, the data provide information about each ad's content, including text and images, in the form of a "storyboard" created by TNS Media Intelligence/CMAG for each unique ad. A storyboard from the same Bush ad is shown in Figure 4.2. The storyboard contains transcripts of all audio and a still capture of every fourth second of video.

TNS Media Intelligence/CMAG gathers such data by using a market-based tracking system, deploying "Media Watch" in each of the 100 largest media markets in the United States. In addition to all local advertising activity, these detectors track advertisements on the major national networks as well as national cable networks. The system's software recognizes the electronic seams between

	creative	market	spotleng	station	affiliat	date	airtime	programn	
199	PRES/BUSH FORWARD	Wilkes Barre	30	WBRE	NBC	12-MAR-2004	16:12:31	OPRAH WINFREY SHOW	S
200	PRES/BUSH FORWARD	Manchester, NH	30	WMUR	ABC	12-MAR-2004	16:24:04	OPRAH WINFREY SHOW	S
201	PRES/BUSH FORWARD	Ft. Myers	30	WINK	CBS	12-MAR-2004	16:24:25	OPRAH WINFREY SHOW	S
202	PRES/BUSH FORWARD	Toledo	30	WTVG	ABC	12-MAR-2004	16:24:56	PYRAMID	S
203	PRES/BUSH FORWARD	Harrisburg	30	WGAL	NBC	12-MAR-2004	16:25:38	OPRAH WINFREY SHOW	S
204	PRES/BUSH FORWARD	Burlington	30	WVNY	ABC	12-MAR-2004	16:26:19	WHO WANTS/MILLIONAIRE	S
205	PRES/BUSH FORWARD	Phoenix	30	KTVK	IND	12-MAR-2004	16:27:47	INSIDE EDITION	S
206	PRES/BUSH FORWARD	Orlando	30	WFTV	ABC	12-MAR-2004	16:33:11	OPRAH WINFREY SHOW	S
207	PRES/BUSH FORWARD	Pittsburgh	30	WTAE	ABC	12-MAR-2004	16:33:48	OPRAH WINFREY SHOW	S
208	PRES/BUSH FORWARD	Jacksonville	30	WJXX	ABC	12-MAR-2004	16:34:58	ELLEN DEGENERES SHOW	S
209	PRES/BUSH FORWARD	Las Vegas	30	KVBC	NBC	12-MAR-2004	16:37:07	HOLLYWOOD SQUARES	S
210	PRES/BUSH FORWARD	Wilkes Barre	30	WNEP	ABC	12-MAR-2004	16:37:38	WHO WANTS/MILLIONAIRE	S
211	PRES/BUSH FORWARD	Dayton	30	WHIO	CBS	12-MAR-2004	16:40:00	PYRAMID	S
212	PRES/BUSH FORWARD	Madison	30	WMTV	NBC	12-MAR-2004	16:41:09	JEOPARDY	S
213	PRES/BUSH FORWARD	Philadelphia	30	KYW	CBS	12-MAR-2004	16:41:17	NEWS	S
214	PRES/BUSH FORWARD	Detroit	30	WXYZ	ABC	12-MAR-2004	16:41:58	OPRAH WINFREY SHOW	S
215	PRES/BUSH FORWARD	Miami	30	WFOR	CBS	12-MAR-2004	16:48:07	OPRAH WINFREY SHOW	S
216	PRES/BUSH FORWARD	Paducah	30	WPSD	NBC	12-MAR-2004	16:48:38	WHO WANTS/MILLIONAIRE	S
217	PRES/BUSH FORWARD	Tucson	30	KGUN	ABC	12-MAR-2004	16:48:39	NEWS	S
218	PRES/BUSH FORWARD	Milwaukee	30	WTMJ	NBC	12-MAR-2004	16:48:40	NEWS	S
219	PRES/BUSH FORWARD	Columbus	30	WCMH	NBC	12-MAR-2004	16:51:33	ELLEN DEGENERES SHOW	S
220	PRES/BUSH FORWARD	Seattle	30	KING	NBC	12-MAR-2004	16:52:01	OPRAH+ WINFREY SHOW	S
221	PRES/BUSH FORWARD	St Louis	30	KSDK	NBC	12-MAR-2004	16:52:40	OPRAH WINFREY SHOW	S
222	PRES/BUSH FORWARD	Des Moines	30	WHO	NBC	12-MAR-2004	16:54:56	JEOPARDY	S
223	PRES/BUSH FORWARD	Burlington	30	WCAX	CBS	12-MAR-2004	16:55:00	KING OF QUEENS	S
224	PRES/BUSH FORWARD	Orlando	30	WKMG	CBS	12-MAR-2004	16:56:03	EXTRA ENTERTAINMENT MAG	S
225	PRES/BUSH FORWARD	Columbus	30	WBNS	CBS	12-MAR-2004	16:56:57	OPRAH WINFREY SHOW	S
226	PRES/BUSH FORWARD	Albuquerque	30	KRQE	CBS	12-MAR-2004	16:59:27	NEWS	S
227	PRES/BUSH FORWARD	Mobile	30	WEAR	ABC	12-MAR-2004	17:05:15	NEWS	S
228	PRES/BUSH FORWARD	Dayton	30	WDTN	ABC	12-MAR-2004	17:07:54	NEWS	S
229	PRES/BUSH FORWARD	Albuquerque	30	KOAT	ABC	12-MAR-2004	17:08:25	NEWS	S

Data View / Variable View

SPSS Processor is ready

FIGURE 4.1 Example of Advertising Targeting Data from TNSMI/CMAG

PRES/BUSH FORWARD

Brand: BUSH FOR PRESIDENT (B331)
Parent: BUSH FOR PRESIDENT COMMITTEE
Aired: 03/11/2004 - 03/13/2004
Creative Id: 3323470

[Bush] "Over the past three years, Americans have faced many serious challenges.

Now we face a choice. We can go forward with confidence, resolve,

and hope, or we can turn back to the dangerous illusion that terrorists are not

plotting and outlaw regimes are no threat. We can continue to create jobs, reform education,

and lower the cost of healthcare. Together, we're moving America

forward. I'm George W. Bush and I approved this message."

[Approved by President Bush and paid for by Bush-Cheney 2004, Inc.]

    AdDetector **tns**

www.PoliticsOnTV.com

Copyright 2004 TNS Media Intelligence/CMAG

 **tns** media intelligence./cmag

1- 866-559-CMAG

FIGURE 4.2   Example of Storyboard from TNSMI/CMAG

programming and advertising and identifies the "digital fingerprints" of specific advertisements. When the system does not recognize the fingerprints of a particular spot, the advertisement is captured and downloaded. Thereafter, the system automatically recognizes and logs that particular commercial wherever and whenever it airs.

The Wisconsin Advertising Project coded virtually every political advertisement broadcast in the top 75 markets in 2000 and in the top 101 media markets from 2001 to 2004. In this process, teams of coders documented the advertisement's tone (positive, negative, or contrast), objective (issue ad or election spot), and sponsorship (party, candidate, or interest group). The coders also recorded the issues raised in the ad, the presence of commonly used adjectives, and a number of other attributes. (The complete coding sheets for 2000 and 2004 can be found in Appendixes D and E.)

To create the complete dataset, the coded data from storyboards were merged with a larger dataset containing information about the market, time, and show on which every ad was broadcast. In the final dataset, the unit of analysis is the individual airing of a single ad, or a "broadcast instance." This means that a given ad produced by a campaign may appear dozens, even hundreds of times in the dataset. Each case also contains information about the date and time of the ad's airing, the television station and program on which it was broadcast, and the complete coding of its content.

These data improve on the six approaches to political advertisement analysis discussed in Chapter 3 in several fundamental ways. Because the unit of analysis is a broadcast instance, with information on the timing (both the day and time of day), the show on which it appeared, and the media market in which it aired, scholars can tell precisely how many ads (in whatever category of tone, sponsor, or other classification) aired on particular days in particular markets or were sponsored by particular political actors. These data can then be aggregated to the level of the unique ad, and by market, ad type, or other desired variable. As a result, we have the ability to provide a uniquely detailed, accurate portrait of campaign advertising at the market level.

Coding Advertising Tone

One of the most important codes was an indicator of ad tone: whether an ad was positive, negative, or contrast. In 2004, for example, 1,376,458 spots aired in federal races during the general election. Wisconsin Advertising Project coders assessed 40 percent as positive, 35 percent as completely focused on the opponent ("pure" negative), and 25 percent as contrast ads focused on both the sponsor and his or her opponent. Ads in the presidential race were significantly more negative than ads in House and Senate contests. Over four in ten (42 percent) ads aired in the presidential race were pure negative ads, and over one in four (27 percent) were contrast spots.

Figures 4.3, 4.4, and 4.5 provide three examples of ads that were coded as contrast. The first is an ad aired by John Kerry's campaign that talks about the problems faced by working families under President Bush. The second one, aired by Democratic Senate candidate Ken Salazar in Colorado, paints his opponent, Pete Coors, as out of touch. The third ad was broadcast by Tim Michaels, a Republican Senate candidate from Wisconsin, who criticizes his opponent's

PRES/KERRY JOHNSTOWN

Brand:	KERRY FOR PRESIDENT (B331)
Parent:	KERRY FOR PRESIDENT COMMITTEE
Aired:	09/09/2004 - 09/10/2004
Creative Id:	3545543

[Announcer]: In 2000, George Bush never bothered to come to Johnstown.

Now he's here promising to "take the side of working families."

But, we know what matters: facts not promises. Healthcare costs are skyrocketing

and family wages are down $1500 dollars. It's time for a new direction.

John Kerry: a real plan to cut middle class taxes and reduce healthcare

costs. John Kerry: stronger at home, respected in the world.

[Kerry]: "I'm John Kerry and I approved this message. [PFB]: Kerry-Edwards '04 Inc.

AddDetector

www.PoliticsOnTV.com

Copyright 2004 TNS Media Intelligence/CMAG

1-866-559-CMAG

FIGURE 4.3   John Kerry Contrast Ad

support for abortion rights. Despite drawing contrasts between the candidates, these spots clearly have significant negative content.

It is worth noting that, unlike scholars who look at the mix of positive and negative "statements" (Finkel and Geer 1998; Geer 2006) or "idea units" (Jamieson, Waldman, and Sherr 2000), we focus here on the ad itself as the unit of analysis. Any negative statement about an opponent resulted in a spot being coded as either a contrast or a pure negative ad. We think such an approach makes particular sense when one is making causal inferences about the impact of an ad, as viewers are more likely to think about an ad in more or less global terms rather than in terms of its constituent parts (although the two measures are clearly

USSEN/CO SALAZAR MIDDLE CLASS

Brand:	POL-US SENATE (B332)
Parent:	POLITICAL ADV
Aired:	09/24/2004 - 09/25/2004
Creative Id:	3566474

[Coors]: "I don't know what a common man is." [Announcer]: And that's Pete Coors problem. He doesn't understand

that middle class families are stuggling with high health care costs. [Coors]: "I don't know what a

common man is." [Announcer]: Coors has no plan to lower drug costs and opposes

letting you buy cheaper drugs from Canada. Ken Salazar disagrees,

he's got solutions that really help people. As Attorney General,

he's already shown the guts to take on the big drug companies for price fixing, and won.

That's experience money just can't buy. [Salazar]: "I'm Ken Salazar and I approved this message." [PFB: Salazar for Senate]

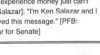

FIGURE 4.4 Ken Salazar Contrast Ad

USSEN/WI MICHELS ABORTION

Brand:	POL-US SENATE (B332)
Parent:	POLITICAL ADV
Aired:	10/15/2004 - 10/17/2004
Creative Id:	3595719

[Michels]: "I'm Tim Michels and I approved this ad. Our Senator is attacking me for being pro-life.

I was in the delivery room when our three children were born and I believe that every life is precious.

Congress isn't deciding whether to keep abortion legal, but they are considering

laws that would stop abortion as late as the 9th month. Senator

Feingold voted seven times against the ban on partial birth abortion,

he even voted against a law which would make it illegal to kill an unborn baby

during a violent crime. Senator, you're right we do have different beliefs." [PFB: Tim Michels for US Senate]

FIGURE 4.5 Tim Michels Contrast Ad

related). Consistent with this argument, when our coders were not given the "middle" choice of contrast in a randomly selected selection of 100 spots from the 2000 and 2004 elections, in 88 percent of the cases they coded the spot as negative. In other words, contrast ads contained a mix of positive and negative statements, but they almost universally were deemed negative by coders.

Creating an Exposure Measure

Advertising tracking data do an excellent job of describing the volume, content, and timing of political advertising in a given media market. In the following chapter, we employ these data to understand how advertising is targeted, using advertising volume and tone as dependent variables to be explained. Still, our ambition in this book is loftier: We seek to examine the effects of advertising on individual-level attitudes and behavior. Our primary objective is to understand the effect of advertising as an independent variable, not simply as an outcome. In the following section, we demonstrate how we employ—and how future scholars can use—the Wisconsin Advertising Project data to create a measure of individual-level exposure. We use this basic method in subsequent chapters to examine how political advertising affects individual behavior.[2]

The Wisconsin Advertising Project dataset records the media market in which each spot aired, allowing us to aggregate the data to that level. Given an interest in a certain type of advertisement (positive ads, or ads by a particular sponsor, for example), one can determine how many spots of that type aired in each media market. And provided that surveys contain information on respondents' zip codes, counties of residence, or area codes, one can effectively determine the number of ads aired in the viewing location of most survey respondents. The potential therefore exists to create very specific exposure measures—exposure to party negative ads versus candidate negative ads, for example.

The aggregate market-level counts can be thought of as the upper limit on the number of ads a respondent possibly could have seen over the course of the campaign. However, it is obviously unrealistic to assume that every respondent in a given media market has seen every ad aired during a campaign. Even in an era of bowling alone or not at all (Putnam 2000), people do take part in activities other than television watching. Moreover, even while watching television, few people can watch more than one channel at a time. And while some people watch a great deal of television, others watch very little or even (gasp!) none at all. Thus, to operationalize an effective exposure measure that will differentiate among viewers in a given media market, one needs additional information on the viewing habits of each respondent.

Such information can come in multiple forms. Many surveys, for example, include questions about television watching in general or attention to news programs in particular. But the most useful television-viewing questions ask about

TABLE 4.1   General Election Campaign Ads by Television Program, 2000 and 2004

2000		2004	
Show	Number of ads	Show	Number of ads
Local news	294,376	Local news	513,715
the *Today Show*	29,934	the *Today Show*	49,171
Good Morning America	24,876	*Good Morning America*	38,650
the *Early Show*	15,933	the *Early Show*	28,837
Wheel of Fortune	12,999	*Jeopardy!*	21,186
Jeopardy!	11,778	*Wheel of Fortune*	20,881
the *Oprah Winfrey Show*	11,292	the *Oprah Winfrey Show*	20,162
Live with Regis and Kelly	10,205	*Dr. Phil*	19,658
Judge Judy	10,036	*Live with Regis and Kelly*	18,797
Nightline	9,357	*Judge Judy*	13,910
Other programs	239,820	Other programs	477,663
Total	670,606	Total	1,222,630

Note: 2000 data based on ads broadcast in the 75 largest media markets; 2004 data based on ads broadcast in the 100 largest media markets.

the frequency with which respondents watch the television shows on which campaign advertising actually airs. As Table 4.1 illustrates, the majority of general election campaign advertising in the presidential, U.S. House, and U.S. Senate races in 2000 was broadcast on a relatively small number of shows. A plurality of all ads—more than 43 percent—was broadcast on local news programs, and another 10.5 percent were broadcast during local slots on the network morning news shows (the *Today Show, Good Morning America,* and the *Early Show*). An additional 4 percent of advertising appeared on *Jeopardy!* and *Wheel of Fortune* (which, in many markets, constitute the transition between local news and the much more expensive prime-time programming), and four other shows (the *Oprah Winfrey Show, Live with Regis and Kelly, Judge Judy,* and *Nightline*) were home to at least 1 percent of total advertising (no other single show on television garnered as much as 1 percent). All told, these ten sources of programming accounted for 64 percent of all federal campaign ads in 2000 (patterns of advertising in nonfederal races were not much different, particularly in their reliance on local news).

And the story was not much different in 2004, when the advertising data expanded from the top 75 media markets to the top 100. As a consequence, and because advertising in general was more abundant in 2004, general election ad totals were double those of 2000. At the same time, however, nearly the same proportion of ads in 2004 aired during local news broadcasts (42 percent). And the top ten programs were nearly identical, except for the inclusion of *Dr. Phil* and the fact that *Jeopardy!* passed *Wheel of Fortune* in the rankings.

Given the concentration of campaign advertising, survey instrumentation can be designed to measure respondents' propensity to view particular shows, and this is precisely the approach taken by a variety of surveys over the last two cycles, including four used in this book: the 2000 American National Election Studies (ANES), the 2000 DDB Needham[3] "Life Style Study," the University of Wisconsin–Brigham Young University 2004 Election Panel Study, and the 2004 DDB Needham "Life Style Study." For example, in 2000, ANES asked respondents how many times a week they watched *Wheel of Fortune* or *Jeopardy!;* local news (with separate questions for the early and late news); morning news programs such as the *Today Show, Good Morning America,* and the *Early Show;* and daytime talk shows like the *Oprah Winfrey Show.* The other three surveys had a very similar instrumentation for media consumption; Appendix C has the precise coding and questions for the variables used in each survey.

To create our measure of advertising exposure, we first assigned every survey respondent to his or her correct media market using county-of-residence information. Using the tracking data, we then created a file that contained the total number of ads aired in each market during the specific programs that the survey asked viewership questions about (along with those aired on all other shows). This file was then merged with the survey dataset, so that for every respondent there was information on the total number of ads seen on each show in that respondent's media market. We re-scaled the viewership questions to a 0 to 1 interval and multiplied each by the number of ads of particular types aired during the corresponding show. To account for the fact that most viewers do not watch multiple television stations at once, we divided the number of ads aired on the morning, evening, and late evening news show categories by three. (Without this adjustment, the substantive results reported in later chapters would be largely the same.) For those shows with no corresponding exposure question (comprising about a third of all spots broadcast in 2000 and 2004), we used mean viewership as an indicator of general television watching and multiplied this by ads aired on other shows. We then summed results of individual estimates. For example, exposure to all campaign ads in 2000 is measured as:

(number of ads during *Jeopardy* in respondent's market * *Jeopardy* viewing)
+ (number of ads during *Wheel of Fortune* * *Wheel of Fortune* viewing)
+ (number of talk show ads * daytime talk show viewing)
+ (number of morning news ads / 3 * morning news program viewing)
+ (number of early evening news ads / 3 * early evening news viewing)
+ (number of late evening news ads / 3 * late evening news viewing)
+ (number of ads aired during all other programs * mean television viewing)

Because we expect the marginal impact of advertising to decline as people see more ads, in the analyses in this book we take the natural log of our exposure measure. Figure 4.6 depicts the distribution of total ad exposure (between June 1 and Election Day) for respondents in the 2000 American National Election Study. The distribution of exposure appears to be fairly normal except for the large number of respondents (about one-third of the sample) who had no

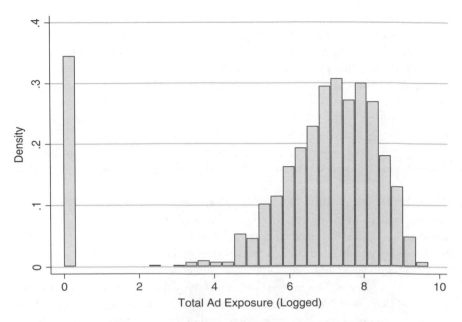

FIGURE 4.6   Distribution of Individual-Level Ad Exposure, 2000 ANES

exposure to advertising at all, either because no ads were aired in their market or they reported watching no television.

Three points are worth noting. First, most surveys do not ask questions about viewing habits for specific television programs. This makes estimating exposure more difficult and less powerful, although not impossible. One substitute for using a battery of show-based measures is to ask about average levels of television viewing, ideally at specific times during the day, referred to in the industry as "dayparts" (Freedman and Goldstein 1999).

Second, our exposure estimate is most appropriately interpreted as a relative measure of advertising exposure. It is most useful for comparing estimated levels of exposure across respondents, rather than saying with certainty precisely how many ads a respondent saw. This is the case primarily because, although a respondent may report regularly watching *Wheel of Fortune,* there is no guarantee that he or she was watching on the evening when a particular ad was aired. Similarly, we have no way of knowing whether a given viewer actually paid attention to a given ad (or ads in general). In the aggregate, we expect such sources of error to be distributed more or less randomly, without disproportionately affecting certain types of respondents or exposure to particular types of advertising.

The final point to note is that the tracking data allow for estimating exposure up to the date of the survey interview. For postelection surveys, this would include all advertising during the course of the election. For preelection interviews, a more precisely tailored measure is possible. If a respondent was interviewed thirty days before Election Day, for example, the data allow one to construct a measure of exposure that excludes ads broadcast after the date of interview.

Thus, these data present researchers with a number of opportunities to test hypothesized links between ad exposure and political attitudes and activity, while avoiding many of the fundamental obstacles inherent in the approaches discussed in the last chapter.

Addressing Potential Critiques

Despite these clear strengths, the Wisconsin Advertising Project tracking data are still imperfect, and there are also issues raised by the combined exposure measures.

One potential criticism of the tracking data is that they are not comprehensive. The TNS Media Intelligence/CMAG system currently tracks advertising in only the 100 largest of the 210 media markets in the United States. These 100 markets cover 86 percent of the television-viewing households in the country (Nielsen Media Research 2002). In 2001, the system tracked advertising in the eighty-three largest television markets, and in 2000 and earlier years the company recorded advertising in the nation's top seventy-five media markets. These seventy-five markets cover 80 percent of the U.S. population, and although there are gaps in CMAG's coverage of the country—advertising in the hotly contested 2002 South Dakota Senate race went untracked, for example—the vast majority of respondents in any nationally representative poll will fall under the system's tracking umbrella. However, for some purposes there may be biases due to noncoverage. For example, people who live in smaller, uncovered media markets are also more likely to live in rural communities and are less likely to live in large cities.

A second line of concern involves questions of validity and reliability. To what extent do the tracking data reflect what was actually aired during the course of a campaign? Would one get the same results by visiting television stations and digging through their logs or billing invoices? And when it comes to coding, would different coders looking at the same ads arrive at similar conclusions? In Appendix A, we report the results of an extensive investigation into the validity of the tracking data. We visited eight television stations in five different media markets to compare tracking data with station logs. In addition, Appendix B reports on a series of analyses of the reliability of our coding of the storyboards. We asked five undergraduate students to recode a sample of ads on several different characteristics. Although agreement with the original coding was not perfect, agreement was high in terms of ad tone, especially for ads originally coded positive. Moreover, agreement was high on other questions, such as whether the candidate narrates his or her own ad.

There are also some legitimate concerns about the validity of individual-level exposure measures like the ones we employ in our analyses and models in this book. For instance, one component of the measure—television viewing—depends on the accuracy of respondent recall, something we expressed doubts about earlier. Several factors, however, lead us to conclude that the recall of television-show viewing is much more accurate than recall of political advertising would be. First, the act of watching a television program is usually intentional, and therefore it is more amenable to recall than the inadvertent exposure to media content such as specific campaign advertising. Second, most television programs last thirty or sixty minutes, in contrast to the thirty or sixty seconds of the typical candidate ad. Moreover, television watching is often a regular and recurring activity, while exposure to a political spot is not. Watching particular programs is part of people's daily or weekly routines, and thus they are more likely to be recalled. Put simply, people should more accurately recall television watching—behavior that they seek out and engage in regularly—than advertising content that they neither deliberately choose nor encounter on a predictable basis.

It is also worth noting that Price and Zaller, two of the main critics of measures of self-reported media use, acknowledged that "it is still possible that they are valid and reliable indicators of simple exposure, even if not of actual reception" (1993, 159). This statement is encouraging given that our purpose in inquiring about media use is not to tap whether people received messages from the media, but to measure potential exposure to advertising when they turned on the television.

Another possible concern with our individual-level measure of advertising exposure is potential endogeneity between watching certain programs and the attitudinal or behavioral outcomes of interest. To the extent that heavy viewers of certain television shows (local news in particular) are more likely to be well informed, highly educated, or especially interested in politics, if we were to find that exposure to advertising leads to increased political information or engagement it could be an artifact of the measure itself. That is, people might appear to be more informed or interested not because of the impact of political advertising, but because informed people are more likely to be exposed to advertising by virtue of the shows they watch.

Fortunately, this is not the case. For the six sets of television shows that comprised our exposure measure in 2000, frequency of watching is positively correlated with a measure of general political information in only one case: evening television news. In three other cases, there is no relationship between political information and viewership, and watching *Wheel of Fortune* and daytime talk shows is negatively correlated with information. Similarly, only news viewership (morning, evening, and late night) is associated with campaign interest (and here only moderately, with correlations in the .15 to .20 range); watching the other shows has no relationship to interest whatsoever.[4] The weak association between local news viewing and campaign interest is not surprising, given the reasons most people watch television news: for information about crime, health, sports, weather, and community information (Pew Research Center 2002). Nevertheless, to be safe, we include local news viewing in our multivariate models in order to control for any remaining association. Finally, in every case, viewership declines with education. In short, we are unencumbered by concerns about selection effects in using these measures to estimate the impact of ad exposure on information and political engagement.

Admittedly, our measure of individual-level exposure to television advertising is not perfect. Some people may change the channel or mute the volume when a political advertisement comes on the air, and others may simply tune out. Our measure does not take into account such idiosyncratic behavior, but neither does any other measure. And reassuringly, a recent article that tested the validity of several measures of exposure to political advertising found that a measure very similar to the one we use in this book—a measure based on reported viewing of several types of television programs—performed the best of the six examined (Ridout et al. 2004). The article revealed that simpler measures of exposure, such as hours of television viewing or the total number of ads aired in a viewer's media market, failed to predict knowledge of facts mentioned in the advertising. But a more sophisticated show-based measure of the type we employ here was a robust predictor of such facts. Of equal importance, this measure did not predict people's knowledge of facts *not* contained within the advertising. These findings provide strong evidence for the validity of our exposure measure.

Finally, some have claimed that the relationship between competitiveness and advertising levels creates an endogeneity problem in which strategic decisions on when and where to advertise are tied to expectations about voter turnout. To get around this supposed problem, some scholars have pointed to a natural experiment made possible by the fact that media markets in the United States—which are where political advertising is bought—can cross state boundaries. This creates a situation in which some viewers or potential voters who normally would not be targeted for advertising in a race (because they live in an uncompetitive state) are hit with advertising targeted toward the competitive state (Krasno and Green 2005; Ashworth and Clinton 2005).

The Philadelphia market is a prime example. This top-ten market in terms of population not only contains viewers and potential voters in Philadelphia and eastern Pennsylvania, but in southern New Jersey and Delaware as well. Because Pennsylvania was a crucial and competitive state in both the 2000 and 2004 presidential elections, massive amounts of advertising were bought on Philadelphia television stations. New Jersey and Delaware were not competitive states, but because many residents of those states lived in the Philadelphia market, many of those states' residents were also exposed to massive amounts of advertising in the presidential races of 2000 and 2004. Of course, this also happens in down-ballot races. Residents of Philadelphia and eastern Pennsylvania were exposed to advertisements from the gubernatorial races in New Jersey in 2005, and northern New Jersey viewers were exposed to thousands of Clinton and Lazio for Senate ads in 2000 that they would not have seen if the media market maps were drawn to correspond to state borders. The difference is that in the presidential races, they were "mistakenly" exposed to ads that were for races they could vote in—uncompetitive ones, but ones with candidates on the ballot.

Endogeneity is certainly a concern when scholars study certain sorts of political activities such as individual-level voter contact. A key variable driving voter contact efforts is a campaign's assessment of a potential voter's probability of voting. To get around this problem when it comes to calculating the effect of voter contact activities, Gerber and Green (2001) executed a number of creative and large-scale field experiments. However, our conversations with campaign professionals and the shotgun method in which advertising is employed revealed that candidates do not target markets because of expectations about aggregate turnout. Rather, television advertising decisions are made on the basis of the distribution of voter preferences for a given (albeit usually not well-specified) level of turnout.

In other words, the problem is not endogeneity—television targeting decisions have little to do with expectations about aggregate turnout in a targeted area—but instead a need for competitiveness to be controlled for properly. As we show in the next chapter, a competitive race in a media market not only leads to more advertising (and more negative advertising), but competitiveness leads to other sorts of things that are likely to influence turnout as well. These include increased media coverage, voter canvass efforts, and greater discussion about the campaign—as well as the perception among potential voters that their vote is more likely to count.

Moreover, the natural experiment is not as clean as some would claim. It is not possible to say that the only difference between voters in the same media market who live in competitive and noncompetitive states is whether or not they saw advertising. Specifically, the fact that media markets cross state boundaries does not set up a situation in which we are able to isolate the relative effects of advertising and voter canvass activities. Like advertising, local news also crosses media markets, and residents of nonbattleground states are likely to see more "spillover" coverage of campaigns as well. It is also not valid to argue that all voters who live in a competitive state have the same likelihood of getting a get out the vote (GOTV) contact. Voter canvass efforts are not targeted at market level, but at the precinct, block, house, and individual level.

In sum, we believe that relative measures of exposure to television advertising can be developed that combine information on what was watched with what was aired. We also believe that endogeneity is not the issue. The other sorts of things that are correlated with increased advertising volume—candidate visits, amount of news coverage—can be included in our models, and variables measuring the closeness of the contest serve to "soak up" or control for the remaining influence of competitive races.

Summary

Whether and how election campaigns and political advertising matter have been the focus of enduring debate. Yet scholars are still far from a resolution to these questions, in part because they have lacked good measures of campaign activity. We have described the Wisconsin Advertising Project data as a basis for measuring the distribution of and exposure to political advertising. The approach has several advantages over other alternatives. In contrast to archival research, the approach allows one to gain an understanding of where, when, and to what extent a particular ad aired. And, in contrast to examining television station records, using tracking data involves much less collection effort and allows for content analysis of the advertisements that did air. The advantage of tracking data over measures of individual recall is the ability to construct measures of exposure based on objective data on ad airings, not the subjective—and error-prone—recollections of survey respondents. Finally, the tracking data outshine experimental methods when it comes to external validity.

In the remainder of this book, we employ Wisconsin Advertising Project data to help us answer questions about the impact of exposure to political advertising on people's levels of political information, their interest in politics, and their political participation. In the next chapter, we employ these data to better understand how strategic decisions are made in an advertising campaign, drawing lessons that we will use when we turn to studying effects.

CHAPTER FIVE

What, When, and Where

Making Sense of Campaign Advertising

O VER THE COURSE OF THE 2000 election season, 970,424 ads advocating for federal candidates aired in the top seventy-five media markets. In 2004, in these same markets, 1,050,630 ads aired on behalf
of presidential, Senate, and House candidates (over 600,000 of which were for
the presidential race). In the top 100 media markets for 2004 (as noted earlier, CMAG expanded its market coverage that year), nearly 1.4 million spots
aired. Ads in both years aired at all times of the day and during scores of different shows, and they were sponsored by candidates, parties, and independent
interest groups.

In order to understand the effects of exposure to all this campaign advertising, it is first necessary to explore the factors that determine the content and
influence the placement of all these ads. In this chapter, we treat political advertising as the dependent variable, focusing principally on the volume, tone,
and targeting of advertisements in the 2000 and 2004 elections. We ask what
factors shaped the ad environment that voters confronted, exploring the roles
of competitiveness, sponsorship, timing, and what we refer to as the "total ad
environment." From these findings, we draw a number of important lessons for
the study of campaign advertising.

Competitiveness

As discussed previously, many studies have looked at campaign advertising using
national-level measures, essentially placing all citizens in the same political context (e.g., Finkel and Geer 1998; Kaid and Johnston 1991). Political advertising,
however, is never evenly distributed throughout the country. There is wide and
systematic variation when it comes to the mix and level of ads broadcast. To a

very large extent, this variance is a function of the degree of political competition in a given media market. More competition almost inevitably means more ads.

As a result, in 2000 and 2004, citizens in different markets were exposed to strikingly different campaigns. Throughout the course of the 2000 campaign in San Antonio, for example, seldom was heard a discouraging ad—or any political ad at all, for that matter. Only 531 election ads were aired during the entire year in the Alamo City. Similarly, Wichita, Oklahoma City, and Baltimore were each home to fewer than 2,000 broadcast political spots during the course of the entire 2000 campaign. What do these markets have in common? They were all in states that were clearly safe for either George W. Bush or Al Gore, and they were all devoid of competitive Senate races.

In contrast, other markets in 2000 drew saturation levels of advertising for months before Election Day. The top markets for election advertising in the country were in states that were not only in play in the presidential race, but that had competitive Senate races and often closely contested House races as well. In 2000, such "perfect storm" markets included Seattle (22,120 general election spots aired), Detroit (21,835), Kansas City (20,528), St. Louis (20,461), Philadelphia (19,347), Spokane (18,406), Flint (18,135), and Grand Rapids (17,341). In Michigan, it was Spencer Abraham versus Debbie Stabenow; in Missouri, John Ashcroft faced Mel Carnahan and then his widow, Jean; and in Washington State, Slade Gorton was successfully challenged by Maria Cantwell. Philadelphia not only drew presidential advertising as a key swing state, but also as a home market for hard-fought Senate races in Pennsylvania, New Jersey, and Delaware. Similarly, New York City made it into the top-twenty most heavily advertised markets (with nearly 16,000 general election spots aired) not because of the presidential race there—there really was none—but on the strength of advertising buys in the Franks–Corzine Senate race in New Jersey and the Clinton–Lazio race in New York.

This pattern holds true for advertising in 2004, albeit with a slightly different set of markets. Table 5.1 shows the top-twenty markets for general election advertising in 2000 and 2004; totals include all general election ads aired on behalf of federal candidates (including party and interest group spots). In 2004, top markets included Tampa (37,252 general election ads), Albuquerque (32,484), Denver (32,396), Las Vegas (32,000), Miami (31,703), and Philadelphia (28,050). Ad buys were so intense in these markets primarily because of the competitiveness of the presidential race, but also because of tight Senate races in Florida and Colorado and competitive House races in Colorado (an open seat to replace Scott McInnis), Nevada (Jon Porter's seat), and New Mexico (a rematch between incumbent Heather Wilson and challenger Richard Romero).

In Table 5.2, we report estimates from three multivariate models where the outcome variable is the number of ads aired in each market for each candidate in House and Senate contests, and the presidential races, in 2000 and 2004.

TABLE 5.1 Top Twenty Markets for General Election Advertising

2000		2004	
Market	Frequency	Market	Frequency
Seattle–Tacoma	22,120	Tampa	37,252
Detroit	21,835	Albuquerque	32,484
Kansas City	20,528	Denver	32,396
St. Louis	20,461	Las Vegas	32,000
Philadelphia	19,347	Miami	31,703
Spokane	18,406	Philadelphia	28,050
Flint	18,135	Orlando	27,860
Grand Rapids	17,341	Milwaukee	27,445
Albuquerque–Santa Fe	17,124	Cleveland	26,321
Orlando	16,767	Green Bay	26,253
Wilkes Barre	16,565	Jacksonville	25,375
Tampa	16,027	Colorado Springs	25,037
Miami–Fort Lauderdale	15,795	Portland, OR	24,902
New York	15,668	Madison, WI	24,330
West Palm Beach	15,444	Toledo	23,748
Louisville	15,433	Cincinnati	23,459
Little Rock–Pine Bluff	14,391	Pittsburgh	21,684
Lexington	14,115	Charleston	21,478
Pittsburgh	12,960	Columbus	21,433
Portland, OR	12,781	Wilkes Barre	20,736

TABLE 5.2 Prediction of Ad Volume

	House	Senate	President
Competitiveness	1140.165 (83.45)*	1220.13 (223.26)*	4611.35 (385.40)*
Democrat	–25.50 (74.65)	221.57 (175.13)	997.42 (353.91)*
Incumbent	66.01 (85.45)	539.07 (214.18)*	—
Open seat	216.25 (108.13)*	1207.33 (261.83)*	—
Electoral votes	—	—	7.77 (14.56)
Margin of victory (previous election)	—	—	–33.78 (28.19)
2004	76.25 (75.44)	245.89 (180.33)	1511.91 (401.95)*
Constant	340.58 (90.65)*	438.73 (220.30)*	2174.40 (793.58)*
N	495	222	222
Adj. R-squared	0.3041	0.3423	0.5026

*$p < .05$—OLS estimates with standard errors in parentheses. Dependent variable is the number of all ads on behalf of a candidate; model excludes candidates with no advertising in the market.

We excluded races and candidates where there were no ads whatsoever. For House races, this excluded a significant number of House contests, as many candidates—because of either the inefficiency of airing television ads or the lack of a significant challenge—chose not to hit the airwaves. Almost all Senate seats (with CMAG coverage) had at least one ad aired on either the Republican or Democratic side, but the presidential candidates (and their party and interest group allies) skipped a significant number of media markets in our sample. Still, there was at least one presidential ad in more than fifty markets in 2000, and either John Kerry or George W. Bush was on the air in more than sixty markets in 2004.[1] Thus, the models were designed to demonstrate the determinants of ad volume, conditional on the presence of at least some minimal advertising activity.

We combined all general election ads from candidates, parties, and interest groups into our measure of ad volume, and we controlled for the competitiveness of the race (a dummy variable), the party of the favored candidate, whether the candidate was an incumbent (for the House and Senate models), and whether the race was for an open seat (for the House and Senate models).[2] For the presidential models, we added variables for the number of electoral votes in each state covered by the market and the presidential margin of victory in each market for the previous election.[3] We also included a dummy variable for 2004, using the 2000 election as the base category.

We included this set of variables to test competing hypotheses about what drives advertising volume. Do open seat House and Senate races see more advertising than races with an incumbent, as conventional wisdom would suggest? Do incumbents air more ads than challengers? And do Republicans flood the air with more ads than Democrats? In the presidential contests, we tested to see whether candidates hit the airwaves in the states with the richest return of electoral votes, whether they concentrated on markets that were tight in previous elections, or whether they aired a similar volume of ads in all markets (Geer 2006; Shaw 1999).

As the results from Table 5.2 demonstrate, competitiveness is the primary factor driving the level of political advertising. A Senate candidate in a competitive market aired, on average, more than 1,200 more ads than a Senate candidate in a noncompetitive market; a House candidate in a competitive market aired about 1,100 more ads than a candidate in a noncompetitive market; and the presidential candidates aired well over 4,000 more ads in competitive markets than they did in noncompetitive markets.

There are other significant findings across the three models. For example, Senate incumbents aired about 540 more ads (per market) than challengers, but candidates for open seats aired about 1,200 more ads than incumbents and candidates challenging an incumbent. This open-seat effect is also present in the House context, where open-seat candidates aired 216 more ads than all other candidates. In the presidential model, Democrats Gore and Kerry each aired nearly 1,000 more ads than Bush, all else equal. And presidential advertising was more abundant in 2004 (with over 1,500 more ads per market).

The importance of competitiveness speaks to the "bang for your buck" gained with each dollar spent on television advertising. As Shaw (2006) noted, in states with few electoral votes, for example, the cost of a presidential candidate's time of visiting the state in person can be very high, because the effect is amortized over fewer voters than in visits to larger states. With television advertising, however, that cost comes only in payment for the airing of the ad, and in smaller markets that cost will not be exorbitant. As such, presidential candidates stand to gain a lot by advertising in competitive states—especially small ones—where the price tag, both in candidate time and resources, is not significantly higher across geographical constituencies.

Competitiveness and Tone

Equally important, it is not only the volume of spots that varies by the competitiveness of races in particular markets. As Table 5.3 illustrates, the competitiveness of a race has a significant influence on the tone of advertising.

In competitive Senate races in 2000, there was a fairly even distribution in terms of the tone of ads, with 35 percent positive, 34 percent contrast, and 31 percent negative. In noncompetitive U.S. Senate races, more than two in three (69 percent) were positive, only 20 percent were contrast, and 11 percent were negative. For House races, competitive and noncompetitive races had roughly equal proportions of broadcast contrast ads, but competitive races had more than twice the proportion of negative ads (45 percent to 21 percent) and about half as

TABLE 5.3   Competitiveness and Tone in 2000 and 2004 Congressional Races

	2000		2004	
	Competitive	Noncompetitive	Competitive	Noncompetitive
House races				
Attack	45%	21%	44%	17%
Contrast	23%	18%	23%	20%
Promote	32%	61%	33%	63%
Total spots	161,270	54,359	95,253	89,582
Senate races				
Attack	31%	11%	27%	13%
Contrast	34%	20%	27%	18%
Promote	35%	69%	46%	69%
Total spots	149,834	51,752	119,082	76,209

Note: Includes all ads sponsored by candidates, parties, and interest groups; columns sum to 100%. Data in both years based on ads broadcast in the 75 largest media markets.

TABLE 5.4   Prediction of Percentage of Negative Ads in a Race

	House	Senate	President
Competitiveness	.203 (.035)*	.084 (.031)*	.014 (.054)
Democrat	−.036 (.026)	.001 (.023)	−.045 (.039)
Incumbent	−.117 (.030)*	−.042 (.029)	—
Open seat	−.096 (.038)*	.005 (.036)	—
Total ads (1,000s)	.043 (.016)*	.037 (.009)*	.001 (.007)
Electoral votes	—	—	−0.001 (.002)
Margin of victory (previous election)	—	—	.003 (.003)
2004	−.044 (.027)+	−.066 (.024)*	.083 (.045)+
Constant	.261 (.032)*	.134 (.020)*	.422 (.088)*
N	495	222	221
Adj. R-squared	.1802	.2576	.021

*$p < .05$; +$p < .10$—OLS estimates with standard errors in parentheses. Dependent variable is the proportion of all ads on behalf of a candidate that are negative; model excludes candidates with no advertising in the market.

many positive ads (32 percent to 61 percent). These proportions held in 2004, where 44 percent of competitive House ads were negative, and competitive Senate ads were twice as negative as ads in noncompetitive races (27 percent to 13 percent).

We report in Table 5.4 the results of three multivariate models (for House, Senate, and presidential races) predicting the percentage of ads aired that are negative (total negative ads are the numerator; negative, contrast, and positive ads are the denominator). We controlled for the same variables as in the volume models from Table 5.1; the unit of analysis was a candidate in a media market.[4] We also added a variable that controlled for the total volume of the ads for the candidate in the market (the dependent variable from Table 5.1). The results demonstrate that the competitiveness of the race drives up negativity in both House and Senate contests. More specifically, competitive House candidates were about 20 percent more negative than noncompetitive candidates, and competitive Senate races were about 8 percent more negative.

A number of the other variables are also significant. In the House context, incumbents (by almost 12 percent) and open-seat candidates (by about 10 percent) were less negative than those candidates challenging an incumbent. And as ad volume increased, negativity went up (for every 1,000 ads aired in the media market, the candidate was about 4 percent more negative). Interestingly, House races in 2004 were about 4 percent less negative than in 2000. In the Senate context, ad volume again predicted higher levels of negativity (by about 4 percent per 1,000 ads aired), and candidates in 2004 were about 6 percent less negative than candidates in 2000.

There appears, however, to be no relationship between tone and competitiveness in the presidential race, although we are not particularly surprised by such a finding. In general, negativity for presidential candidates tends to be part of a more national strategy, as opposed to a market-by-market phenomenon (unlike ad volume, as reported earlier). As such, the importance of competitiveness in predicting tone seems rooted in House and Senate races. The only significant effect ($p < .10$) for the presidential model was the dummy variable for 2004, which indicated that Bush and Kerry were about 8 percent more negative than Bush and Gore in 2000 (this is counter to the trend in the 2004 House and Senate races, where negativity appeared to decline, all else equal). In truth, however, the pooled data for the presidential model masked some important variation within each year. When looking at the data for each election separately, we found that Gore had a higher percentage of negativity than Bush (about 23 percent), but Bush was significantly more negative than Kerry (by about 35 percentage points, all else equal).

These findings have important implications for studies of tone and turnout. Because competitive races are also more likely to draw increased campaign activity and increased voter interest, it is crucial for studies of turnout to take into account the competitiveness of races. If they do not, the higher turnout that comes about in competitive races could be spuriously attributed to increased negativity. Put differently, a negative campaign can obscure the effects of electoral competition.

Sponsorship

Although candidates themselves aired the majority of spots in the 2000 and 2004 campaigns, parties and interest groups were active players in many contests. The previous discussion combined candidate, party, and interest group ads into two dependent variables (total ad volume for candidates in different markets, and the percentage of that volume that was negative), but it is critical to recognize the great diversity of ad sponsorship in many campaigns. Sponsorship of ads has become one of the enduring controversies surrounding debates over campaign finance reform.

A little background on the issue is in order. Before passage of the Bipartisan Campaign Reform Act of 2002 (BCRA), parties and interest groups could raise unregulated and unlimited amounts of "soft money," funds that could be used in advertisements that mentioned or pictured federal candidates, but did not expressly advocate their election or defeat. These amounts were over and above the standard "hard money" expenditures that were (and remain) tightly regulated by campaign finance law.

For parties, the use of these funds was intended to build the party's image and help spread partisan (but not candidate-specific) messages; for interest groups, soft-money provisions were intended to allow interest groups to make political and issue-based (but again, not candidate-specific) messages intended to educate or mobilize citizens for or against policies or issues. The standard used to distinguish hard and soft money public communications developed into a "bright-line" test based on whether the communication mentioned so-called "magic words."[5] For ads without these magic words, money raised outside the limits of campaign finance laws was permitted—thus allowing parties to raise, and interest groups to spend, millions from corporate and labor union treasuries (Herrnson 2004, Corrado 2005).

In the elections between 1996 and 2002, parties and interest groups used this method, simply avoiding the use of magic words, to fund advertisements for or against candidates; hence, ads that urged citizens to call or contact a politician became more frequent than ads telling citizens to vote for or against a candidate.[6] Indeed, soft money ads became so commonplace, they often surpassed the use of hard (or regulated) money in competitive congressional races (Magleby and Monson 2004, specifically Chapter 1). All told, parties broadcast 34 percent and interest groups aired 10 percent of all campaign spots in federal contests in 2000. Interest group and party activity comprised an even greater proportion of spots aired in competitive races. For example, in the forty-five most competitive House races in 2000, candidates aired fewer than half the spots. Parties aired 33 percent and interest groups aired 21 percent of spots in these competitive House races.

All of this was supposed to change with the passage of the BCRA.[7] First, the new law banned parties from using soft money in federal elections (except for a small $10,000 exemption for voter mobilization, known as Levin Funds). This shifted the fund-raising strategies of parties from raising hundreds of millions in soft money (often from a few large donations) to intense hard-money solicitation (from thousands of small donations). According to FEC reports, Democrats raised over $580 million in hard money in the 2004 election cycle, and Republicans raised over $630 million. Both totals exceeded the parties' combined hard- and soft-money fund-raising in 2000 ($450 million total for the Democrats and $611 million for the GOP). This change in the source of party money was an intended effect of the new law.

Second, for interest groups, the "magic word" test was replaced with a candidate-mention test, where the new distinction between issue and express advocacy was whether the ad mentioned or pictured a candidate for federal office. In addition, any interest-group-sponsored ad airing within sixty days of the general election or thirty days of a primary had to be funded with hard money.

The intention behind the party-soft-money ban and the new rules on interest-group express advocacy was to reduce the level of unregulated money in federal elections. It also was meant to force interest groups and parties to fund election season ads with regulated and publicly disclosed hard money. But, as with all things involving campaign finance, new "loopholes" developed. Most notably, interest groups with a specific IRS classification, known as Section 527 groups, exploded on the political scene.

Section 527 classification is a broad category encompassing all campaign organizations with a stated political purpose (including FEC-registered political action committees [PACs], and candidate campaign committees), but some 527s have carved out a special place that allows the continued use of unregulated soft money for issue advocacy close to Election Day. These are 527s that only raise money from individuals, have no stockholders, and proclaim a primary interest in issue (not candidate) advocacy (Weissman and Hassan 2005). For these groups, soft money ads that mention or picture candidates are permissible, though "magic word" ads are not.

The most famous of these 527s in 2004 was probably the Swift Boat Veterans for Truth. According to IRS reports, Swift Boats raised nearly $26 million in 2004, and they spent almost every penny on campaign activities attacking the Vietnam War record of Democrat John Kerry. This included over 6,600 ads aired in August, September, and October.

Despite the flood of media reports that elevated the profile of the group's claims, however, their ad buys paled in comparison to pro-Kerry 527s. The Media Fund, for example, aired over 50,000 ads attacking Bush and supporting Kerry, and MoveOn.org sponsored over 37,000.[8]

The larger message for this analysis is that the sponsorship of political ads changed with the passage of BCRA, but this in no way eliminated the presence of parties and interest groups in the air war. These patterns are evident in Figures 5.1 and 5.2, where we show the nationwide sponsorship of Gore, Kerry, and Bush ads in the last two presidential elections.

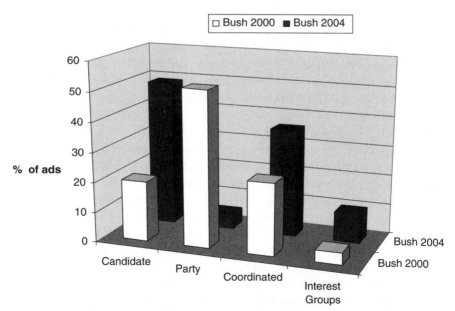

FIGURE 5.1   Sponsorship of Bush Advertising

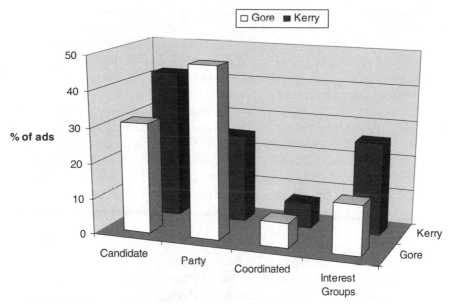

FIGURE 5.2   Sponsorship of Gore and Kerry Advertising

As the figures make clear, the Bush and Gore campaigns in 2000 had different patterns of ad sponsorship. Over half the ads (52 percent) aired on behalf of Bush in 2000 were paid for by the Republican National Committee. And although it is difficult to identify the exact mix of funds that were used to pay for these ads, most of it was certainly from soft-money sources. In contrast, the Bush–Cheney campaign committee aired only one in five of the spots that were broadcast in support of the Texas governor's candidacy. Another 24 percent were aired in coordinated fashion using hard party money and funds from the candidate. Notably, interest groups were not major players for the Bush campaign in terms of the television air war, airing only 4 percent of all Bush ads.

It was a different story on the Gore side, where the former vice president's interest-group allies aired 14 percent of all the ads that were broadcast in support of his campaign. The two biggest interest-group supporters of the Gore campaign in terms of spot advertising were Planned Parenthood and the AFL-CIO, broadcasting 5,851 and 5,320 spots respectively. For the Democratic candidate, party expenditures also exceeded the amount spent by the actual campaign, with the Democratic National Committee sponsoring nearly half (48 percent) of the ads aired for the Democratic presidential ticket and the Gore–Lieberman campaign paying for slightly more than three in ten spots (31 percent).

Four years later there were different patterns of sponsorship for both major candidates. Bush sponsored nearly 50 percent of ads favoring his candidacy. Party-sponsored spots plummeted to fewer than 5 percent, while coordinated ad buys (involving the party but still controlled by the Bush campaign) jumped to about 35 percent. Interest groups ads, of the Swift Boat variety, accounted for just fewer than 10 percent of pro-Bush ads. On the Kerry side, the pattern was somewhat similar—candidate-sponsored spots and interest-groups ads increased, while the share of party ads declined. A notable difference between the Bush and Kerry campaigns in 2004 was the lack of any significant coordinated campaign between Kerry and the Democratic Party.

The pattern was slightly different in House and Senate campaigns of 2004. Because of the high-profile presidential race, and because most observers expected control of Congress to remain in GOP hands, party and interest group presence in congressional races declined from 2000. For example, only 18 percent of 2004 Senate ads were sponsored by parties or interest groups (down from 27 percent in 2000), and only 26 percent of House ads were sponsored by parties and interest groups in 2004 (down from 39 percent four years earlier).

There is one final point. Sponsorship is also relevant for understanding the tone of campaign ad wars. Table 5.5 shows the distribution of general-election positive, negative, and contrast ads in 2000 and 2004 by sponsorship. As the table makes clear, the majority of candidate-funded ads in both years were positive (57 percent in 2000 and 2004). Party ads, however, tended to be contrasting or negative (only 25 percent of party-sponsored ads were positive in 2000; only 10 percent were positive in 2004), and a large majority of interest group ads were purely attack oriented (about 70 percent in both years). Notably, coordinated campaigns became more negative between 2000 and 2004: In 2000, 39 percent of the nearly 38,000 coordinated ads were positive; this declined to 17 percent in 2004. As such, the percentage of coordinated ads that were purely negative rose from 29 percent in 2000 to 44 percent in 2004.

TABLE 5.5   Tone of General Election Ads by Sponsor

Sponsor	Attack	Contrast	Promote	No. of airings
2000				
Candidates	14%	29%	57%	323,156
Parties	45%	31%	25%	229,722
Interest groups	70%	5%	25%	75,304
Coordinated party and candidate	29%	32%	39%	37,938
2004				
Candidates	20%	23%	57%	708,550
Parties	70%	20%	10%	210,203
Interest groups	73%	14%	13%	160,743
Coordinated party and candidate	44%	39%	17%	140,550

Note: Percentages are raw percents. 2000 data based on ads broadcast in the 75 largest media markets; 2004 data based on ads broadcast in the 100 largest media markets.

These data make a fundamentally important point: An accurate inventory of political advertising not only must include candidate-sponsored ads, but interest group, 527, and party advertising as well. This is important not only for describing the advertising environment of a given campaign, but also for making inferences about the impact of this environment on viewers.

Timing

Political advertising not only varies by the competitiveness of the race and by sponsorship, but in timing. While Labor Day has traditionally marked the start of the "fall campaign," tuning in to advertising in September means missing a great deal of crucial ad activity. To get an accurate reading of the complete information environment confronting voters means monitoring the airwaves far in advance of Labor Day. This is even more evident in the wake of campaign finance reform, because interest groups can still air issue-advocacy ads (with unregulated money) outside the sixty-day general election and thirty-day primary windows.

For example, in 2000 (when the sixty-day and thirty-day provisions were not yet law) only twenty-seven interest groups sponsored federal candidate ads before the sixty-day benchmark; they accounted for 17,064 spots, or 6.7 percent of all ads during the run-up to the fall campaign. In 2004, the total number of groups (airing ads before the sixty-day cutoff) rose to forty-three, accounting for 97,554 ads (or 20.2 percent of the ads aired). In contrast, advertising after the sixty-day cutoff actually declined for interest groups in 2004, from 12.4 percent of all ads in the fall of 2000 to just under 8 percent in the fall of 2004.

The early start is also evident in ads for the presidential candidates. In 2000, Gore and Bush (and their allies) were on the air throughout the summer (especially Gore, who aired about 2,500 ads a week beginning in June). And in 2004, with Kerry and Bush eschewing federal matching funds—thereby allowing them to spend their huge primary-election war chests before the conventions—the candidates flooded the air with general-election spots as early as mid-March.

To display these trends more clearly, Figure 5.3 shows the cumulative proportion of ads aired by week over the course of the 2000 and 2004 campaigns. The x-axis shows the number of weeks until the election, and the y-axis tallies the percentage of all election year ads aired up to that week. With about nine weeks until Election Day in both years—roughly when the sixty-day provisions of BCRA kick in—nearly 40 percent of all ads had already aired. The cumulative percentages in 2004 were a bit higher because of the issues noted above—a particularly early start to the presidential campaigning that year and interest-group adaptation to new rules on timing.

All told, then, the larger lesson is that studies of advertising must take into account the extended campaign period. If we just look at post–Labor Day advertising, we will not correctly gauge the volume or mix of advertising activity.

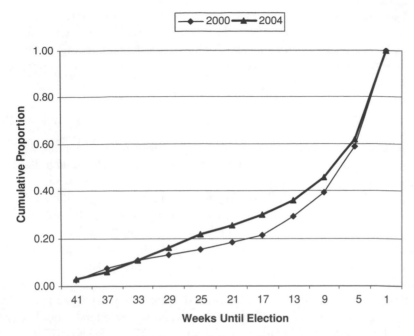

FIGURE 5.3   Cumulative Proportion of Ads by Week

Total Advertising Environment

Although crowded ballots are common to many states, election contests can vary
in competitiveness from state to state (and even within states), thus drawing more
or less advertising. As a result, a market that is uncompetitive in one contest might
be extremely competitive in another. In 2000, for example, the commonwealth of
Virginia saw no advertising from the presidential candidates, but it was deluged
with a flood of more than 25,000 ads from its hotly contested Senate race. The
same was the case in New York, where citizens were bombarded with thousands
of ads from the competitive Senate races in New York and New Jersey, but
they saw no presidential ads. By contrast, in Ohio and Wisconsin, the Senate
races were yawners, but citizens were targeted with high levels of presidential
advertising. The bottom line is that understanding advertising's effects (on voter
turnout, for example) demands that one take into consideration the full range
of electoral competition with which voters are confronted. Doing otherwise—
looking only at presidential advertising, for example—means risking significant
measurement error when it comes to descriptive and causal inferences about
political advertising.

Yet this simple fact has been consistently overlooked in the extensive literature on campaign advertising. For example, most empirical work on the impact
of campaign advertising on voter turnout has considered ads from only a single

race at a time. Whatever the methodology—experimental or survey based—
and regardless of whether researchers have taken into account the market- and
state-level nature of campaigns, previous scholarship has looked at discrete presidential, Senate, or gubernatorial elections without considering the cumulative
effects of multiple ads from multiple races (e.g., Finkel and Geer 1998; Goldstein
and Freedman 2002; Kahn and Kenney 2000).

This strategy may make sense when looking at the persuasive effects of ads
in a particular race, but it is problematic when the focus is on turnout, interest
in the campaign, or political efficacy. Although citizens may be drawn to the
polls to vote in one or two particular races, and although some races may have a
bigger influence on turnout than others, citizens usually vote for all races on the
ballot, and all races contribute to the full campaign environment. As a result, no
citizen can avoid being bombarded with advertisements from the full range of
races, regardless of whether he or she plans to vote in a given contest.

To demonstrate the heterogeneity of ad volumes for different races within
media markets, we plot in Figures 5.4 and 5.5 the number of presidential ads in
each market against the number of congressional ads for 2000 and 2004. There
is no discernable linear trend to the data; in some markets there was a high
concentration of presidential ads with little else, while in other markets there
was a lot of congressional advertising with little from the presidential candidates.

For example, in 2000, while a number of markets had rough parity in number
of presidential and congressional ads (Albuquerque had 8,000 congressional and

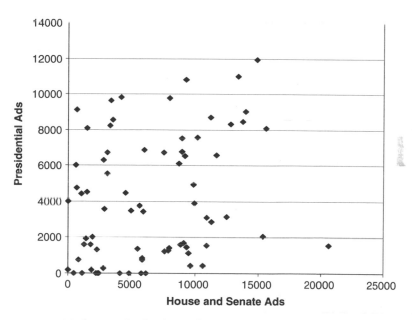

FIGURE 5.4   Market-Level Ad Volumes for 2000

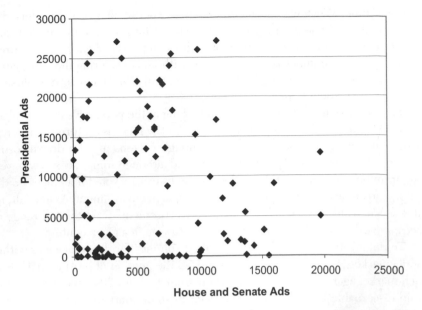

FIGURE 5.5 Market-Level Ad Volumes for 2004

9,700 presidential ads; Detroit had 13,000 congressional and 11,000 presidential spots), a number of markets fell significantly off the diagonal (Minneapolis saw over 15,000 congressional ads, for example, but only 2,000 presidential spots; by contrast, Portland, OR, had nearly 10,000 presidential ads, but only 3,300 congressional spots). The variability was more significant in 2004. Consider Columbus, Ohio, where television stations hosted over 21,000 presidential ads, but only 1,300 congressional spots; or Lexington, Kentucky, where congressional candidates (and their allies) sponsored over 15,000 ads, but no one was heard from in the presidential race.

These findings indicate that presidential advertising is not highly correlated with congressional ads; one cannot reliably infer a high level of one from a high level of the other. Therefore, it is essential to have independent data about all types of ads, from all sorts of sponsors.

Summary

Our analysis of the ad tracking data in recent elections has provided us with a number of lessons important for the study of advertising effects.

The first is that competitiveness drives advertising volume. The level of political competition in a race explains a large part of the variation in the volume of advertising across markets. Competitiveness is also a primary determinant of the tone of the advertising campaign in a particular state or congressional district. To a great extent, close races are associated with higher levels of negativity. The

lesson here is a simple but important one: Competitiveness must be incorporated into virtually any model looking at advertising effects. Failure to do so risks attributing all the effects of everything that goes on in a competitive contest (increased media attention, mobilization activity, citizen interest) to advertising.

Second, who airs ads matters. Even in the post-BCRA era, interest groups and parties remain important players in the advertising air war, and the kinds of ads broadcast by parties and interest groups differ dramatically from those sponsored by candidates. They are less likely to be positive, promotional spots, and far more likely—particularly in the case of interest groups—to be pure attack ads. Ignoring noncandidate advertising not only leads to an inaccurate depiction of the volume of advertising aired and the competitive balance of campaign advertising, but also of the tone of the race.

Third, the timing of political advertising matters. Political campaigns and political advertising are commencing earlier in the campaign year—and in some cases, in the year preceding an election year. In 1995, Bill Clinton began airing ads in anticipation of the November 1996 election contest. In the 2004 contest, the Bush and Kerry campaigns, along with their interest-group allies, began airing a sustained barrage of campaign commercials in early March, seven months before Election Day. Yet scholars have often only begun their search for election effects after Labor Day, the traditional start of the campaign. The typical strategy is to compare surveys taken in September and surveys conducted just after Election Day. Using September data as a preelection baseline, however, is to miss the mark entirely. In modern campaigns, the starting date is closer to St. Patrick's Day than Labor Day. Scholars who began their search for advertising effects in September 2004 would have missed the airing of over half a million political advertisements in the presidential race alone.

Our fourth and final point is a crucial one: In order to understand the nature and impact of campaign advertising, it is essential that one take into account the complete advertising environment and not simply pay attention to the race at the top of the ballot. Although crowded ballots are common to many states, election contests can vary in competitiveness from state to state (and even within states), thus drawing more or less advertising. As a result, a market that is uncompetitive in one contest might be extremely competitive in another. The bottom line is that understanding advertising's effects (on voter turnout, for example) demands that one take into consideration the full range of electoral competition confronting voters. Doing otherwise—looking only at presidential advertising, for example—means risking significant measurement error when it comes to descriptive and causal inferences about political advertising.

With these lessons in hand, we shift gears in the next four chapters to explore the impact of advertising exposure at the individual level. We begin in Chapter 6 with an exploration of the effects of exposure on the amount of information respondents have about the candidates running in federal races.

CHAPTER SIX

What Did They Know and
When Did They Know It?

THERE ARE PROBABLY few people (besides the four of us) who sit down in front of their television sets during election season and say, "Let's watch some campaign ads!" Rather, advertising comes to people uninvited and mostly unwelcome. But campaign ads do not appear automatically and are not distributed randomly. Ad exposure varies geographically—as described in Chapter 5, the most advertising shows up in the most competitive markets, for example. Ad exposure also varies individually—a citizen who steers clear of local news, for example, devoting all of his or her television-watching time to movies on premium cable channels, simply will not bump into many political ads, no matter how competitive the presidential (or Senate or House) race in his or her state or district. But for a neighbor who watches local news broadcasts and talk shows, daily exposure could be considerable.

What effect does ad exposure have on individual citizens? Do the ads these neighbors see matter when it comes to what they know about politics or whether they take part in the political process? Does someone living in a "perfect-storm" market, such as Detroit in the 2000 campaign, who has seen hundreds of ads from the more than 30,000 aired in the Motor City market, know more about the candidates and have a higher interest in the campaign than her sister living in Corpus Christi, Texas, where not a single ad aired?

Consider the respondent in the 2000 American National Election Studies who had the highest estimated exposure to campaign ads. She was a forty-year-old woman living in the St. Louis media market (we do not, of course, know her name) who reported watching a morning news program, the national news, the early local news, and *Wheel of Fortune* every day in the week before she was interviewed. She also reported watching late local news five times, daytime talk shows three times, and *Jeopardy!* once in the previous week. Obviously, she was a very heavy television viewer. Moreover, she lived in a media market that saw over 30,000 ads aired between January 1 and Election Day. More than 6,000 of these were aimed at the various U.S. House races in the St. Louis area, and over 7,000 were aired for Missouri's tightly contested U.S. Senate contest. Another 6,000-some ads were aired for Missouri's gubernatorial contest, and over 8,500 ads were aired in the presidential contest—both for the primaries and the general election. Might our respondent have learned at least something given all of her considerable ad exposure?

Three of our main hypotheses, presented in Chapter 2, suggest that increasing exposure to political ads affects individual voters embedded in particular campaign environments. First, the information hypothesis holds that citizens exposed to campaign advertising actually will learn something about the candidates and their messages. Second, the differential effects hypothesis suggests that these effects will be greatest among those who need the information most: citizens who have lower levels of political information at the outset. Finally, our partisan hypothesis asserts that the effects of advertising will be greatest among those least set in their ways when it comes to politics: political independents. In this chapter, we begin the process of testing these hypotheses.

The Informational Content of Advertising

Conventional wisdom suggests that political advertising is a distraction, diverting viewers' attention away from issues that matter by deluging them with meaningless, irrelevant, or bogus information. Ads, in this view, are primarily venues for candidates to sling mud at each other, tearing each other apart while dragging democracy down in the process. But as we noted in Chapter 2, scholars of political communication have been much less willing to accept this conventional wisdom, with some going as far as to suggest that people actually learn more from advertising than television news broadcasts (Patterson and McClure 1976).

So how much informational content is there in political advertising? Our analysis of the Wisconsin Advertising Project data showed that in the 2000 general election presidential campaign, 69 percent of all ads focused on policy matters and fewer than 7 percent focused solely on the personal characteristics of the candidates. Another 24 percent focused on both, according to the coders. These findings are quite consistent with those of Geer, who found that about 80 percent of negative appeals and 70 percent of positive appeals in presidential ads in 2000 were issue based (2006, 61). Clearly, candidates are not avoiding discussion of policy issues. Moreover, more than two-thirds (68 percent) of all ads during the 2000 election provided some supporting source, such as a newspaper article or a Congressional vote, either in the visual or the text of the ad.

However, as West noted, there is a difference between an ad that contains only a policy mention—perhaps a candidate's vague statement that he will "grow the economy"—and one that contains an action statement, "a clear statement of past positions or expectations about future action" (2005, 45). In fact, action statements are quite prevalent in the universe of thirty-second campaign ads. For instance, in August 2004, John Kerry's campaign aired a spot that criticized Bush for his lack of a plan to address health-care insurance and then offered his own proposal for reform, including "tax credits to help small businesses provide health insurance" and "reimbursing employers for catastrophic costs." Included in the ad was a link to a website—www.KerryHealthPlan.com—which gave details of Kerry's health insurance initiative. Similarly, in an ad from the 2004 nomination season, Democrat Richard Gephardt spoke of his economic proposals, mentioning specifically his support for repealing Bush's tax cuts, imposing an international minimum wage, and raising the minimum wage in the United States. Such examples are common; ads frequently offer voters clear, policy-based information that, if received, would allow them to differentiate between the candidates when called on to do so on Election Day.

Models and Data

To investigate the potential for ads to inform, we turned once again to the Wisconsin Advertising Project data described in Chapter 4, which provided information on the content, volume, and targeting of political advertising in 2000 and 2004. We combined these data with the 2000 American National Election Studies, the 2000 DDB Needham "Life Style" panel study, and the UW–BYU 2004 Election Panel Study to test our main hypotheses.[1] These studies provided a rich array of political, psychological, and demographic instrumentation along with measures of television-viewing habits. (See Appendix C for more information about each survey.) Because exposure to political advertising is a function of both what was watched and what was aired, we merged these questions with information on the content, volume, and targeting of political ads to create a measure of exposure to various sorts of political ads. (See Chapter 4 for a more extensive discussion about creating these exposure measures.)

We tested the information hypothesis in several different ways, using all three datasets. In the 2000 ANES, we examined whether respondents were able to recall the name of one of the House candidates running in their district, as well as the accuracy of their reports, along with their ability to place correctly the presidential candidates on a series of issue positions. We also examined the number of "likes" and "dislikes" respondents were able to offer for each of the major-party presidential candidates. Respondents were asked, "Is there anything in particular about Vice President Al Gore [Texas Governor George W. Bush] that might make you want to vote for [against] him?" and they were allowed to give up to five responses. Someone who said, for instance, that she liked Bush's plainspokenness, that he is a Christian, and that he opposes gun control would have been recorded as having offered three Bush "likes." Past research has established the importance of candidate affect for understanding vote choice as well as turnout, and the ANES "likes" and "dislikes" battery taps into cognitive as well as affective engagement with the candidates (Holbrook et al. 2001; Jacobson 1997; Kelley 1983; Marcus and MacKuen 1993).

The DDB Needham "Life Style" data allowed us to test the extent to which citizens acquired more specific knowledge about George W. Bush and Al Gore in 2000. Respondents were asked a series of eight factual questions, half of which concerned facts mentioned in the candidates' ads, half of which did not. (We describe these questions in detail later.)

The 2004 UW–BYU panel study let us look at the impact of advertising on respondents' knowledge of U.S. Senate candidates. Following Bartels (1986), we operationalized knowledge as the ability to render an opinion when asked: "Is your opinion of [incumbent, challenger, or open-seat U.S. Senate candidate] very favorable, somewhat favorable, somewhat unfavorable, unfavorable, undecided, or haven't you heard enough about [candidate's name] yet to have an opinion?"

We investigated the differential effects hypothesis by interacting a measure of general political knowledge (described below) with each of our exposure measures, and we examined the partisan hypothesis by interacting a measure of partisanship (is the respondent an independent or not?) with each exposure measure. These interactions allowed us to test whether lower information respondents and independents experience a unique effect from advertising exposure (one we expect to be positive) in comparison to respondents who are more politically aware and engaged.

Each of our models included a measure of campaign ad exposure as the primary explanatory variable. Ad exposure was operationalized in a number of ways, depending on the dependent variable. For questions that were asked on the ANES postelection survey (such as voter turnout), we used our estimate of exposure to advertising from June 1, 2000, through Election Day.[2] For questions asked on the preelection survey (such as House-candidate recall), we used our measure of exposure to ads from June 1 up to the date of the respondent's preelection interview (thus the end date varies by respondent). In 2004, we estimated ad exposure using data from March 3 (the day after John Kerry effectively wrapped up the Democratic nomination) to Election Day. Our start date was much earlier than in 2000 because candidates began their general-election advertising much earlier in 2004 than in past years (as discussed in Chapter 5).[3]

Additionally, depending on the model, we used exposure to advertising of one of three types: presidential ads, U.S. Senate ads, or U.S. House ads. For example, in our questions of presidential knowledge, we include only exposure to presidential advertising. In later chapters, when we ask questions about interest in the campaign, turnout, and trust in government, because these questions are broader and not race-specific, we include exposure to all political advertising.

In each model we controlled for variables that could plausibly affect the outcome measures, including education, gender, age, race, income, education, strength of partisanship, newspaper reading, and a measure of general political information. Following the logic laid out by Zaller (1992) and Price and Zaller (1993), we measured generalized political information in the ANES with a familiar battery of questions asking respondents to identify the "job or office" held by William Rehnquist, Trent Lott, Tony Blair, and Janet Reno, along with questions about partisan control of the House and Senate. A total of six questions were used to construct this knowledge scale. The mean number of correct answers was 2.1. A quarter of respondents answered none of the questions correctly, and fewer than 4 percent got all six answers correct.

Our measure of political information in the 2004 UW–BYU study was constructed similarly, except respondents were asked to identify the job or office held by Bill Frist instead of Trent Lott and John Ashcroft instead of Janet Reno. Unlike the 2000 ANES, this study did not inquire about partisan control of each house of Congress. The average number of correct responses to the knowledge questions in this study was 1.4. Just under 30 percent of respondents answered none of the questions correctly; just under 10 percent got all four correct.

Political information was measured in the 2000 DDB Needham "Life Style" data by a seven-question scale:

1. Which political party is more liberal?
2. Which political party holds a majority in the U.S. Senate?
3. Which political party holds a majority in the U.S. House?
4. To which political party does Trent Lott belong?
5. To which political party does Tom Daschle belong?
6. Which political party opposes a 72-hour waiting period for handgun purchases?
7. Which political party voted in higher numbers for the recently passed tax cut?

The distribution of this variable was fairly uniform. The average number of correct responses was 3.6; 15 percent of respondents answered none correctly, and another 15 percent of respondents answered all seven correctly.

In all of our models, we also included measures of the competitiveness of the House, Senate, and presidential races in the districts and states in which each respondent lived. This was to account for the possibility that electoral competition leads to higher levels of information and engagement for reasons other than increased advertising, as discussed in Chapter 5 (see also Rosenstone and Hansen 1993; Jacobson 1997).[4] These competitiveness measures were based on rankings assigned by the *Cook Political Report* prior to the election. We operationalized competitiveness as a series of binary measures, one each for the Senate, House, and presidential race.

In addition, we included in each model an individual-level measure of campaign contact—a dummy variable coded "1" if a respondent reported having

TABLE 6.1   Standard Model Predictors

Campaign ad exposure
House race competitiveness
Senate race competitiveness
Presidential race competitiveness
Campaign contact
Television-news viewing
Age
Race
Education
Gender
Income
Strength of partisanship
Newspaper use
Generalized political information

been contacted by a political party or someone from a campaign. Including this contact variable in the model helped to ensure that it was ad exposure doing the explanatory work and not another form of mobilization to which high-ad-exposure citizens also might be subject.

Notwithstanding the assurances about endogeneity discussed in Chapter 4, we also included in all of the models the respondent's level of television news viewing to control for the possibility that people who watch television news are learning about the campaigns from such programming—during which many ads air—and not from the advertising itself. Together, these controls should allay any concern about endogeneity in our models; that is, they allowed us to capture the impact of campaign ad exposure on our measures of information and engagement without undue concern that those who were already engaged and informed would find themselves more exposed to campaign ads.

Table 6.1 specifies the statistical model that we use in this chapter. Unless noted otherwise, this is the model used in the remainder of the book as well.

Informational Effects in Presidential Elections

Our first test of the informational effects of advertising focused on five measures of knowledge about the presidential candidates in 2000. To reiterate the question, do people learn from the advertising they are exposed to during a political campaign? And if so, are these learning effects more evident in presidential or subpresidential campaigns like Senate and House races? On the one hand, we might expect to find large advertising effects in presidential campaigns because of the massive volume of advertising in these races. On the other hand, because the presidential candidates are initially much better known than candidates for lower office, the potential for advertising to have an impact is smaller.

Our first measures of information, from the 2000 presidential campaign, involved perceptions of the candidates themselves. Specifically, we looked at people's ability to articulate likes and dislikes about the major party presidential candidates. ANES asked respondents whether there was anything in particular that would make them vote for each of the major party presidential candidates; up to five mentions were accepted for each candidate, including everything from past experience and leadership ability, to physical appearance and other personal qualities. Respondents also were asked whether there were reasons to vote against each of the candidates. Again, up to five responses—ranging from comments about the candidate's character to criticisms of his policy positions— were accepted. On average, respondents were able to offer slightly more than one reason for liking each of the presidential candidates, for a combined mean of 2.2 mentions (out of a maximum of 10). They could provide slightly fewer reasons for disliking the candidates (an average of two out of a maximum of ten).

Most important for our purposes, presidential-candidate likes and dislikes rose with exposure to campaign advertising, as the positive and statistically significant coefficients in Table 6.2 reveal.[5] Note, we only report the effects for advertising exposure (which will be our approach in this and the remaining three empirical chapters), but where appropriate, we will note in the text the effects of relevant control variables. For example, in these initial models, individual-level controls (see Appendix C for coding) work much as one might expect, with both likes and dislikes increasing with education and general political information. Strong partisans are somewhat more likely to mention something that they like (but not dislike) about the presidential candidates, and women tend to mention more likes (but not dislikes) than men.[6]

To give a sense of exposure's impact, we used the models' estimates to predict the number of likes and dislikes that a "typical" respondent would offer given a change in levels of exposure to presidential advertising. We defined a typical respondent here, as we do throughout the book, as a thirty-year-old nonblack female living in an area without a competitive presidential or congressional

---

TABLE 6.2   Effects of Ad Exposure on Presidential Candidate Knowledge

	Presidential candidate likes	Presidential candidate dislikes	Know facts in ads	Know facts not in ads	Bush-Gore info
Ad exposure (2000 ANES)	.020 (.009)*	.051 (.009)**	—	—	.020 (.009)*
Ad exposure (2000 DDB Needham)	—	—	.039 (.022)+	.015 (.022)	—

Entries are coefficients (with standard errors in parentheses) from separate equations estimated using a generalized linear model with a binomial link function. All exposure measures are logged, as described in the text.
$+p < .10$; $*p < .05$; $**p < .01$

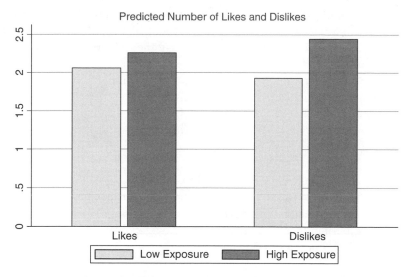

FIGURE 6.1 Predicted Number of Presidential Likes and Dislikes by Ad Exposure

campaign. She had not been contacted by a party or campaign encouraging her to vote, and she had average levels of local-news viewing and newspaper reading. Moreover, her level of education, income, generalized political knowledge, and partisanship were all set at the mean for the sample.

Figure 6.1 shows the impact of increasing this typical respondent's exposure to presidential ads from one standard deviation below to one standard deviation above the mean. It was not possible to express this change precisely in terms of a number of ads because exposure depended not only on the number of ads aired, but the individual's viewing habits as well. The two-standard deviation increase raised the number of likes offered ever so slightly, by around a fifth of a mention, from 2.06 to 2.26. The effect of this same change in exposure on dislikes was more pronounced, rising by about half of a mention. At low exposure, we predicted the typical respondent would offer 1.93 candidate dislikes, whereas at high exposure, we predicted 2.44 mentions would be made. To put this effect of advertising into perspective, we calculated the impact of a candidate or party contact using the same assumptions. A contact raised the predicted number of likes by 0.28 and increased the predicted number of dislikes by 0.37. The impact of advertising on information, then, was roughly similar to the impact of a party or candidate contact.

Thus, even controlling for everything else in the model, additional advertising exposure increased the number of comments, both positive and negative, that people made when asked to report whether there was anything they liked or disliked about Bush and Gore. This finding added one piece of evidence for our contention that advertising can have a positive impact on voter knowledge of the candidates, but our case is not yet closed.

The next bit of evidence concerns what people can learn about candidates and issues by viewing campaign ads. If advertising really does have the potential to increase voters' knowledge beyond increasing their ability to say something about the candidates, exposure to advertising should also increase citizens' ability to remember facts featured in the ads. At the same time, ad exposure should have no impact on the recall of facts not mentioned in ads. Fortunately, we had four questions in the 2000 DDB Needham "Life Style" data tapping facts about the presidential candidates that appeared in their advertising. Respondents were asked which candidate, Bush or Gore

1. favored allowing young people to devote up to one-sixth of their Social Security taxes to individually controlled investment accounts;
2. favored providing targeted tax cuts to a particular group;
3. favored drilling for oil in Alaska's Arctic National Wildlife Refuge;
4. served as a journalist in Vietnam.

Each of these facts was mentioned in advertising sponsored by the candidates, the parties, or their interest-group allies. For instance, Gore aired a contrast ad in which he criticized Bush's $1.6-billion tax-cut proposal because most of the benefits would go to the wealthiest Americans and highlighted his own plan, which would offer a $10,000 tax deduction for college tuition. This ad aired in several swing states in October. Another Democratic National Committee ad, which aired in Florida right before Election Day, highlighted Bush and Cheney as "two former oil executives" who favored "drilling in Alaska's pristine Arctic wilderness."

We also had four questions tapping facts about the two candidates that did not appear in their advertising. Respondents were asked which candidate, Bush or Gore

1. had a brother who was currently a state governor;
2. gave a dramatic kiss to his wife at the national nominating convention;
3. used to be partial owner of a major league baseball team;
4. favored a 72-hour waiting period for gun purchases at gun shows.

The average number of correct responses to the questions about facts in the ads was 2, while the average number of correct responses to the questions about facts not in the ads—many of which received widespread media attention on the news or the late-night talk shows—was 2.7.

Table 6.2 shows again that advertising has an impact—and in the way expected. Increased exposure to advertising was positively associated with knowledge of facts mentioned in the candidates' advertisements.[7] Just as important, increased exposure did not predict knowledge of the second set of facts—those not mentioned in the candidates' advertising. If our exposure measure were simply picking up general political awareness or engagement, there would have been positive effects even for those pieces of information not contained in the advertising. We are encouraged, therefore, by this indication of the discriminant validity of our exposure measure.

The substantive impact of advertising exposure in this case, however, is quite modest. Moving from low exposure (one standard deviation below the mean) to high exposure (one standard deviation above the mean) increased the predicted number of correct answers from 1.95 to 2.09. Though this change was not dramatic (it is less than the 0.54 increase predicted by moving from minimum to maximum newspaper exposure, for example), we still consider it noteworthy for several reasons. First, people acquire campaign information through many different sources, including newspapers, local television news, radio, the Internet, nightly news broadcasts, and interpersonal communication. That advertising still has an educative impact in this crowded message environment is important. Second, as discussed in Chapter 2, the conventional wisdom holds that ads are devoid of informational content and thus should contribute nothing to learning. Our findings show that this is clearly not the case.

Our final test of advertising's impact at the presidential level investigated the ability of survey respondents to place Gore to the left of Bush on a series of issue scales. Specifically, we examined whether respondents were able to place "correctly" the candidates along a range of eight issues, including abortion, gun control, environmental protection versus jobs, environmental regulation, government spending and services, defense spending, aid to African Americans, and government job guarantees.[8] To illustrate with an example: Respondents were asked to place both Bush and Gore on a government-spending scale that ranged from one to seven. At the low end was the position that government should provide far fewer services; at the high end was the position that government should provide many more services. Those who gave Gore a higher number than Bush (indicating they believed Gore favored more government services than Bush) were deemed correct; those who scored the two politicians evenly or gave Bush a higher number than Gore were deemed incorrect. The variable was operationalized as the number of correct placements (placing Bush to the right of Gore). On average, respondents got a little over three placements correct.

That said, correct placements varied widely by issue: Only 13 percent of respondents, for example, were able to order correctly the candidates on the question of defense spending, but 62 percent could identify Gore as being more amenable to restrictions on gun sales, and almost two-thirds could identify Bush as being more supportive of restrictions on abortion than Gore.

We regressed the number of correct placements for each respondent on the independent variables in the models reported above. The model's estimates, reported in the last column of Table 6.2, show that ad exposure was positively and significantly related to correct issue placements at the .05 level. Put simply, respondents exposed to more advertising were better able to place the candidates on issue scales correctly.[9]

Overall, our evidence is clear: Exposure to advertising increases people's knowledge of the presidential candidates. And although the magnitude of the effects is relatively modest, recall that this is in line with our prior expectations. The important point is that citizens do, in fact, seem to be learning from campaign ads.

Learning from Ads in Senate and House Races

We next turned our attention to other races on the ballot, specifically the House races from 2000 and the Senate races of 2004. We first examined the effect of exposure on respondents' ability to recall the candidates running in their district in 2000 for the U.S. House of Representatives. We estimated two models, one for citizens' claims about knowing the names of the candidates, and one for the accuracy of their reports. Respondents first were asked if they happened "to remember the names of the candidates for Congress—that is, for the House of Representatives in Washington—who are running in the November election from this district?" Respondents who answered affirmatively were then asked to name those candidates. Not surprisingly, given the social desirability of being politically informed, a higher percentage of citizens said they knew who was running (26.6 percent) than were able to correctly name those candidates when put on the spot (14.8 percent).

As the first two columns of Table 6.3 illustrate, both reported knowledge of House candidate names and the accuracy of recalling those names increased with exposure to congressional campaign advertising.[10] The substantive impact of these effects is illustrated in Figure 6.3, which shows how the predicted probability of both recall and accuracy increase as exposure increases. Moving from no exposure to maximum exposure doubled the probability of House name recall from just under 0.1 to almost 0.2. Increasing exposure had a smaller

TABLE 6.3   Effects of Ad Exposure on House and Senate Candidate Knowledge

	House name recall	Recall accuracy	Senate challenger recall	Senate open-seat recall	Senate incumbent recall
Ad exposure (2000 ANES)	.104 (.031)**	.116 (.039)**	—	—	—
Ad exposure (2004 UW–BYU)	—	—	.113 (.034)**	.104 (.058)+	−.210 (.156)

Entries are coefficients (with standard errors in parentheses) from separate equations estimated with logistic regression, with the exception of the fourth model (candidate recall in open Senate seats), estimated using ordered probit. All exposure measures are logged, as described in the text.
$+ p < .10; *p < .05; **p < .01$

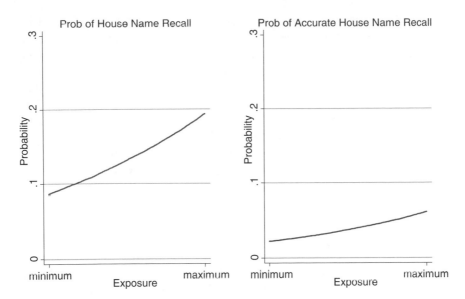

FIGURE 6.2   Predicted Probability of House Candidate Recall

effect on the accuracy of recall, but it is still evident in the second panel of Figure 6.2, in which the probability of correct name recall increased by about 0.05 across the range of exposure. (See again Figure 4.6 in Chapter 4 for an illustration of the distribution of exposure in the 2000 ANES. Because a nontrivial number of respondents are estimated to have no political advertising exposure, we consider this a decent baseline. Although few respondents were exposed to the maximum exposure, there are a number of respondents who approach that level of saturation. To visualize a more modest exposure effect, consider the middle-third of any plotted probabilities.)

Finally, using the data from the postelection wave of the 2004 UW–BYU survey, we examined whether total advertising exposure was a predictor of respondents' knowledge of the names of three different types of candidates in U.S. Senate races: incumbents, challengers, and candidates in open-seat races. As noted earlier, knowledge was gauged by respondents' ability to give an opinion of the candidate. Respondents who indicated they had an opinion or were undecided were coded 1, while those who said they did not have enough information to have an opinion were coded 0.[11]

As one might expect, knowledge of incumbents was highest; about 92 percent of respondents held an opinion of the incumbent. Knowledge of challengers was much lower; only 63 percent of respondents indicated they were able to form an opinion of a challenger. Knowledge in open-seat races was somewhat higher. Of the 284 respondents living in states with no incumbent senator, 73 percent expressed an opinion of both candidates, and another 20 percent expressed an opinion of one candidate, leaving only 7 percent of respondents unknowledge-able about both. Clearly, knowledge of nonincumbents was higher in open-seat races than in races featuring an incumbent, probably a result of the large amount of resources that candidates and parties put into such campaigns.

Returning to Table 6.3, we again find evidence that exposure to advertising increases knowledge of candidates. Increased exposure significantly improved respondents' abilities to express an opinion of both challengers and candidates in open-seat races.[12] The one condition in which advertising had no impact was for incumbents. This might be expected, though, given that incumbent senators tended to be well known going into a campaign. There was just not that much learning for the voter to do about an incumbent senator who had served a state for almost six years or, in some cases, several decades.

The substantive impact of exposure is illustrated in Figure 6.3, which depicts the probability that our same hypothetical respondent expressed an opinion of a challenger and opinions of both open-seat candidates, varying levels of exposure. Advertising appears to have had a substantial impact on knowledge of challengers. Moving from no exposure to maximum exposure increased the probability of knowing the challenger by about 0.2, from 0.6 to 0.8. To put this in perspective, this rise in the probability of knowing the challenger was almost exactly the same as predicted by increasing the respondent's level of general political information from its minimum to its maximum. The second panel in the same figure illustrates that impact of advertising was just as strong on knowledge of candidates in open-seat races. Moving from no exposure to

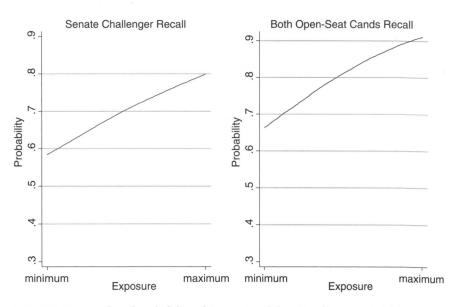

FIGURE 6.3   Predicted Probability of Senate Candidate Recall

maximum exposure increased the probability of knowing both candidates in the race by over 0.2.

We originally speculated that advertising effects might be more evident in U.S. House and U.S. Senate races than in the race for president. After all, citizens know so much more about the candidates running for president thanks, in part, to all of the free media that they generate. Yet, in this chapter, we find that exposure to advertising is associated with political knowledge in races at all levels.

This is encouraging evidence and an affirmation of our information hypothesis. And it is worth noting once again that these specific effects are not the primary goal of candidates and campaign consultants. As we have said repeatedly, the effects we are looking for are spillover effects from the game of gaining votes on Election Day. That voters are more informed about House, Senate, and presidential candidates after exposure to intense barrages of political advertising (even if those effects are modest) implies that television advertising can have a healthy influence on the electorate.

Of course, our empirical investigation has only begun and there are still important questions to consider; one such question is reviewed in the next section.

Differential Effects Hypothesis

To what extent are these effects evenly distributed across the electorate? Does exposure to campaign ads have the same sorts of effects on all citizens, or are there systematic differences? Recall that the differential effects hypothesis holds that advertising should have the greatest impact on those lowest in general political information. After all, these are the voters who need campaign information the most. What's more, because political advertising is relatively easy to comprehend (in fact, it is designed to be easily digestible and even entertaining), lower initial levels of political sophistication should not be a significant barrier to message retention (as it might be with more complex political information, such as print media or in-depth investigative journalism).

To test this, we divided our respondents into low versus high categories based on their general information score, and used a dummy variable to create an interaction with estimated ad exposure (as always, logged). Thus, we were able to observe the impact of exposure separately for respondents "low" versus "high" on the general political information scale.[13]

Of the ten models we estimated (the top halves of Table 6.4 and Table 6.5), we found a positive coefficient on seven of the interaction terms, indicating that low-information respondents learned at higher rates than high-information respondents. In four of those seven instances, these differences were statistically significant. As described below, however, the results are hardly definitive support that low information respondents consistently learn more than high-information counterparts.

TABLE 6.4 Differential Effects of Ad Exposure on Presidential Candidate Knowledge

	Presidential candidate likes	Presidential candidate dislikes	Know facts in ads	Know facts not in ads	Bush-Gore info
Ad exposure (2000 ANES)	.008 (.012)	.038 (.012)**	—	—	.029 (.012)*
Ad exposure × low information	.016 (.014)	.030 (.014)*	—	—	−.016 (.014)
Ad exposure (2000 DDB Needham)	—	—	.054 (.025)*	.034 (.025)	—
Ad exposure × low information	—	—	.026 (.023)	.041 (.024)+	—
Ad exposure (2000 ANES)	.018 (.009)*	.055 (.009)**	—	—	.024 (.009)**
Ad exposure × Independents	.020 (.020)	−.041 (.021)*	—	—	−.041 (.021)*
Ad exposure (2000 DDB Needham)	—	—	.040 (.022)+	.013 (.022)	—
Ad exposure × Independents	—	—	−.011 (.026)	.011 (.027)	—

Entries are coefficients (with standard errors in parentheses) from separate equations estimated using a generalized linear model with a binomial link function. All exposure measures are logged, as described in the text.
$+ p < .10;$ $^*p < .05;$ $^{**}p < .01$

TABLE 6.5 Differential Effects of Ad Exposure on House and Senate Candidate Knowledge

	House name recall	Recall accuracy	Senate challenger recall	Senate open-seat recall	Senate incumbent recall
Ad exposure (2000 ANES)	.154 (.039)**	.182 (.053)**	—	—	—
Ad exposure × low information	.080 (.039)*	.089 (.049)+	—	—	—
Ad exposure (2004 UW–BYU)	—	—	.170 (.047)**	.123 (.061)*	−.220 (.171)
Ad exposure × low information	—	—	−.089 (.050)+	−.060 (.050)	.015 (.110)
Ad exposure (2000 ANES)	.106 (.031)**	.126 (.039)**	—	—	—
Ad exposure × Independents	−.025 (.051)	−.118 (.071)+	—	—	—
Ad exposure (2004 UW–BYU)	—	—	.122 (.035)**	.100 (.059)+	−.232 (.175)
Ad exposure × Independents	—	—	−.112 (.072)	.023 (.060)	.044 (.124)

Entries are coefficients (with standard errors in parentheses) from separate equations estimated with logistic regression, with the exception of the fourth model (candidate recall in open Senate seats), estimated using ordered probit. All exposure measures are logged, as described in the text.
$+ p < .10;$ $^*p < .05;$ $^{**}p < .01$

To aid with interpretation of the two tables, consider this simple advice: The coefficient estimate on "ad exposure" represents the effect for high-information respondents. With that estimate as a baseline, the interactive coefficient tests for whether the politically uninformed are significantly affected to a greater or lesser extent. The total effect for the low-informed then is the main effect plus the interactive effect.

First, consider the case of reported presidential candidate dislikes. As the results in Table 6.4 demonstrate, both low and high-information voters are responsive to increased levels of advertising exposure, but the interactive co-efficient shows that the politically uninformed receive an added boost. For high-information respondents, the coefficient is 0.038, but for low-information respondents, the effect of ad exposure is 0.068 (0.038 + 0.030). Thus, under conditions of heavily saturated ad exposure, a low-information respondent would have learned more (relative to where that person started) than a political sophisticate with the same level of exposure.[14]

In the same table, we also see that exposure to advertising was more useful to those low in political information in being able to recall facts not mentioned in presidential advertising. Granted, this finding was a bit perplexing given that exposure to ads should have had no impact on knowledge of facts not in those ads. It is possible that campaign-ad exposure inspired at least some of these low-information respondents (to whom the effect is isolated in this case) to seek out additional campaign information (and thus score higher on these measures), while their ill-informed and underexposed counterparts were content to remain ignorant of all campaign-related information. This explanation is only speculative, however.

Ad exposure also aided respondents' recall of House candidates, and the accuracy of that recall, significantly more among low-information respondents than among high-information respondents (Table 6.5). We expand on this below.

We find inconsistency, however, in exposure effects for recall of Senate challengers. Contrary to our expectations, the effect of advertising on recall was greater for people high in general political information than for people low in information. However, this does not mean that low-information respondents are unaffected by ad exposure, only that the effect is slightly steeper for political sophisticates. Figure 6.4 illustrates this. The panel on the left reveals, first, that general political information had a considerable impact on a person's knowledge of a Senate challenger. The probability of a high-information individual expressing an opinion of a Senate challenger was considerably greater than the probability for a low-information individual. Second, the panel shows that advertising mattered more for high-information respondents (the top line, which rises more steeply). Nonetheless, both sets of respondents gain from exposure.

The panel on the right in Figure 6.4 shows the effect of ad exposure on the ability of both high- and low-information respondents to be able to state an opinion about both open-seat candidates. This panel looks similar to the panel for

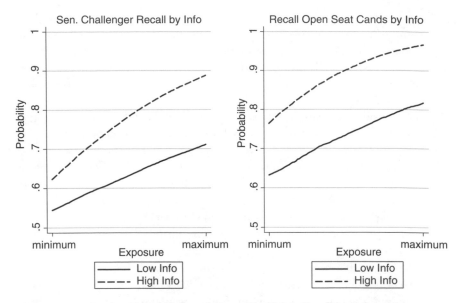

FIGURE 6.4   Predicted Probability of Senate Candidate Recall by Information

challengers, except that both lines are higher, indicating that people, in general, knew more about open-seat candidates than they did about challengers. Still, the gap in knowledge between high-information and low-information people was evident in these races as well. (Note, however, that the interaction for low-information respondents was insignificant in this case, so the lines are roughly parallel here.)

Figure 6.5 concerns U.S. House races and depicts the predicted probability of candidate-name recall and the accuracy of recall, again varying levels of exposure from their minimum to the maximum in our data and again using the same hypothetical respondent. In the first panel, it is evident that increased exposure led to increased recall for both low- and high-information respondents, but, more to the point, exposure aided the learning of low-information individuals more. Although it may be difficult to discern with the naked eye, this is also the case in the second panel, which concerns the accuracy of House recall. Exposure mattered more (in relative terms) for low- than high-information individuals.

And so, we are left with conflicting evidence relative to the differential effects hypothesis. We are not dismayed, however. In truth, the expectations for differential effects were very specific—higher rates of learning for those lower in initial stores of political information. Even in the case of Senate recall where the lower informed learned at lower rates, it was still the case that these respondents ended the campaign with more relevant political information.

Keep in mind the alternative. It is entirely possible for political ignorance to act as a barrier to sincere campaign learning. This is certainly what many scholars

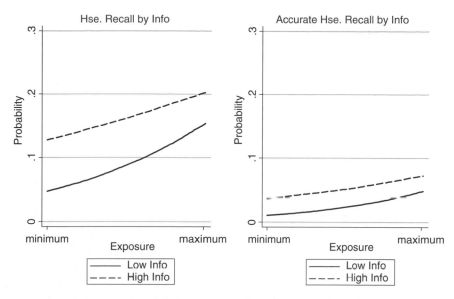

FIGURE 6.5 Predicted Probability of House Candidate Recall by Information

expect to find, arguing that being politically unaware blocks message retention (see again Chapter 2). We find no evidence of this, however, in the realm of political advertising exposure. Despite mixed support for the notion that low-information respondents learn at higher rates, we are comforted to know that they at least are still learning.

Partisanship

Finally, we also hypothesized that the effects of advertising might be greater for political independents, people who tend to be less attached to the political system in general. To explore this possibility, we interacted a dummy variable indicating the respondent was a pure independent with each respondent's level of ad exposure.[15] This is the identical approach taken for differential information effects in the previous section, but now the distinction is for partisans and independents. As such, the main effect is the exposure effect for partisan respondents, and with that as a baseline, the interactive coefficient tests for whether independents are significantly, more or less, affected by ad exposure.

Our expectations about the effects of this interaction term were wholly unsupported by our analyses (bottom halves of Table 6.4 and Table 6.5). In only three instances was the interaction term a significant predictor: for accurate recall of House candidates, for presidential candidate dislikes, and for placements of Bush and Gore on the information scales. And in all three of these instances, and contrary to the partisan hypothesis, pure independents were less influenced by advertising than were those who felt at least some attachment to a political party. In total, these results do not indicate that independents are confused by political advertising, only that the positive effects for partisans are not similarly present for independents. Put simply, the balance of the evidence in this section is suggestive that independents (at least compared to partisans) learn little from political advertisements.

Summary

We argued in Chapter 2 that there are good theoretical reasons to suspect that campaign ads—rich in information and laden with emotional content—have the potential to bring about a more informed citizenry. Television advertisements can help increase the aggregate store of politically relevant information that voters have at their disposal, which in turn can help activate the heuristics that voters use in making decisions and making sense of the political world.

The empirical evidence supports the notion that advertising can inform citizens. Specifically, our findings show that exposure to campaign advertising produces citizens who know more about the candidates—and not just at the presidential level. These effects are evident in presidential, U.S. House, and U.S. Senate races—and in both 2000 and 2004 elections.

The conventional wisdom of most pundits and some scholars has been that ads serve to confuse viewers and disengage potential voters. None of our evidence supports such a claim. There is no hint that these ads serve to distract or obfuscate. Rather, this chapter has demonstrated that ads can provide a small but significant amount of information to citizens—and frequently that assistance is provided to those who most need it: those low in political information. The question remains, however, whether the positive impact of advertising on knowledge of candidates overflows into other areas, including people's interest in the campaign, feelings of efficacy, and other democratic attitudes. We examine these relationships in the next chapter.

CHAPTER SEVEN

Campaign Advertising and Voter
Attitudes toward the Political Process

A S WE DEMONSTRATED in the previous chapter, campaign advertisements have the potential to inform citizens. More specifically, we showed that exposure to campaign advertising was related to informational gains in the context of presidential, House, and Senate races. Still, while ads may inform, critics also contend that they create a toxic atmosphere, turning people away from politics and making governing and accepting election results more difficult.

As said by Kay McFadden of *The Seattle Times*, in 2004:

> Study after study reveals, commercials for Republican President George W. Bush and Democratic challenger Sen. John Kerry have emerged as the No. 1 source of data to voters. Increasingly, campaign ads also frame how the news media report stories. Depending on how you look at it, the result is a civic-affairs tragedy or a realpolitik adjustment to citizens with less time and shorter attention spans.

She goes on to cite communications scholar David Domke, who raises the following question: "We could say ads are the worst possible source, because of the spinning and distortion. Or we could say they're the modern version of the Greek assembly, where we hear competing arguments and then make up our minds" (McFadden, 2004).

In this chapter, we investigate the question: if ads represent the modern version of the Greek assembly, might exposure to ads boost citizen assessments of the electoral process? Specifically, we ask whether citizens exposed to campaign advertising are more interested in the campaign, care more about the outcome of an election, judge the electoral process as fair, trust government, and feel efficacious about their role in politics.

As noted, most critiques of campaign ads simply assume that any such attitudinal effects are negative—that exposure to campaign commercials leads to lower levels of engagement and trust. In keeping with our more sanguine view of the impact of campaign advertising, we are suspicious about these claims and put them to the empirical test here. In contrast, we suspect that exposure to television ads actually might boost trust in government and interest in campaigns. We refer to these effects collectively as the system support hypothesis.

As with the information hypothesis, such a normatively pleasing link between television campaign ad exposure and attitudes about politics and government runs counter to conventional wisdom. As we noted in Chapter 2, one of the reasons proffered for why so many Americans eschew social engagement these days—expressed as a society where everyone bowls alone (Putnam 2000)—is the negative impact of television. Robinson (1975) called the attitudinal effect of this "videomalaise," although he referred only to the impact of television news on public attitudes (see also Norris 2000). Mutz and Reeves made the following point in their treatment of the role of televised incivility on assessments of trust in government:

> More general theories suggesting that television bears some responsibility for negative attitudes toward politics and politicians have received enthusiastic receptions over the years. For some, the root of the problem is the cynicism of game-centered political coverage and journalists' ongoing denigration of politicians' motives; for others, it is simply the conflict-oriented, adversarial nature of political coverage. The timing of the well-documented decline in trust toward governmental institutions initially gave these theories great plausibility, but documenting a causal link between political *television* and negative public attitudes has proven quite difficult. This difficulty stems from a lack of certainty about which aspects of political television are most likely to produce negative attitudes, and from problems inherent in studying media effects (2005, 2—emphasis in original).

We come at this question from the perspective of televised campaign advertising.[1] Although there is some evidence that "videomalaise" is real and accelerated by exposure to television news (Mutz and Reeves [2005], for example, find that uncivil television debates lower viewers' trust in government), it is not self-evident that televised political ads work the same way.

In fact, one study of incivility in political advertising found few effects of any substance on measures of trust, interest, and efficacy (Brooks and Geer 2007). We will focus more explicitly on the tone of ads in Chapter 9 (allowing us to speak directly to the findings from the above study), but our analysis here focuses on the complete information environment that voters are exposed to on television. As such we include all ads broadcast by candidates, parties, and interest groups, and we combine positive, negative, and contrast ads. Under conditions of high exposure to this total environment, we expect that ads help assessments of elections and government, and they boost campaign interest. To be sure, we do not expect these effects to be massive. As we discovered in the last chapter, the informational effects of campaign ad exposure tend to be relatively modest. Advertising is likely to matter mainly at the margin.

We begin by discussing a variety of political attitudes that advertising might potentially influence. These dependent variables are culled from a number of different surveys conducted over the course of multiple elections. We then examine the impact of television advertising exposure on citizen attitudes. As in the previous chapter, we first examine exposure in the aggregate before searching for differential effects of advertising among those high and low in political knowledge, and among those who identify and do not identify with a political party.

Models and Data

As in the previous chapter, we relied on three separate surveys from 2000 and 2004, but we also add a fourth in this chapter: the 2004 DDB Needham "Life Style" study. In this chapter, we explore the impact of advertising exposure on eight dependent variables, representing a diverse range of attitudinal responses:[2]

Campaign engagement:

1. How interested was the respondent in the election (2000 ANES)? We used a measure from both the preelection and postelection surveys. Respondents could answer by saying that they were "not much interested," "somewhat interested," and "very much interested" in the campaign.
2. Did the respondent care about the outcome of the presidential election (2000 ANES)? Here, respondents could answer by saying they cared "a great deal," or they did "not care very much."

Evaluations of elections:

1. Did the respondent feel that the election process was fair (2004 DDB Needham "Life Style")?
2. Did the respondent feel that the country needed serious electoral reform (2004 DDB Needham "Life Style")?
3. Did the respondent feel that money decided elections (2004 DDB Needham "Life Style")? For each of these questions, respondents could answer on a six-point scale ranging from "definitely disagree," "generally disagree," and "moderately disagree," to "moderately agree," "generally agree," and "definitely agree."

4. Did the presidential campaign make the respondent feel more or
   less confident that campaigns are truthful (2004 UW–BYU)?
   Respondents could answer with "less confident,"
   "no effect," or "more confident."

Trust and efficacy:

1. How often did the respondent trust in the federal government (2000
   ANES)? Response categories included "just about always," "most of
   the time," "only some of the time," and "never."
2. How much political efficacy did respondents exhibit? That is, how
   competent did they feel when it came to taking part in politics, and
   how responsive to their concerns did they consider the government
   to be?
   a. 2000 NES: An additive scale of two questions, coded from one
      to five (agree strongly to disagree strongly): "Public officials
      don't care much what people like me think"; and "People like
      me don't have any say about what the government does."
   b. 2000 DDB Needham "Life Style" and 2004 DDB Needham
      "Life Style": An additive scale of three questions, coded from one
      to six (definite disagreement to definite agreement): "People like
      me don't have a say in government decisions," "People like me
      can solve community problems," and "No matter whom I vote
      for, it won't make any difference." The variables were recoded so
      that higher scores represented more efficacious responses.

To investigate the effects of campaign ad exposure in 2000 and 2004 on the above
attitudes, we estimated a series of models employing the same model specification we used in the previous chapter (see Table 6.1). We included variables
that measured the respondent's media consumption habits, including local-news
viewership and newspaper reading, along with measures of education, age, gender, race, income, strength of partisanship, and general political knowledge. We
also controlled for whether respondents lived in competitive media markets and
whether they were mobilized by a campaign or political party.

Campaign Engagement

Table 7.1 contains results from a number of models predicting interest in the
election and concern for the outcome of the presidential contest. As in the previous chapter, we show only the coefficient estimates on the exposure variables.
Once again, our expectations were that campaign advertising would have positive effects when it came to political interest and concern for the outcome of
the presidential race. The estimates reported in the table provide only mixed
support for this hypothesis, however.

TABLE 7.1   Effects of Advertising on Campaign Engagement

	Preelection interest in campaign	Postelection interest	Cares about the outcome
Ad exposure (2000 ANES)	.029 (.015)+	.015 (.017)	−.022 (.031)
Ad exposure × low interest (2000 ANES)^	—	.043 (.020)*	—
Ad exposure (2000 DDB Needham)	—	.000 (.019)	—

Entries are coefficients (with standard errors in parentheses) from separate ordered probit and logit models. All exposure measures are logged.
$+ p < .10$; $*p < .05$; $**p < .01$
^ Effect for respondents with low interest in the preelection wave.

First, exposure to political advertising did positively affect interest in the preelection 2000 ANES, but it had no direct impact on respondents' interest in the postelection survey, nor did it have an impact on whether they cared about the outcome of the presidential election. Television ad exposure also failed as a predictor of postelection interest when we estimated a model using the 2000 DDB Needham "Life Style" data.

Note, however, that exposure did increase postelection interest among respondents in the 2000 ANES—but only among those who reported low levels of interest in the preelection wave of the study. Of the 334 respondents who reported being "not much interested" in the campaign during the preelection interview, 157 reported being somewhat interested, and 34 reported the highest level of interest during the postelection wave (in other words, between the pre- and postelection season, 57 percent of those respondents who reported no interest moved out of that category).[3] The evidence suggests that it was advertising exposure that drove many of these respondents into the higher interest category.

It is important to note that a number of control variables were also significant predictors of campaign interest. For example, older and more educated respondents reported higher levels of interest; and media consumption (local news and newspapers), generalized political information, strength of partisanship, and campaign and party mobilization were associated with greater campaign interest.

In Figure 7.1, we show predicted probabilities generated from the pre- and postelection interest models. As with Chapter 6, we defined a typical respondent as a thirty-year-old nonblack female living in an area without a competitive presidential, U.S. Senate, or U.S. House campaign. She had not been contacted by a party asking her to vote, and her local-news viewing and newspaper reading were average for the sample of respondents. She also had average levels of education, income, generalized political knowledge, and partisanship.

As the figure shows, increasing exposure to political ads from the lowest levels to the highest (from zero to ten on the logged exposure measure) raised the probability that a respondent would be "very much interested" in the election (in the preelection survey, where most interviews were in Sept.) from about 0.15 to about 0.20. In contrast, the probability a respondent would report being "not

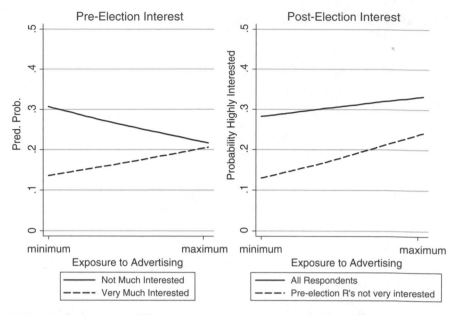

FIGURE 7.1   Predicted Effects of Advertising on Campaign Engagement

much interested" dropped from about 0.30 to about 0.20. Compare this to the effects of party mobilization in the preelection model. With exposure at its mean, a respondent not contacted by a political party had a 0.17 probability of being highly interested in the election. With a party contact, the probability rose to 0.25.

For the postelection models (the right panel of the graph), the solid line indicates the effect of ad exposure for all respondents. The impact of exposure was positive (the coefficient is 0.015, compared to 0.029 in the preelection model), but, as the table demonstrates, insignificant. In essence, exposure to campaign ads had no discernible effect on campaign interest reported at the end of the election.

However, as noted above, if one looks more closely at respondents who reported having low levels of interest before the election (that is, in the first wave of the ANES), the effects of campaign ad exposure were positive and significant (see the dotted line in the right panel in Figure 7.1). For these citizens, campaign ads did indeed serve to stimulate interest in the election. The probability that these respondents reported being "very much interested" increased from 0.15 to 0.24; this was even greater than the impact of ad exposure on pre-election interest. Thus, campaign ads mattered in two ways when it came to interest in the election: First, they increased interest in the aggregate, prior to the election; second, they gave an added boost to those who started out least interested.

In contrast, Figure 7.2 illustrates the impact of exposure on whether respondents reported caring about the outcome of the 2000 presidential election.[4]

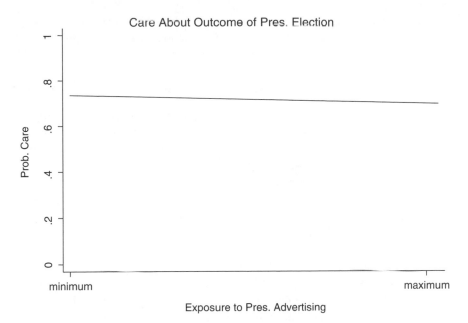

FIGURE 7.2 Predicted Effects of Advertising on Campaign Concern

Because the question related specifically to the presidential election, we included the respondent's exposure only to presidential-election ads. As the figure demonstrates, exposure had almost no impact whatsoever on how much respondents cared about whether Bush or Gore won—the line is essentially flat. One possible explanation for this null effect is that, even with no exposure, our "average" respondent already had a predicted probability of caring about the outcome of over 0.70, which left little room for a growth in concern (indeed, 1,402 of 1,799 respondents—78 percent—reported caring about the election).

Although this respondent had little room to move higher, it is important to note that there was considerable room for her concern about the presidential election's outcome to decline. Critics of campaign advertising might expect additional ad exposure to be associated with growing disengagement and lower levels of concern about the outcome. In fact, although the direction of the relationship was slightly negative, the effects statistically were indistinguishable from zero.

Indeed, up to this point, we have found no significantly negative relationships between exposure and our outcome variables (either in this chapter or the previous chapter). It is important to reinforce this point. We are looking explicitly for significantly positive relationships, but even in the context of null findings, we have a compelling story. To be sure, one should be cautious in inferring too much from insignificant effects, but it is hard to deny that the evidence thus far has done very little to reinforce the conventional wisdom that campaign ads are harming American democracy.

Evaluations of Elections

In this section, we take advantage of a number of interesting survey items that tap respondents' assessments of the electoral process and relate them to television ad exposure. Are elections fair? Does the electoral process need reform? Does money decide elections? Finally, are campaigns truthful? We used a series of questions from the 2004 DDB Needham "Life Style" study, and one question from the 2004 UW–BYU survey. To repeat a point made earlier, the ability to leverage numerous surveys in two presidential-election years bolsters the confidence we place in the larger conclusions about the impact of political ads.

The distribution of responses to these items demonstrated some important variation. First, only a small number of respondents were highly confident about the health of American elections. For example, only 8 percent of survey respondents definitely agreed that the election process was fair; only 6 percent definitely disagreed that money determined election outcomes, and 4 percent definitely disagreed that we needed serious change in the way elections were run; finally, only 9 percent of respondents in the UW–BYU survey agreed that the presidential election made them feel more confident that campaigns were truthful. Despite the general lack of intense optimism, there was a more even distribution of respondents in all other categories (including the more pessimistic responses). The only exception was campaign truthfulness, where 56 percent of respondents said the presidential campaign made them feel less confident in the truthfulness of campaigns (34 percent said the campaign had no effect). Is it conceivable that exposure to campaign ads might move people into more optimistic categories?

Findings appear in Table 7.2, and again, we see modest but significant effects of advertising exposure. In the first three models, negative coefficients indicated growing disagreement with the beliefs that elections were fair, that

TABLE 7.2   Effects of Advertising on Evaluations of Elections

	Elections are fair	We need election reform	Money decides elections	Campaign truthfulness
Ad exposure (2004 UW–BYU)	—	—	—	$-.000$ (.016)
Ad exposure (2004 DDB Needham)	.018 (.027)	$-.065$ (.028)*	$-.062$ (.028)*	—

Entries are coefficients (with standard errors in parentheses) from separate ordered probit models. All exposure measures are logged.
$+ p < .10$; $*p < .05$; $**p < .01$

changes were needed in the way elections were run, and that money decided election outcomes. For the "campaign truthfulness" model, negative coefficients indicated an increased sense that campaigns were NOT telling the truth. In line with the system support hypothesis, therefore, we expected positive coefficients in the "elections are fair" and "campaign truthfulness" models, but negative coefficients in the reform and money models.

In the middle two models of Table 7.2, ad exposure worked exactly as expected. Higher exposure reduced perceptions that money decided elections and that the United States needed serious changes in the election process. At the same time, exposure had no direct impact on assessments of the presidential campaign's truthfulness nor the assessment of the fairness of elections.

With respect to our control variables, African Americans were much more pessimistic about elections than whites or Latinos (in the first three models), as were respondents in competitive races (disagreeing in higher numbers that elections were fair, and agreeing more often that we needed reform and that money decided elections). Curiously, older people thought elections tended to be fair, but they were also worried about the impact of money and advocated serious reform; by contrast, higher-income respondents were ambivalent about election fairness and the need for reform, but (perhaps not surprisingly) they disagreed in higher numbers that money determined election outcomes. There were no effects for media consumption, party mobilization, education, or gender.[5] Finally, there were some interesting effects for generalized political information, which we will address later in this chapter.

Predicted probabilities on exposure for the first three models are reported in Figure 7.3. For our average viewer, with no exposure, the predicted probability that she strongly agreed with the claim that money determined elections fell from 0.25 to just under 0.20; the probability that she strongly disagreed rose from nearly 0 to just about 0.07. At the same time, the probability that she strongly agreed that the country needed serious electoral change (and what constitutes "serious" was left to the respondent) fell from over 0.40 to about 0.30; the probability that she strongly disagreed rose only slightly.

What's going on here? Are we to believe that exposure to campaign advertising leads citizens to feel better about the health of the American electoral process? Absolutely, and for two reasons. First, exposure was not moving respondents—in significant numbers—to more strongly disagree with these negative claims. As we have seen, those changes in probabilities were modest (and the probability that respondents strongly disagreed was already low). Instead, they had their strongest impact on reducing the probability that respondents strongly agreed with the negative claim. In this sense, ad exposure made these citizens less certain that things were as bad as they could be.

This is not as far-fetched as it might seem. By exposing viewers to policy debates, to candidate biographies, and, yes, to hard-hitting attacks, campaign ads

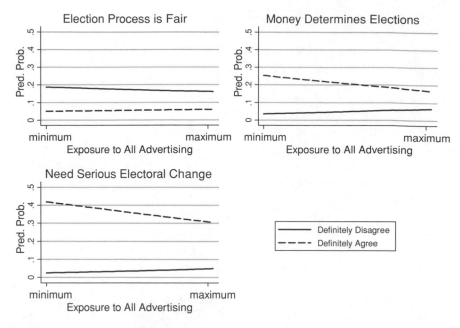

FIGURE 7.3   Predicted Effects of Advertising on Evaluations of Elections

may suggest to citizens that the American electoral system is, in some meaningful sense, working. After all, ads are direct appeals to voters, a constant reminder of voters' own political power. It is not surprising, then, that assessments of elections move in the more democratically healthy direction. Indeed, while it may take money to purchase air time, high levels of advertising convey the claim that money does not decide elections—voters (and viewers) do.

Trust and Efficacy

Thus far, we have seen modest but positive effects of exposure on respondents' interest in the campaigns and assessments of electoral politics. These results reinforce our general claim that advertising exposure is neither the cause nor cure for what ails American politics. It has, at worst, a neutral impact, and, at best, a positive, if modest, effect. But can the system support hypothesis be extended further? Does ad exposure move respondents to feel better about the health of American government?

We measured this in two ways. First, we examined the relationship between exposure and trust in government; second, we investigated the extent that ads made respondents feel more or less efficacious. We included efficacy here because it related to the extent to which a citizen felt that her political participation could have an impact. The results of these analyses are reported in Table 7.3.[6]

TABLE 7.3   Effects of Advertising on Trust and Efficacy

	Trust in government	External efficacy
Ad exposure (2000 ANES)	.031 (.017)+	.016 (.015)
Ad exposure (2000 DDB Needham)	—	−.005 (.150)
Ad exposure (2004 DDB Needham)	—	.093 (.071)

Entries are coefficients (with standard errors in parentheses) from separate ordered probit and OLS models. All exposure measures are logged.
+ $p < .10$; $^*p < .05$; $^{**}p < .01$

As the table shows, respondents with higher ad exposure reported having greater trust in government—although these effects were very modest and only significant at the $p < .10$ level. In contrast, exposure had no effect on reported external efficacy—people's beliefs about how responsive government is to citizens.[7] This result was the most consistent of all our measures of citizen attitudes, in that we were able to examine it in three surveys over two elections. In each case, ad exposure had no effect on political efficacy.

We show predicted probabilities in Figure 7.4. For respondents with high exposure, the probability that they reported trusting government only some of the time was lower than for respondents with low or no exposure (falling

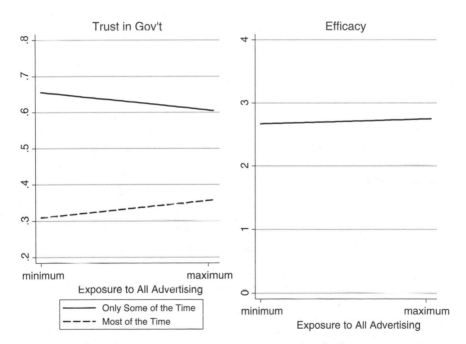

FIGURE 7.4   Predicted Effects of Advertising on Trust and Efficacy

Source: Efficacy estimates are from 2000 ANES model

from about 0.65 to just over 0.60 over the range of exposure). In contrast, the probability that respondents reported trusting government "most of the time" rose from just over 0.30 to over 0.35.

In many ways, we should have expected the smallest effects here. Very few political ads make appeals in broad terms that might directly inspire trust or external efficacy. But if ads can make respondents feel better about elections (as the results in the previous section appear to suggest), they could be having some spillover effects into broader assessments. We see that with the results for the trust in government model (Figure 7.4).

Differential Effects

All told, the evidence suggests that in addition to informing and educating citizens, ads are reaching voters with emotional and attitudinal appeals. Citizens who see lots of ads are more interested in the campaign, more likely to assess elections as fair and properly functioning, and more likely to trust government. But so far we have looked at these effects only in the aggregate, across the wide spectrum of citizens in our surveys. A key motivation in all our analyses is the sense that advertising effects are most likely to be concentrated among certain subgroups.

But which subgroups? In Chapter 6, the choice was obvious: Those with low levels of political knowledge should be most susceptible to informational appeals (partly because they need that information the most, but partly because the thirty-second spot is easy to digest—indeed, little is required of the informationally poor in order to process television ads). But are those with low levels of political information also more likely to receive messages that result in a change in attitudes? The results from Tables 7.4, 7.5, and 7.6 suggest not.[8]

Across all sets of results—campaign engagement, evaluations of elections, and trust and efficacy—we found only three instances in which low-information respondents got a significantly bigger boost than their high-information

TABLE 7.4   Heterogeneity Effects on Campaign Engagement

	Preelection interest in campaign	Postelection interest	Cares about the outcome
Ad exposure (2000 ANES)	.002 (.018)	−.014 (.020)	−.065 (.049)
Ad exposure × low information	.046 (.018)**	.049 (.017)**	.058 (.049)
Ad exposure (2000 ANES)	.003 (.016)	−.011 (.019)	−.063 (.040)
Ad exposure × Independents	.062 (.018)**	.057 (.018)**	.074 (.047)
Ad exposure (2000 DDB Needham)	—	.001 (.019)	—
Ad exposure × Independents	—	−.000 (.023)	—

Entries are coefficients (with standard errors in parentheses) from separate ordered probit and logit models. All exposure measures are logged.
$+ p < .10$; $^*p < .05$; $^{**}p < .01$

TABLE 7.5   Heterogencity Effects on Evaluations of Elections

	Elections are fair	We need election reform	Money decides elections	Campaign truthfulness
Ad exposure (2004 DDB Needham)	.018 (.027)	−.062 (.029)*	−.064 (.028)*	—
Ad exposure × low information	−.0004 (.017)	−.012 (.018)	.010 (.017)	—
Ad exposure (2004 UW–BYU)	—	—	—	.017 (.018)
Ad exposure × low information	—	—	—	−.031 (.015)*
Ad exposure (2004 UW–BYU)	—	—	—	−.000 (.016)
Ad exposure × Independents	—	—	—	−.000 (.021)

2004 DDB Needham "Life Style Study" did not contain a party identification variable, which explains the missing heterogeneity model relative to independents. All exposure measures are logged.
$+ p < .10;\ ^*p < .05;\ ^{**}p < .01$

counterparts. The first two were in the pre- and postelection interest models. In the postelection model, the coefficient on the exposure by low-information interaction term was positive and statistically significant ($p < .01$). Recall that in Table 7.1, the effects of total exposure were insignificant. The result reported here indicates that low-information respondents were more influenced by advertising (in the postelection assessment) than those with high levels of political information (who were unaffected). The relationship was similar in the preelection model. The final instance was in the trust model (see Table 7.6); while the interaction term was not significant, the total effect for low information respondents (main effect + interaction) was weakly significant ($p < .10$).[9] This suggests that lower-information respondents were more responsive than sophisticates with regard to assessments of trust in government.

TABLE 7.6   Heterogeneity Effects on Trust and Efficacy

	Trust in government	External efficacy
Ad exposure (2000 ANES)	.026 (.019)	.013 (.017)
Ad exposure × low information	.007 (.016)	.004 (.015)
Ad exposure (2000 ANES)	.038 (.019)*	.018 (.017)
Ad exposure × Independents	−.017 (.018)	−.006 (.016)
Ad exposure (2000 DDB Needham)	—	−.017 (.149)
Ad exposure × Independents	—	.064 (.056)

Entries are coefficients (with standard errors in parentheses) from separate ordered probit and OLS models. All exposure measures are logged.
$+ p < .10;\ ^*p < .05;\ ^{**}p < .01$

For all other models, low-information respondents behaved similarly to those with higher levels of generalized political information. Of course, the story is a bit more complicated, in part because it is not clear that the politically unsophisticated are most in need of attitudinal boosts. Indeed, we started the analysis with the presumption that low-information citizens would be less inclined to approach elections with interest or trust (and that they would be less likely than high-information respondents to trust government more generally). It turns out, however, that we were only partly correct; there were interesting differences in how levels of generalized political information related to our attitudinal dependent variables.

In Table 7.7, we report the coefficient on general political information from all of the models in Tables 7.1, 7.2, and 7.3. The table demonstrates that those with higher generalized political information held more positive attitudes about politics and elections (care, efficacy, and interest). But higher political information led to lower assessments of the health and truthfulness of campaigns.

We translated four of these effects into predicted probabilities in Figure 7.5. This figure shows that higher information led to significant gains in interest and care, but it lowered trust (by about 0.10) and raised the probability that respondents saw a need for serious electoral change (definite agreement rose by almost 0.10).

What does this mean? On the one hand, those with higher levels of political knowledge had a strong commitment to political participation (as Table 7.7 indicates, they had a high interest in elections); and these were voters also more likely to consume political material, as well as to discuss and debate politics with friends and family (such political engagement is the focus of the next chapter).

TABLE 7.7 Impact of General Information

Dependent variable	General info
Care	.282 (.061)**
Efficacy (2000 ANES)	.052 (.022)*
Preelection interest	.234 (.025)**
Postelection interest	.228 (.026)**
Trust	−.054 (.025)*
Election fairness	−.009 (.021)
Need election reform	−.042 (.022)+
Money decides elections	−.024 (021)
Campaign truthfulness	−.140 (.028)**

Entries are coefficients and standard errors (for the general political info control) from *separate* regression models; results are from models estimating effects of total exposure. For election fairness, need election reform, and money decides elections, negative coefficients indicate movement from disagreeing to agreeing.
$+p < .10; *p < .05; **p < .01$

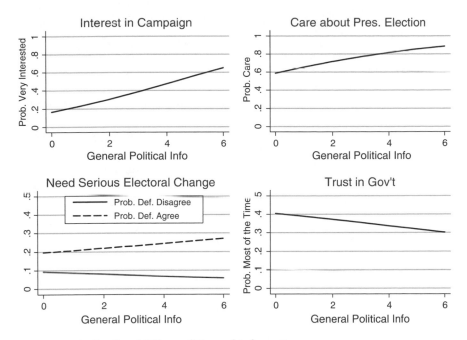

FIGURE 7.5   Predicted Effects of General Information

But on the other hand, political knowledge brought with it greater concern about potential defects in the political system. These were the respondents, despite a deeper commitment to politics, most likely to worry about the structure of elections (i.e., was the presidential outcome in 2000 fair? Were ballots counted properly? Were some African Americans denied voting rights?) or to distrust the government's ability to solve important problems. This pattern of results should make sense to those who consider themselves politically aware and knowledge-able. They watch Sunday morning political talk shows; they read the newspaper and perhaps participate on political blogs. But they also are most likely the ones shouting at talking heads on television and feeling dissatisfied with the course of political debate in Washington, D.C.

As such, although we have argued that low-information voters are those most in need of the health benefits that can come from political ads, this was not the case for all of our attitudinal variables. In some cases, those rich in po-litical information are the ones in greatest need. As such, the significant main effects reported in Table 7.5 (on the need for election reform and the impor-tance of money) were encouraging; these were the coefficient estimates for high-information respondents. Indeed, holding all else constant and varying ex-posure by two standard deviations (from one below to one above the mean of exposure) raises the probability by 0.03 that high-information respondents def-initely disagree with the statement that money determines elections (from 0.08

to 0.11); it lowers the probability that the respondent definitely agrees by 0.04 (from 0.15 to 0.11).

Keep in mind, however, that in these two cases the interactive effect for low information respondents was insignificant and small. This implies that the politically uniformed also received an attitudinal boost from campaign-ad exposure. Indeed, varying levels of exposure in the same way shows similar gains for the lower informed.

And so we are left with a similar story in this chapter as with Chapter 6, relative to the differential effects hypothesis. Sometimes the politically uninformed are influenced by ads at greater rates than their high-information counterparts (in this case, for interest in the election and trust in government), and sometimes they are influenced at the same rate (for evaluations of election fairness and money's role in election outcomes). And while this is not definitive evidence in favor of our heterogeneity expectations, we are comforted to know that at least lower initial stores of generalized political information are not acting as a barrier to the healthy effects of campaign ad exposure.

Partisanship

Finally, we investigated the differential effects hypothesis for political independents. These findings are also reported in Tables 7.4, 7.5, and 7.6. Perhaps this subgroup, unaligned with a political party, got a unique attitudinal boost from political advertising. More specifically, as reported in this chapter, in almost all of the attitudinal models, strength of partisanship predicted more interest in the campaigns and a healthier evaluation of elections. Independents, in this sense, may have "needed" the attitudinal boost provided by campaign advertising.

As our findings demonstrated, only in the 2000 ANES pre- and postelection interest models did independents get a unique lift from exposure (in relation to partisans), and those effects were even a bit larger than the boost felt by low-information respondents.

These results stand in contrast to the findings from Chapter 6, where we found some negative interactive effects for independents. In that case, the interactions indicated not that independents were (all else equal) negatively affected by exposure, but that the main effects were confined to partisans. More specifically, because the main effect and interactive effect in those cases were nearly equal and opposite in size, the total effect for independents was essentially zero.[10] In the interest models in this chapter, the interaction effect was positive and significant, while the partisan main effect was insignificant. This is an indication that independents got a unique attitudinal boost in relation to those tied to a political party.

Despite these two effects, however, the evidence for the partisan hypothesis is very weak. Over the course of the last two chapters, while finding that the weakly informed were sometimes more affected, and often as affected, as high-information respondents, there is only scattered evidence here that the dynamic works in the same way for independents.

Summary

At this point, we have spoken only of the effect of ads on the citizens who remain seated on their couch. At the very least, ads are increasing the store of (accurate) information about campaigns, and we learned in this chapter that there is limited evidence that ads serve to improve assessments of politics and campaigns.

We present one final summary of impact. In Figure 7.6, we show the average probability of being in the top categories of the four dependent variables where we found advertising effects. We assigned each respondent to two conditions—one in which exposure was zero, and one in which exposure was at its maximum—and we predicted the probability for each respondent, using the reported values of the control variables.

Thus, for example, after estimating the model for preelection interest, we only changed the respondent's exposure measure. If every respondent had no exposure, for example, the average probability (across all respondents) of being somewhat or very much interested in the election was about 0.25. When every respondent was exposed to a high level of ads, by contrast, the average probability of being highly interested in the campaign rose to over 0.35.

In a hypothetical world where no respondents in the 2004 DDB Needham "Life Style" study were exposed to any campaign advertising, there would be widespread discontent about the state of American elections—an average

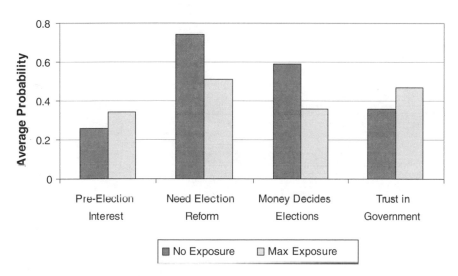

FIGURE 7.6 Average Probabilities for Varied Exposure.

Note: Probabilities for interest are for "somewhat" and "very interested"; for election reform and money in elections, probabilities are definite and general disagreement; trust is "just about always" and "most of the time."

probability of perceiving the need for election reform of about 0.80, and an average probability of perceiving money's damaging impact on elections at near 0.60. In a world of pervasive and widespread political ads, however (one that reaches nearly everyone), these damning assessments of American elections fall to about 0.50 and just under 0.40, respectively. This simulation obviously presents an exaggerated picture of the magnitude of advertising's effects, but it nonetheless illustrates that a proliferation of advertising is not necessarily democratically disturbing.

Finally, with no exposure, trust in government (the probability of trusting government "just about always" and "most of the time") would be just below 0.40. In a world in which every citizen saw the maximum set of ads, however, the probability of high levels of trust would increase to nearly 0.50.

It seems likely that viewers exposed to ads that inform and raise campaign interest also will be more likely to get off the couch and participate in the political process. Indeed, almost every theoretical and empirical model of political participation predicted that the effects of information and many of the attitudinal variables considered here would be positive and large. We suggest, then, that exposure to advertising can indirectly boost levels of political action.

But what sorts of direct effects does advertising have on various forms of participation? We interpret the null results from the efficacy models as an appropriate transition into the next chapter. Ads may help people feel better about elections and government, which might lead them to increased political participation, but ads also might lead them to believe that their participation matters. As the results from this chapter demonstrate, however, it seems ads have no effect on assessments of the impact of one's participation. It remains an open question, then, whether ads have the ability to increase engagement and participation in the political process. This is the question to which we turn in the next chapter.

CHAPTER EIGHT

Campaign Advertising and Citizen

Participation

D URING THE 2004 CAMPAIGN season, 3.4 percent of Americans adults did campaign work for a candidate or party; 7.6 percent attended a campaign meeting, rally, or speech; 9.6 percent contributed money to a candidate; 20.6 percent displayed a campaign sign or bumper sticker; 48.5 percent tried to influence the vote of someone else; [1] and, according to the U.S. Census Bureau, 58.3 percent of the voting-age population voted. While participation in many political activities, such as doing actual campaign work, was very low, a large number of Americans talked to their friends and neighbors about the elections, and even more people made it to a polling place on Election Day.

What explains these disparate patterns of participation? According to the "civic voluntarism" model of Verba, Schlozman, and Brady (1995) and most models of political participation (Rosenstone and Hansen 1993; Teixeira 1992), there are three essential sets of factors. The first is motivation or engagement; citizens must want to be active in the political process (and believe that their participation can make a difference). The second is capacity; citizens must have access to the resources and skills necessary to participate in politics. These can include the time to travel to a polling place, the financial resources to contribute money to a political candidate, or the informational resources to write a letter to a member of Congress or to cast an informed vote. The final factor influencing participation is political mobilization: the simple fact of whether someone has asked you to participate. People embedded in large social networks and people with more organizational ties are more likely to be asked to participate, and, thus, are more likely to do so.

How does political advertising factor into all of this? Can advertising affect people's motivation to participate in politics, their capacity to do so, or their probability of being mobilized—all things that should make participation more likely, according to the civic voluntarism model? To be sure, there is a vast literature linking the tone of a political campaign—and the tone of television advertising in particular—to voter turnout. We reviewed much of that literature in Chapter 2 and will analyze the specific effect of advertising tone on a wide range of attitudes and behaviors including turnout in the following chapter. But our question here concerns the effects of political advertising more generally (regardless of tone), on voter turnout and political participation.

We have already seen in Chapter 6 that exposure to television advertising increases one's store of information about the candidates, a valuable resource if one is heading to the voting booth. In Chapter 7, although the results were less conclusive, we found a positive relationship between ad exposure and both political interest and trust in government, two factors that may motivate political participation. We also found some evidence that advertising might improve attitudes about the election process itself by making people less likely to believe that money decides elections and that the American electoral system requires reform. Holding positive views such as these about American democracy also might increase someone's motivation to participate politically. What then is the net effect of exposure to campaign ads? Does it make political participation more likely?

Our primary hypothesis in this chapter is that increased exposure to political advertising should be associated with increased political participation. This is precisely because advertising affects other precursors of participation, including information, political interest, and trust in government. That said, we expect that the size of the impacts will be small; given the many different factors that influence political participation, that advertising should have massive direct effects does not make sense to us. As in previous chapters, we also test the differential effects hypothesis, which posits that the impact of ad exposure will be greatest among those with lower levels of political information at the outset. Finally, we test whether the effects of advertising will be the greatest among those least set in their ways when it comes to politics: political independents (our partisan hypothesis).

Models and Data

Again, we used Wisconsin Advertising Project tracking data combined with survey data to build the same measures of ad exposure we employed in earlier chapters. Our four surveys are the same used previously.

We estimated several models with exposure to political advertising as the primary predictor variable. Our dependent variables were voter turnout, several individual acts of political participation (including attending a political rally, displaying a campaign bumper sticker or yard sign, circulating a petition for a candidate or issue, and contacting a public official), and several types of political "chatter" (including talking with friends about politics, talking with family about politics, holding a political discussion with someone with whom you disagree, and encouraging someone to register to vote). The predictor variables in each model were the same as in previous chapters.

In all of the datasets, turnout was measured with a simple indicator variable, with one indicating the respondent reported having cast a vote and zero indicating he or she failed to do so. The DDB Needham "Life Style" data in both 2000 and 2004 asked whether respondents had engaged in several types of political participation in the previous three months. These were tapped through a scale that ranged from one to eight, with one indicating no instances of the activity in the past three months, two indicating one instance of the activity in the past three months, and on up to eight, indicating more than twenty-five instances of the activity in the past three months. The political chatter variables were coded in the same way; for example, someone who reported talking about politics with friends five times in the past three months received a score of five on this variable.

Unfortunately, a common feature of survey research is substantial overreporting of voter turnout. Surveys like the ANES typically find reported turnout among the sample at ten, 20 or more percentage points higher than official turnout figures. One reason for this is that turnout is a socially desirable behavior, and so people are reluctant to admit they have not voted. Another reason for this is that we used panel studies in which respondents who had been previously interviewed were being interviewed again. Generally, it is those least interested in the topic of the survey (in our case, politics) who are least likely to agree to additional interviews, and thus it is those who are least likely to vote who are dropping out of the survey. Finally, in panel studies such as the ones we examined here, there may have been some mobilizing effect from having participated in the earlier wave of the survey.

Among the surveys we used, the incidence of overreporting was lowest in the 2000 ANES, in which 76 percent of respondents reported having voted, compared to official statistics that placed turnout rates at just under 55 percent of the voting-age population.[2] The 2000 DDB Needham "Life Style" study pegged voter turnout at 87 percent. That same percentage of respondents reported having voting in the 2004 DDB Needham "Life Style" study, a year in which about 58 percent of the voting-age population showed up to vote.[3] In the UW–BYU study, an astounding 91 percent of respondents reported having voted.

Though overreporting of turnout is common, Verba, Schlozman, and Brady (1995, 613–17) made a convincing case that this overreporting should not substantially bias one's results, as those who were most likely to report incorrectly that they had voted closely resembled those respondents who actually voted. Thus, even though our descriptive statistics may give a biased picture of the population, as legions of scholars have done, we can still estimate unbiased parameters in our statistical models assuming that people's propensity to overreport turnout is uncorrelated with their actual propensity to turn out to vote.

There is one additional dataset that we employed in this chapter. It is a county-level dataset onto which we merged data on voter turnout levels in each county along with the volume of television advertising aired in each county for which we had Wisconsin Advertising Project tracking data. In 2000, we were able to analyze 1,590 of the 3,000 counties in the United States; that number jumped to 2,008 in 2004 because we had access to advertising data for 25 additional television markets, 100 in all. We used these county-level data to estimate turnout models, which were quite parsimonious.[4] For instance, in estimating the rate of turnout in each county in 2004, we included only four predictors: the volume of advertising in that county, the rate of turnout in the 2000 general election, an indicator of whether there was a competitive U.S. Senate race in the state, and an indicator of whether the presidential election was competitive in that state.

Turnout

We looked first at the impact of political advertising on voter turnout (Table 8.1). Our results emphatically rejected the oft-heard claim that advertising is causing voters to stay home on Election Day, and, consequently, is destroying American democracy. In none of the six datasets we used to estimate a model of voter turnout was advertising a significant predictor of lower turnout and in three of the data sets—the 2000 ANES, the 2000 county-level data, and 2004 county-level data—advertising was positively correlated with turnout.[5]

What is the substantive impact of advertising on turnout? Figure 8.1 begins to speak to this by displaying a voter's predicted probability of turning out to vote based on his or her exposure to advertising, using data from the 2000 ANES. Clearly, the effects were quite substantial. We predicted that an "average" person exposed to no advertising, either because he or she watched no television or lived in a place in which no ads were aired, had just under a 0.5 probability of turning out to vote.[6] When we increased that same person's exposure to advertising to the maximum found in the dataset, the predicted probability of voting jumped by 0.2 to 0.7.

TABLE 8.1   Effects of Ad Exposure on Voter Turnout

Total exposure (2000 ANES)	.101 (.038)**
Total exposure (2004 UW–BYU)	−.146 (.093)
Total exposure (2000 DDB Needham)	−.033 (.131)
Total exposure (2004 DDB Needham)	−.067 (.073)
Thousand ads (2000 county data)	.038 (.020)+
Thousand ads (2004 county data)	.081 (.011)**

Entries are coefficients (with standard errors in parentheses) from different logit models. All exposure measures are logged.
$+ p < .10$; $^{*}p < .05$; $^{**}p < .01$

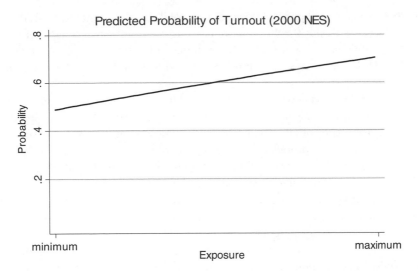

FIGURE 8.1   Predicted Effects of Ad Exposure on Turnout

A similar story emerged at the county level. The first panel of Figure 8.2 shows the estimated effect on turnout within a county by increasing ads aired during the course of the 2000 election. The effects were significant, but relatively modest: According to this model, an increase of 10,000 ads broadcast increased voter turnout only a small amount, about three-tenths of a percentage point. Considering that Seattle-Tacoma—the most heavily targeted market

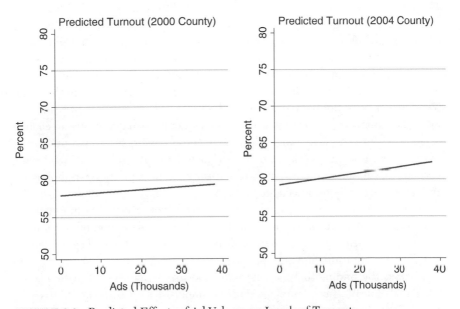

FIGURE 8.2   Predicted Effects of Ad Volume on Levels of Turnout

in 2000—received about 22,000 ad airings total, these findings appeared even more modest. To put this effect in perspective, the influence of advertising in 2000 was only about one-quarter the influence of living in a state with a competitive U.S. Senate race (which was predicted to raise turnout 1.1 percentage points).

The 2004 county-level model (illustrated in the second panel of Figure 8.2) pointed to considerably larger effects. Here, an increase of 10,000 ads led to an increase in turnout of about eight-tenths of a percentage point. We estimated that (all else equal) turnout was about 3 percent higher in the market that saw the most advertising in 2004—Tampa–St. Petersburg, Florida, with over 37,500 ads—than in a media market such as San Antonio, Texas, or Wichita, Kansas, that received no advertising. This effect was quite a bit larger than the effect of living in a state with a competitive Senate race, which was predicted to boost turnout only about 0.5 percentage points in 2004.

Taken as a whole, the turnout models suggested that campaign advertising has a positive impact on voter turnout, and they lent no support to the claim that campaign advertising serves to reduce turnout. Admittedly, though, our results were somewhat modest. Advertising does not have the capacity to boost voter turnout to universal levels; to the extent that ads help citizens cast a ballot, it is on the margins and in small doses.

Moving Beyond Turnout

The next outcomes we examined were for four different types of political participation, including attending a political meeting or rally, displaying a bumper sticker or yard sign, circulating a petition for a candidate or issue, and contacting a government official. We asked whether increased exposure to political advertising might encourage forms of political participation beyond showing up at the ballot box, working through increased information and interest. With the DDB Needham "Life Style" data, we regressed, using OLS, an eight-point scale indicating how many times in the past three months citizens had engaged in each of these activities. The scale ranged from zero (no times) to seven (twenty-five or more times). With the ANES data, we estimated a logit model in which having participated in one of the activities or not (circulating a petition was not asked about) was the dichotomous dependent variable.

Our findings, reported in Table 8.2, showed that advertising in almost all instances had absolutely no direct impact on people's likelihood of engaging in these four political activities. There was only one statistically significant relationship between exposure and participation in either year, and it was an unexpected one: It was the finding that increased ad exposure was associated with a lower likelihood of displaying a campaign sign or bumper sticker (using the 2000 ANES

TABLE 8.2   Effects of Ad Exposure on Political Participation

	Attend rally	Display sticker	Circulate petition	Contact official
Total exposure (2000 ANES)	−.073 (.060)	−.087 (.048)+	—	−.013 (.036)
Total exposure (2000 DDB Needham)	−.021 (.031)	−.038 (.061)	.003 (.021)	.050 (.047)
Total exposure (2004 DDB Needham)	−.050 (.053)	.041 (.028)	−.006 (.022)	—

Entries are coefficients (with standard errors in parentheses). We used logit models with the ANES data and OLS models with the DDB Needham "Life Style Study" data. All exposure measures are logged.
$+ p < .10; {}^{*}p < .05; {}^{**}p < .01$

data). This one negative coefficient is very weak evidence, however, for the oft-heard claims about the deleterious effects of political advertising.

Finally, we examined whether advertising might be associated with political "chatter." That is, might television advertising provide people with more political information and increase their interest in politics, leading them to talk more about politics? Do the effects of ad exposure on interest and information make it more likely that citizens will take up the issues addressed in ads in discussions, conversations, and arguments with friends, family members, or coworkers?

To test this hypothesis, we estimated four models of the frequency of political discussion, including talk with friends, talk with family, talk with political opponents, and, finally, encouraging others to vote. The variables were coded on the same eight-point scale used for some of the participation variables: Zero indicated no discussion, and seven indicated twenty-five or more discussions in the past three months. Table 8.3, which reports the estimates obtained from our four models, reveals there was no relationship whatsoever between exposure to political advertising and political chatter. None of the six coefficient estimates, two from the year 2000 and four from 2004, was significantly different from zero. Exposure to ads does not stimulate people to talk more about politics.

TABLE 8.3   Effects of Ad Exposure on Political Chatter

	Talk with friend	Talk with family	Talk with opponents	Encourage to vote
Total exposure (2000 DDB Needham)	.017 (.049)	.022 (.047)	—	—
Total exposure (2004 DDB Needham)	−.024 (.027)	−.028 (.028)	.023 (.029)	−.028 (.028)

Entries are coefficients (with standard errors in parentheses) from different ordered probit models. All exposure measures are logged.
$+ p < .10; {}^{*}p < .05; {}^{**}p < .01$

Informational Heterogeneity

Although the only direct effect of advertising that we have identified is for turnout, we wanted to explore whether advertising's impact might be evident for certain subgroups of the population, specifically those low in political information and those who are political independents. Our thinking was that people low in political information and political independents, lacking the anchor provided by a partisan attachment, might be more susceptible to the influence of advertising. And, unlike the more complicated information story from the last chapter (where higher levels of generalized political information led to a higher interest in elections but more pessimistic assessments of electoral fairness), in all of our models for this chapter, higher levels of general political information and stronger partisanship were associated with more political participation.

Considering first advertising's impact on turnout, our hypothesis that ad effects might be more evident among those low in political information received only limited support (Table 8.4). The interaction of information with ad exposure was a statistically insignificant predictor of voter turnout. Indeed, the significant main effect from the 2000 ANES shows that political sophisticates were influenced by political ad exposure. At the same time, however, the very small and insignificant interactive effect demonstrates that those respondents low in generalized political information were also motivated to vote under conditions of high exposure. As in Chapters 6 and 7, we take this to be confirming evidence that the politically ignorant are not insulated from ad messages. Consider these predicted effects: Varying levels of ad exposure from minimum to maximum changes the probability of voting for high-information respondents by 0.13 (from 0.74 to 0.87). But for low-information respondents, because their initial probability of

TABLE 8.4   Interactive Effects of Ad Exposure on Voter Turnout

Total exposure (2000 ANES)	.089 (.040)+
Total exposure × low information	.017 (.043)
Total exposure (2004 UW–BYU)	−.122 (.100)
Total exposure × low information	−.031 (.058)
Total exposure (2000 DDB Needham)	−.027 (.135)
Total exposure × low information	−.018 (.073)
Total exposure (2000 ANES)	.099 (.036)**
Total exposure × Independents	.015 (.042)
Total exposure (2004 UW–BYU)	−.222 (.099)*
Total exposure × Independents	.127 (.057)*
Total exposure (2000 DDB Needham)	−.044 (.134)
Total exposure × Independents	.034 (.065)

Entries are coefficients (with standard errors in parentheses) from different logit models. All exposure measures are logged.
$+p < .10$; $*p < .05$; $**p < .01$

TABLE 8.5   Interactive Effects of Advertising on Political Participation

	Attend rally	Display sticker	Circulate petition	Contact official
Total exposure (2000 ANES)	−.064 (.073)	−.121 (.058)*	—	−.019 (.044)
Total exposure × low information	−.004 (.075)	.014 (.053)	—	.021 (.039)
Total exposure (2000 DDB Needham)	−.029 (.031)	−.052 (.065)	−.002 (.022)	.046 (.046)
Total exposure × low information	.016 (.013)	.026 (.023)	.010 (.011)	.008 (.018)
Total exposure (2000 ANES)	−.072 (.061)	−.084 (.048)+	—	−.003 (.036)
Total exposure × Independents	−.012 (.097)	−.050 (.082)	—	−.078 (.046)
Total exposure (2000 DDB Needham)	−.022 (.032)	−.045 (.061)	−.002 (.021)	.051 (.047)
Total exposure × Independents	.005 (.014)	.037 (.020)+	.025 (.010)*	−.004 (.019)

Entries are coefficients (with standard errors in parentheses). We used logit models with the ANES data and OLS with the DDB Needham "Life Style Study" data. All exposure measures are logged.
$+ p < .10; * p < .05; ** p < .01$

voting is already lower, exposure moves their predicted probability by 0.24 over the range of exposure (from 0.48 to 0.72).[7]

As for acts of political participation (Table 8.5), in none of the seven reported models was the impact of advertising different for those low and high in political information. Again, though, the negative main effect on displaying a sticker (recall, this is the only significant negative effect from exposure that we have found thus far) implies that those rich in political information are negatively affected; but the small interactive effect implies a similar demobilizing trend for those low in political information. For example, across the full range of exposure, political sophisticates see a 0.04 drop in the probability that they

TABLE 8.6   Interactive Effects of Advertising on Political Chatter

	Talk with friend	Talk with family
Total exposure (2000 DDB Needham)	.013 (.050)	.023 (.048)
Total exposure × low information	.008 (.019)	−.003 (.019)
Total exposure (2000 DDB Needham)	.030 (.071)	.041 (.158)
Total exposure × Independents	−.035 (.102)	−.025 (.280)

Entries are coefficients (with standard errors in parentheses) from different ordered probit models. All exposure measures are logged.
$+ p < .10; * p < .05; ** p < .01$

report displaying a sign or sticker during the 2000 election (from 0.07 to 0.03); that effect is comparable for low information respondents (from 0.06 to 0.03).

Indeed, the bottom line is this: when it comes to political participation, advertising had no greater or lesser impact on the poorly informed than on the well informed. This is confirmed again in Table 8.6. The information interaction term also failed as a predictor of political chatter.[8] In the conclusion to this chapter, we will expand on these results and put them in the context of the other tests for differential effects discussed in the previous two chapters.

Partisan Heterogeneity

We also examined the partisan hypothesis, which asserts that political independents might be more influenced by advertising than political partisans. We have found little evidence to that effect in the previous chapters, and there was almost no support for that hypothesis in our model estimates here. With regard to voter turnout, we found that independents in the 2004 UW–BYU study (Table 8.4) were uninfluenced by exposure to advertising, compared to partisans who were demobilized. But in the context of the 2000 NES, partisans (see the main effect) and independents (because of the small and insignificant interactive effect) are similarly mobilized. This inconsistency weakens any larger claims we can make about differential partisan effects.

With regard to other types of participation, we found that the impact of advertising was slightly greater for political independents for predicting the frequency of displaying bumper stickers and yard signs and circulating a petition

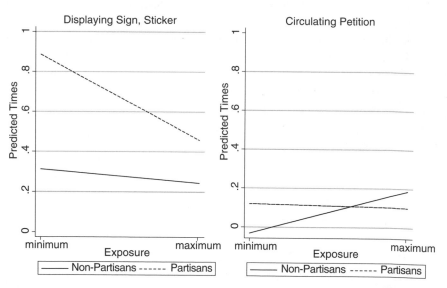

FIGURE 8.3   Predicted Effects of Ad Exposure on Political Activities by Partisanship

for a candidate (see the 2000 DDB Needham "Life Style" effects in Table 8.5). One must be careful, however, not to read too much into these last two findings; the results are displayed graphically in Figure 8.3. What is important to note in the first panel is that even though ad exposure (the main effect) had a negative (though statistically insignificant) impact on the frequency of displayed signs or stickers, this relationship was barely evident for political independents. This implies that political independents were less likely to be demobilized in this way by advertising in comparison to partisans. In the second panel, advertising had virtually no impact for partisans on the reported frequency of circulated petitions, but the effects for nonpartisans were positive.

Summary

This chapter provides reasonable evidence for the conclusion that if exposure to political advertising has any impact on voter turnout, it is a positive one. One of our four individual-level models, along with our county-level models from 2000 and 2004, confirmed a positive relationship between increased exposure and increased turnout, and the remaining three models found no relationship at all.

The impact of advertising, however, is confined to turnout. In none of the other instances of participation that we examined—ranging from putting up a yard sign, circulating a petition, or chatting with a neighbor about politics—did we find direct impacts of advertising. This pattern of results made some sense to us given that advertising may provide the information and positive attitudes toward the system that may push someone who is on the cusp of voting to the polls. Yet voting is a relatively simple act of participation—something that the majority of Americans did in the last election—so the benefits of advertising appear not to extend to more difficult types of political participation.

As important, we have uncovered very little evidence that political advertising is a demobilizer, that it reduces people's likelihood of circulating a petition, displaying a candidate bumper sticker, or talking about politics with their friends or family. Different sources of data from different years back this claim. The naysayers appear to be wrong: Political advertising does not cause people to be less engaged in politics.

Of course, up to this point, we have focused on only one aspect of the advertising environment: the volume of advertising to which citizens are exposed. In the next chapter, we disaggregate advertising into two types, positive and negative, to examine whether the democratic consequences are different depending on the tone of the advertising.

Before proceeding, however, it is important to consider the weight of evidence relative to the information and partisan hypotheses. We do so here because we do not take these up in the next chapter. What are we to make of the balance of evidence relative to the notion that independents and the politically ignorant are more affected by political ads? The answer is that the weakly informed are, in fact, influenced by campaign-ad messages. They learn important campaign information from them; they respond with higher reported interest in the election and more optimism about democracy generally; there is even some evidence to suggest that they are also more likely to vote. Sometimes this effect outpaces the gains felt by political sophisticates. and sometimes it does not. But, on balance, there is little evidence to suggest that being politically uniformed blocks message retention in the ways measured here. This makes sense knowing what we know about the content of political ads and the relative ease with which someone can intake that information. We are encouraged by these results, even if they are not overwhelming evidence of our expectation that lower-informed respondents would be the primary beneficiaries of ad exposure.

As for the partisan hypothesis, we feel it is safe to say that the evidence implies almost no unique effects for independents. For learning, the results suggest partisans are far more responsive. For attitudes, there is some evidence to suggest that independents are more interested in the election than partisans under conditions of heavy exposure, but that's it. And for participation, any unique gains are isolated to the probability of circulating a petition. In short, we can conclude nothing of substance relative to these differential partisan effects. If there is any differential story in these rich sets of findings, it is for the lower-informed.

We turn now to our final empirical investigation and the test of our negativity hypothesis.

CHAPTER NINE

Advertising Tone and Political Engagement

W E HAVE SEEN IN the previous chapters that exposure to political advertisements can have important effects on what voters know, as well as on their attitudes about the political process. In this chapter, we look at whether different types of advertisements have different effects on what potential voters learn, think, and do. More specifically, we ask whether the tone of advertising matters.

Critics of campaign advertising have reserved their harshest attacks for attack ads themselves. One of the main problems with campaign advertising, according to the critics, is that it is too negative. As we saw in Chapter 2, negative ads are thought to alienate the public, causing people to become disenchanted—if not disgusted—with the candidates, disengaged from the political process, and, ultimately, less likely to turn out on Election Day.

We disagree. We argued in Chapter 2 that campaign ads function as crucial information shortcuts—vitamin supplements that help citizens to make sense of the political world—and in the previous chapters, we showed that people can and do learn from campaign ads and become engaged in politics because of their exposure to them. What kinds of ads provide the best shortcuts for voters looking for cues? There are several reasons to suspect that negative ads better serve this function than positive ads.

First, and as we noted in Chapter 2, with thousands of ads aired in competitive races and heaps of political and nonpolitical information available (even if largely unavailed of), negative ads simply have a greater chance of being noticed. Their characteristic jarring graphics, ominous soundtracks, and aggressive messages are more likely to make an impression. Consider the following negative message from an ad captured and coded by the Wisconsin Advertising Project.

It was sponsored by the Democratic National Committee and comes from the 2000 presidential campaign:

> Announcer: "Whose side is George W. Bush on? As governor, he pushed through a big tax cut for the oil industry but opposed health insurance for 220,000 more children. He failed to fund school lunches for hungry children. Under Bush, Texas has fallen from 29th to the 48th worst state in America to raise a child. Second to last in children's health insurance. Last in health insurance for families. Ask yourself, are George W. Bush's priorities our priorities?"

Next, consider a positive ad aired on behalf of George Nethercutt's Senate campaign in Washington State in 2004, which is shown in Figure 9.1. Although it attempts to be light-hearted (and make a favorable impression on viewers), which ad is truly more compelling? Which is more likely to make viewers perk up their ears, put down their pizza, and listen? We argue that negative ads, such as the first one, are more likely to convey that sense of urgency.

In addition, it seems that negative advertising is a component of the television campaign that is here to stay. As Franz, Rivlin, and Goldstein (2006) noted, the level of negative and contrast advertising remained relatively unchanged between the presidential election years of 2000 and 2004—this despite major campaign finance reform meant, in part, to curb the negativity of political advertising by requiring that candidates "stand by their ads." Because advertising tone is driven by fundamental factors like electoral competitiveness, there will always be incentives that compel candidates, interest groups, and parties to go on the attack.[1]

If negative ads do, in fact, provide the most direct and compelling informational shortcuts for citizens, potential voters exposed to more negative advertising should be more likely to cast their ballots. Furthermore, if this theoretical account is correct, voters exposed to negative advertising not only should be more likely to vote, but they should know more about the candidates, be more interested in the campaign, care more about outcomes, and feel more efficacious. This is the negativity hypothesis introduced in Chapter 2.

We also bring evidence to bear on a crucial, underexplored nuance in the debate over negative advertising. Knowing that some negative ads contain policy information while others contain vicious personal mudslinging, what are the effects of these very different types of negative ads?

The Informational Content of Negative Ads

As a preliminary step, we compared the informational content of positive, contrast, and negative ads. Given that many negative ads are often condemned as

USSEN/WA NETHERCUTT COMMERCIAL

Brand: POL-US SENATE (B332)
Parent: POLITICAL ADV
Aired: 10/28/2004 - 10/30/2004
Creative Id: 3611537

[Nethercutt]: "You know it's not easy taping a commercial with your wife."

[Mrs. Nethercutt]: "Well, I'll let them tell me what to.." [Nethercutt]: "You know, I've been though this a lot."

[Nethercutt]: "I'm asking for your vote to restore that tradition of la.. stro.....Shoot"

[Mrs. Nethercutt]: "That was awful. No. Bad. Too Stiff." [Nethercutt]: "Sorry guys, I apologize for that."

[Mrs. Nethercutt]: "Would you tell him to stop telling me how to say it?"

[Mrs. Nethercutt]: "Is this good?" [Nethercutt]: "It's perfect."

[Mrs. Nethercutt]: "What's the deal here?"

[Nethercutt]: (laughter) "I'm George Nethercutt and I approved this message."

[PFB]: Nethercutt for Senate

AdDetector **tns**
www.PoliticsOnTV.com

Copyright 2004 TNS Media Intelligence/CMAG

tns media intelligence./cmag
1-866-559-CMAG

FIGURE 9.1   George Nethercutt Positive Ad

"mudslinging," one might surmise that they contain less substantive information than positive ads, that they focus on personal attacks at the expense of real issues, and that they provide little in the way of useful information to help voters make informed choices. None of these charges turned out to be true.

First, we defined a positive ad as one that solely promoted the featured candidate and focused on positive attributes, including policy stands and personal characteristics. Ads that included criticism of an opposition candidate, we considered negative. If an ad dealt exclusively with the opponent, we considered it a pure negative or attack ad. Ads that mentioned both the opponent and the sponsor—even if only a fleeting mention—were coded as contrast ads.

In addition to assessing the tone of the ad, coders of the 2000 and 2004 ad data were asked to assess whether the primary focus of the ad was the personal characteristics of either candidate, their public policy stances, or some combination of both (as initially discussed in Chapter 6). Some research has suggested that viewers are more likely to accept criticisms of an opponent based on a candidate's issue positions or voting record, and reject ads that focus on candidates' personal characteristics as uncalled-for "mudslinging" (Kahn and Kenney 1999). Our coders also recorded up to four campaign themes in each unique ad. For ads classified as solely about personal characteristics, for example, common thematic mentions included the background and personal values of the candidate, as well as his or her honesty and integrity. For policy ads, the most common themes included taxes, education, Social Security, health care, and Medicare.

Obviously, a policy ad might include an implicit reference to personal characteristics: for example, a suggestion that opposition to the privatization of Social Security is a moral failure. More than 33,000 of the 570,000 policy spots broadcast in 2000 mentioned the background of the sponsoring candidate, and issues of honesty and integrity were referenced in just over 2 percent of strict policy ads. In addition, some ads coded as primarily dealing with personal characteristics also mentioned some policy issue. In 2000, about 6 percent of all "personality" ads mentioned health care, about 10 percent mentioned education, and 15 percent referred to taxes.

Finally, ads that mention neither policy nor personality tend to be focused on getting out the vote or reminding voters of Election Day. These ads accounted for only 1 percent of all federal airings in 2000, for example, and over 30 percent of these (about 3,000 aired spots) were sponsored by interest groups.

The findings presented in Table 9.1 are based on an analysis of 2,084 individual ads broadcast in federal races (House, Senate, and presidential) in 2000, and 2,842 ads broadcast in federal races in 2004. The table shows the percentage of ads, broken down by tone, that were focused on policy matters, the personal characteristics of the candidates, both, or neither.[2] The first thing to note is that attack ads and contrast ads were quite similar in terms of their discussion of policy issues. Sixty-two percent of attack ads and 65 percent of contrast ads in 2000 were primarily focused on questions of policy; no more than 10 percent of each were focused on the characteristics of the candidates. By contrast, fewer than half of the positive ads had a distinct policy focus, and 14 percent emphasized personal traits.

In 2004, the pattern was just as pronounced. Around 60 percent of both negative and contrast ads were policy focused, compared to only 42.7 percent of positive ads. And while over a fifth (21.5 percent) of positive ads focused on the characteristics and personalities of the candidates, only 16.8 percent of negative ads and only 11.5 percent of contrast ads did. Similarly, in his analysis

TABLE 9.1   Storyboard Policy Content by Ad Tone, 2000 and 2004

	Attack	Contrast	Promote
2000			
Policy	62.4%	65%	46.8%
Candidate characteristics	10.1%	8.5%	13.7%
Both	25.0%	26.3%	36.6%
Neither	2.5%	0.2%	2.9%
2004			
Policy	58.9%	60.0%	42.7%
Candidate characteristics	16.8%	11.5%	21.5%
Both	22.1%	28.4%	33.2%
Neither	2.2%	0.2%	2.5%

Note: Figures are column percentages.
2000: N = 2,084
2004: N = 2,842

of advertising in presidential contests from 1960 to 1988, Geer showed that negative spots were much more likely to talk about issues than positive ones (2006, 62).

Clearly, negative and contrast ads are more likely to focus on questions of policy than are positive spots. Of course, an ad focusing on a candidate's personal characteristics may contain information useful to voters. But policy-based information is, on the whole, certainly more useful to voters than claims touting a candidate's integrity, compassion, and love of family. The claim that negative ads are devoid of policy content is simply wrong.

Thus far we have differentiated between "pure" negative and "contrast" ads. However, the latter are, by definition, negative ads that include at least some positive statement (even if fleeting) about the sponsor. Elsewhere we noted that when one investigates negativity at the level of the campaign (for example, Senate campaigns between 1998 and 2002), there is strong correlation between measures of pure negative spots versus combined negative and contrast spots (Ridout and Franz forthcoming). In this sense, when candidates, parties, and interest groups "go pure negative," they also "go contrast negative." (And as our inter-coder reliability tests discussed in Appendix B demonstrate, differentiating between pure negative and contrast spots was not as reliable as defining positive spots.)

Contrast ads contain the attention-grabbing elements of negative ads; they play into voters' aversion for risk by highlighting the potential dangers of electing the opposing candidate, and, like pure negative ads, they tend to focus on policy appeals, not personal characteristics. For all intents and purposes, contrast ads are a subspecies of negative ads, and, as such, in all of the models in this chapter, we estimated combined exposure to negative and contrast ads.[3]

What, then, is the effect of negative advertising on the dependent variables explored in the last three empirical chapters? We organize this chapter around four sets of results. First, we examine the impact of tone on levels of information, using the dependent variables from Chapter 6. Second, we explore the relationship between tone and attitudes, as in Chapter 7. Third, we examine whether higher exposure to negative/contrast ads is related to higher political participation by citizens, as in Chapter 8. Finally, we split negative/contrast ads into those that contain some policy content and those that mention only the personal characteristics of candidates. We ask whether these two different forms of tone exposure have different effects on information, attitudes, and participation.

Tone and Information

Our first set of results, which speak to the relationship between ad tone and citizen knowledge, is shown in Table 9.2.[4] Our expectation was that exposure to negative advertising would be positively related to our measures of campaign knowledge, and we found some, though far from universal, supporting evidence.

The first two models predicted knowledge of facts in and not in ads, measures we discussed in Chapter 6. When measured separately, we found no significant effects of exposure to negative or positive ads on knowledge. But the next set of models, which spoke to the number of likes and dislikes that respondents reported about the presidential candidates in 2000, revealed an interesting effect of ad tone. Exposure to negative and contrast advertising was a statistically significant and positive predictor of the number of both positive and negative statements that citizens made about the presidential candidates. Indeed, when compared to the magnitude of the effects of total ad exposure in Chapter 6 (see Table 6.2), the effect of negative/contrast ads was four times greater for candidate likes, and twice as large for dislikes. It would appear to be negative (including contrast) ads that served to increase the store of considerations voters had about the candidates.

We demonstrate these effects visually in the top two panels of Figure 9.2, where we varied positive or negative/contrast exposure while holding the other measure constant at its mean.[5] The substantive impact of increasing negative ad exposure was, in fact, quite large. Moving from a low level of exposure (that is, from a respondent with no exposure) to a high level of exposure (a heavy television-watcher living in a market with many ads) increased the number of candidate likes and dislikes that were expressed by well over a full mention, from about two to almost four. By contrast, holding constant exposure to negative/contrast ads, but increasing positive ad exposure, slightly reduced the number of likes and dislikes mentioned.[6]

It is worth reiterating, however, that viewers do not see positive or negative ads in a vacuum. Rather, they are exposed to both—and at levels that are correlated with one another. That is, as exposure to negative ads increases, exposure to positive ads is also likely to increase. Note that the reverse is not always true; in some races where noncompetitive candidates air a nontrivial number

TABLE 9.2 Tone and Information

	Know facts in ads	Know facts not in ads
Negative/contrast exposure (2000 DDB Needham)	.045 (.040)	−.009 (.041)
Positive exposure	−.005 (.040)	.023 (.040)

	Presidential candidate likes	Presidential candidate dislikes	Bush-Gore info
Negative/contrast exposure (2000 ANES)	.083 (.024)**	.102 (.028)**	.066 (.028)*
Positive exposure	−.056 (.024)*	−.044 (.027)	−.042 (.028)

	House name recall	Recall accuracy	Senate challenger recall	Senate open-seat recall	Senate incumbent recall
Negative/contrast exposure (2000 ANES)	−.027 (.039)	−.147 (.047)**	—	—	—
Positive exposure	.178 (.073)*	.220 (.092)*	—	—	—
Negative/contrast exposure (2000 AMES)^	.427 (.435)	.306 (.456)	—	—	—
Positive exposure^	−.467 (.489)	−.330 (.525)	—	—	—
Negative/contrast exposure (2004 UW–BYU)	—	—	.123 (.041)**	.039 (.060)	−.110 (.079)
Positive exposure	—	—	−.117 (.079)	.045 (.094)	−.322 (.219)

Entries are coefficients (with standard errors in parentheses) from different regression models. All exposure measures are logged. Senate total exposure is total challenger or total incumbent exposure.
+ $p < .10$; * $p < .05$; ** $p < .01$
^ Only for respondents in competitive House races

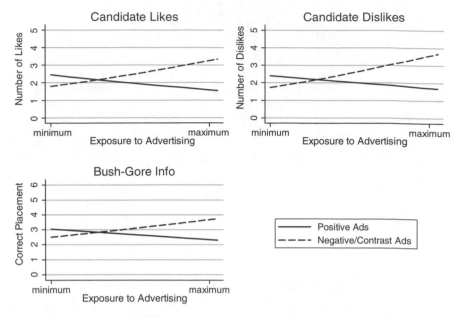

FIGURE 9.2   Predicted Effects of Tone on Information

of ads, viewers might be exposed primarily to positive ads. We consider this in our discussion of knowledge of House candidates, below. Overall, however, it is important to consider the net effect of positive and negative ad exposure on candidate assessments. We take this issue up again when we consider the effect of tone on participation.

Our next test of the hypothesis that exposure to negative advertising can increase people's political knowledge made use of several survey questions in which respondents were asked to place both Al Gore and George W. Bush on an ideological scale for eight different issues. As in Chapter 6, the dependent variable in the model was the number of correct placements, i.e., placing Gore to the left of Bush.

We again found support for the negativity hypothesis, as Table 9.2 shows. Increasing exposure to contrast and pure negative advertising was associated with respondents' making more correct issue placements. And exposure to positive advertising had no significant impact on the number of correct issue placements. Indeed, by disaggregating exposure, the statistical effect for negative/contrast ads was triple the size for total exposure (reported in Chapter 6). Substantively, exposure to negative ads had a large impact on knowledge of Bush and Gore issue positions, holding positive ad exposure at its mean. Moving from a low level of exposure to a high level of exposure increased the expected number of correct placements by one out of the eight possible, as the bottom left panel in Figure 9.2 reveals.

Turning to the House and Senate candidate knowledge models, the evidence became a bit more difficult to interpret. Contrary to the expectations of the negativity hypothesis, Table 9.2 reveals that exposure to negative and contrast ads reduced the accuracy of respondents' recall of House candidates. Exposure to negative ads, however, was unrelated to self-reported recall. What is more, we saw here the information-enhancing effects of positive ads. This is curious, but perhaps it is explained by the nature of advertising in House races.

Unlike presidential advertising, which is almost always focused in competitive markets and states, many House and Senate candidates in noncompetitive races continue to bombard viewers with positive ads. For example, in the 2000 ANES, we estimated the average logged positive and negative/contrast exposure for respondents in competitive House markets to be 4.96 and 5.44, respectively. For respondents in noncompetitive markets, the average exposure was 4.36 and 3.93. As we can see, negative/contrast exposure was a lot lower for respondents in noncompetitive races, but positive exposure was nearly the same. Thus, there was frequently a great deal of positive advertising in noncompetitive House races, races in which a safe incumbent was widely known by voters. As a result, these findings were an artifact of these advertising patterns. Indeed, when we re-estimated the House recall models with only those respondents living in competitive House races, the impact of positive ads disappeared and the signs on the coefficients were consistent with our larger account (the results are shown in Table 9.2).[7]

When it came to Senate elections, the results lent additional support for the negativity hypothesis. In the case of Senate challenger recall, exposure to negative/contrast ads increased the probability that a respondent would be able to remember the name of a challenging candidate (the estimated effect was nearly the same as that for total exposure reported in Chapter 6), and exposure to positive ads had no impact on recall. Exposure, however, was unrelated to recall of Senate candidates in open-seat contests and recall of Senate incumbents.

What can we conclude here? We saw in Chapter 6 that as citizens are exposed to higher levels of political advertising, they generally learn more about political candidates. The results of the current chapter demonstrate that it is primarily exposure to negative and contrast ads that facilitate this increased knowledge.

We turn next to the effect of tone on citizens' attitudes about campaigns, politics, and government.

Tone and Attitudes

As we saw in Chapter 7, exposure to political advertising has demonstrable effects on citizens' interest in and evaluations of campaigns, as well as on trust in government. If negative ads have informational effects, might they also, as

TABLE 9.3   Tone and Attitudes

	Preelection interest in campaign	Postelection interest	Cares about the outcome
Negative/contrast exposure (2000 ANES)	.053 (.033)	.069 (.081)	.003 (.066)
Positive exposure	.006 (.035)	−.055 (.086)	−.027 (.063)
Negative/contrast exposure (2000 DDB Needham)	—	−.015 (.034)	—
Positive exposure	—	.020 (.035)	—

	Election fairness	Need election reform	Money decides elections	Campaign truthfulness
Negative/contrast exposure (2004 UW−BYU)	—	—	—	−.013 (.038)
Positive exposure	—	—	—	.013 (.040)
Negative/contrast exposure (2004 DDB Needham)	−.004 (.018)	−.030 (.019)	−.024 (.018)	—
Positive exposure	.016 (.040)	−.021 (.042)	−.024 (.041)	—

	Trust in government	Efficacy
Negative/contrast exposure (2000 ANES)	.078 (.080)	−.165 (.077)*
Positive exposure	−.051 (.085)	.191 (.081)*
Negative/contrast exposure (2000 DDB Needham)	—	.174 (.201)
Positive exposure	—	−.273 (.311)
Negative/contrast exposure (2004 DDB Needham)	—	.028 (.048)
Positive exposure	—	.047 (.108)

Entries are coefficients (with standard errors in parentheses) from different regression models. All exposure measures are logged.
$+ p < .10$; $^*p < .05$; $^{**}p < .01$

we have argued, stimulate campaign interest and raise evaluations of elections and politics? In other words, to what extent are the results from Chapter 7 the consequence of messages in negative versus positive ads (or, perhaps, both)?

Table 9.3 shows estimates of the impact of negative/contrast and positive ad exposure on pre- and postelection assessments of campaign interest; whether respondents cared about the outcome of the presidential election; how they felt about election fairness, the need for electoral reform, the relationship of money and election outcomes; the truthfulness of campaigns; and finally, whether they trusted government or felt externally efficacious.

In short, we found few statistically significant results. For example, we found that negative ads did not have a significant effect on interest measured during the campaign itself (i.e., on the preelection survey), nor on interest measured retrospectively, after the election was over (the postelection measure). In both models, exposure to positive advertising had no statistically discernible impact on interest in the campaign. Moreover, exposure to positive or negative advertising was unrelated to evaluations of the electoral process. Citizens' levels of exposure to negative and contrast ads (and positive ads, for that matter) were unrelated to their evaluations of election fairness and truthfulness, and to their desire to see election reform and reduce the importance of money in election outcomes.

All told, the modest attitudinal effects observed in Chapter 7 disappeared when disaggregating exposure by tone. Unlike the investigation of tone and information, where the total exposure effects were amplified when looking specifically at negative/contrast ads (allowing us to tie those effects more directly to negativity), the effects from Chapter 7 appeared spread out between positive and negative ads, indicating that the findings in that chapter resulted from total exposure rather than exposure to ads with a particular tone.

These null findings certainly failed to make a strong case on behalf of negative ads; however, they stood in stark contrast to the claims of the most vocal critics of negative campaigning. Negative spots, such critics are quick to assert, must be turning citizens off to politics and the electoral process (recall David Broder's [2002] assertion that political ads are killing our democracy), and they must be an increasing source of discontent for those who hardly can stand to endure the nasty attack ads that bombard them between Double and Final *Jeopardy!* or between weather and sports reports on local news broadcasts. Yet there is little evidence that this is happening.

There is one finding reported in Table 9.3, however, that warranted more careful scrutiny: Exposure to positive ads boosted evaluations of external efficacy, while exposure to negative/contrast ads lowered it. (This effect, however, is only present in one of the three surveys used to test for an exposure/efficacy relationship). Notably, the coefficient estimates on the two exposure variables were nearly equal in size, suggesting that the null results from Chapter 7 were the consequence of viewing experiences in which the effects of positive and negative/contrast ads balanced each other out. Nevertheless, we concede that, when it comes to efficacy, critics of negative advertising may have a legitimate claim. Given the overall dearth of evidence that negative ads harm attitudinal responses, however, we remain suspicious about the robustness of this finding. If true, it certainly would suggest a complex effect for negative ads: a consistent educative function, but one that weakens citizens' belief that greater engagement actually matters politically.

We turn next to a re-investigation of advertising exposure and measures of political participation, looking for indications that exposure to negative/contrast ads might have some mobilizing influence.

Tone and Participation

In Chapter 8, we witnessed the relatively small influence of advertising exposure on political participation. While total exposure (and total ads in our county-level models) did have a modest positive effect on the probability of turning out to vote (as well as on the estimated county-level turnout rate), these effects were limited to turnout. Might we find broader participation effects by disaggregating exposure by tone? In other words, does our total exposure specification mask important mobilizing or demobilizing effects from positive or negative ads?

In this section, we replicate the models from Chapter 8. We examine direct political action, including turnout and levels of political chatter. The results are shown in Table 9.4. In short, we concluded that the effect of tone was weak and, most often, nonexistent.

Indeed, we found statistically significant effects in only two areas. First, we found in the 2000 ANES that exposure to negative/contrast ads was related to turnout. As exposure to negativity increased, turnout increased. Moreover, in the 2004 county-level model, we found that as the proportion of negative/contrast ads aired in a county increased, turnout increased as well. These effects were not seen in any of the other surveys or in the 2000 county-level model (where the coefficient was actually negative, though insignificant). Second, exposure to negative/contrast ads was positively related to the intensity with which citizens encouraged others to vote. This finding was encouraging in that participation effects seemed focused around the act of voting and nowhere else.

To illustrate the effect of advertising tone on turnout, we converted the co-efficients (from the 2000 ANES model) on exposure to advertising into more easily understood probabilities. These are shown in Figure 9.3. As noted earlier, exposure to negative/contrast ads and exposure to positive ads are highly correlated in the real world. Citizens who are blanketed with advertisements very likely see ads of all tones in high numbers. The predicted effects demonstrated in Figure 9.2 held one exposure measure constant and varied the other. This is useful for seeing the isolated effects of only one measure. To see a more realistic set of effects, however, we take a slightly different approach here. We hold all control variables constant, but leave estimated exposure measures unchanged. We then plot predicted effects for the 1,200 NES respondents, where the x-axis is negative/contrast exposure.

As we can see, the positive coefficient on the negative/contrast measure overcame the demobilizing (though insignificant) effect of positive ads; more specifically, at any point along the x-axis, the variation in predicted probabilities is the consequence of varying levels of positive ad exposure. Recall Figure 8.1, where we varied exposure to the total ad environment, holding all else constant. With Figure 9.3, we allow the mobilizing effect to be more variable, depending on each respondent's mix of positive and negative/contrast exposure. All told,

TABLE 9.4 Tone and Participation

	Turnout	Participation index	Attend rally	Display sticker	Sign petition	Contact official
Negative/contrast exposure (2000 ANES)	.413 (.185)*	—	−.099 (.364)	−.186 (.256)	—	−.043 (.175)
Positive exposure	−.318 (.194)	—	.025 (.388)	.107 (.267)	—	.032 (.185)
Negative/contrast exposure (2004 UW–BYU)	−.117 (.109)	—	—	—	—	—
Positive exposure	.034 (.145)	—	—	—	—	—
Negative/contrast exposure (2000 DDB Needham)	−.188 (.186)	.196 (.164)	.064 (.042)	.084 (.086)	.043 (.027)	.029 (.072)
Positive exposure	.227 (.310)	−.310 (.242)	−.121 (.072)	−.178 (.134)	−.063 (.044)	.003 (.089)
Negative/contrast exposure (2004 DDB Needham)	.022 (.058)	.015 (.046)	.024 (.022)	.018 (.019)	−.010 (.015)	—
Positive exposure	−.123 (.114)	.007 (.107)	−.096 (.075)	.017 (.038)	.019 (.029)	—
Thousand ads (2000 county data)	.052 (.024)*	—	—	—	—	—
Proportion negative/contrast ads	−1.13 (.949)	—	—	—	—	—
Thousand ads (2004 county data)	.064 (.012)**	—	—	—	—	—
Proportion negative/contrast ads	1.30 (.379)**	—	—	—	—	—

	Talk with friend	Talk with family	Talk with opponents	Encourage to vote
Negative/contrast exposure (2000 DDB Needham)	.030 (.071)	.041 (.158)	—	—
Positive exposure	−.035 (.102)	−.025 (.281)	—	—
Negative/contrast exposure (2004 DDB Needham)	−.014 (.017)	−.003 (.013)	.011 (.018)	.031 (.018)+
Positive exposure	.011 (.041)	−.008 (.043)	−.038 (.042)	−.069 (.044)

Entries are coefficients (with standard errors in parentheses) from different regression models. All exposure measures are logged.
+ $p < .10$; * $p < .05$; ** $p < .01$

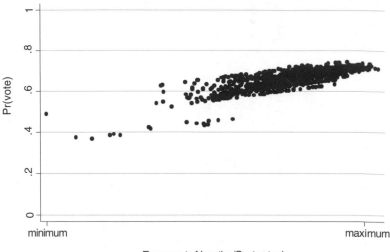

FIGURE 9.3   Predicted Effects of Tone on Turnout.

despite introducing such variation, turnout probabilities moved from about 0.5 (a fence-sitter who had seen zero positive or negative ads) to about 0.7 (a near-certain voter) across the range of negative/contrast exposure. These results were consistent with our findings in Chapter 8.

In sum, we found little evidence here that negative and contrast ads moved voters to be politically active, beyond turning out to vote and encouraging others to do so as well. But the evidence was more clear in rebutting some of the conventional wisdom about negative campaign messages: Negative ads emphatically failed to demobilize the electorate (while at times, slightly mobilizing them).

Tone and Policy Ads

In this final section, we re-examine many of the same dependent variables, but under a new specification of negative ad exposure. We split advertising exposure into three categories—exposure to positive ads, exposure to negative/contrast ads with some policy content, and exposure to negative/contrast ads completely focused on the personal characteristics of the candidates. Recall Table 9.1, in which we showed the relationship between an ad's tone and its policy content. In creating a measure of negative/contrast policy ad exposure, we included all ads with complete focus on policy, along with ads that contained both policy and personal content. Thus, the measure included some personal characteristics of the candidates, but all of the ads had some policy discussion. By contrast, our measure of exposure to negative/contrast personality ads included only those ads with no policy discussion and a complete focus on the personal characteristics of the candidates.

In creating this three-category measure of ad tone, we were distinguishing between what one might consider "mudslinging" ads (those that refer only to an opponent's personal characteristics) and what one might consider to be more "legitimate" negative ads (those that focus on an opponent's policy positions). Our expectation was that the policy-focused negative ads would have a much more powerful effect on the information that viewers received from advertising; but, building on Kahn and Kenney (1999), we were open to the possibility that personality-focused negative ads may have had a negative impact on citizens' democratic attitudes and levels of political participation.[8] Such findings would have been in line with the larger message of the book—ads have, at best, a modest positive benefit for information, attitudes, and participation (and, at worst, a null effect). Plus, those benefits are likely the consequence of the substantive dialogue in political ads—not the result of fancy graphics, humor, or stinging personal insults.

For this analysis, we examined twelve dependent variables from the 2000 ANES. We had three information variables (number of presidential likes and dislikes, and Bush-Gore issue placement), five attitudinal variables (pre- and postelection interest, care about outcome of election, trust in government, and efficacy), and four participation variables (turnout, attending a rally, displaying a sticker, and contacting a public official). The results of all nine models are reported in Table 9.5.

The model estimates demonstrated convincingly that the policy content of negative and contrast ads was the driving force behind the effect of negative/contrast ad exposure. In all three knowledge models, the policy exposure variable was positive and significant, while the personality exposure measure was insignificant and even significantly negative for Bush-Gore issue placements. These findings were consistent with those of Kahn and Kenney (1999), who demonstrated that potential voters were turned off by mudslinging. The substantive impact of exposure to each type of ad is detailed in Figure 9.4. Each line shows the effect of varying one of the measures of exposure while holding the level of the other two exposure measures constant at the mean of the sample. (For ease of interpretation, especially with three exposure measures, we demonstrate effects in this way, instead of as in Figure 9.3.)

As one can see from the figure, the information-enhancing effects of negative and contrast policy ads were evident. Indeed, it even seemed as though negative/contrast personality ads behaved more like positive ads in terms of their effects on voters. Consider the lower left panel of the figure, which speaks to the ability of respondents to correctly place Bush and Gore on an issue scale. High levels of exposure to negative/contrast mudslinging ads lowered the correct issue placement of Bush relative to Gore by nearly a full mention!

TABLE 9.5 Policy and Personality Negativity

	Presidential candidate likes	Presidential candidate dislikes	Bush-Gore info
Positive exposure	−.055 (.024)*	−.041 (.027)	−.030 (.027)
Negative/contrast policy exposure	.075 (.026)**	.112 (.030)**	.089 (.031)**
Negative/contrast personality exposure	.015 (.031)	−.027 (.033)	−.074 (.035)*

	Preelection interest	Postelection interest	Care about outcome	Trust in government	Efficacy
Positive exposure	−.027 (.035)	−.026 (.083)	−.039 (.066)	.039 (.084)	.159 (.082)+
Negative/contrast policy exposure	.065 (.034)+	.045 (.077)	−.021 (.072)	−.083 (.077)	−.138 (.076)+
Negative/contrast personality exposure	−.014 (.024)	−.005 (.022)	.081 (.088)	.018 (.022)	.003 (.021)

	Turnout	Attend rally	Display sticker	Contact official
Positive exposure	−.332 (.206)	.032 (.360)	.136 (.250)	−.007 (.188)
Negative/contrast policy exposure	.445 (.191)*	−.033 (.329)	−.121 (.234)	−.005 (.173)
Negative/contrast personality exposure	−.026 (.053)	−.118 (.077)	−.147 (.063)*	−.001 (.048)

Entries are coefficients (with standard errors in parentheses) from different regression models. All exposure measures are logged. Results are from 2000 ANES.
+ $p < .10$; * $p < .05$; ** $p < .01$

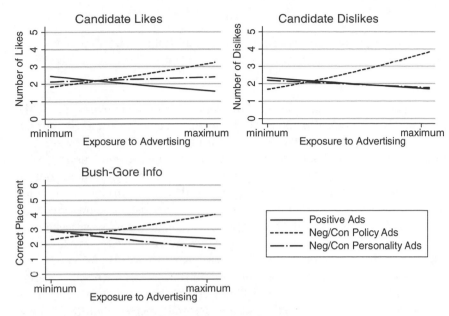

FIGURE 9.4   Predicted Policy Ad Effects on Information

We also saw some limited effects on interest and turnout in Figure 9.5. Exposure to policy-focused negative/contrast ads nearly tripled the probability of being highly interested in the campaign, and it was policy-focused negative ads that accounted for the boost in turnout rates witnessed earlier in Figure 9.3.[9]

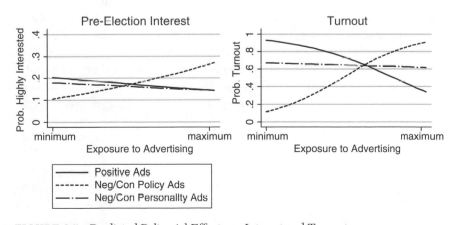

FIGURE 9.5   Predicted Policy Ad Effects on Interest and Turnout

Summary

The results from this chapter complete our empirical investigation of advertising's effects. The goal of this chapter was to see how the tone of advertising matters—the most enduring debate in the existing scholarship on advertising effects.

Our investigation examined all of the dependent variables considered in the previous three empirical chapters. We found first that negative and contrast ads were responsible for higher levels of political information. Thus, at the very least, to say—as we did in Chapter 6—that exposure enriched citizen knowledge was only part of the story. More precisely, it was exposure to negative and contrast ads—with their high levels of policy content and their ability to grab the attention of viewers—that was chiefly responsible for those increases in knowledge.

Second, we found that the tone of advertising had little to do with changing attitudes. Indeed, in the only statistically significant effect we reported, citizens who saw higher levels of negative/contrast ads had lower reported levels of efficacy. In contrast, efficacy was higher for citizens seeing increased levels of positive ads, all else equal. In terms of interest, trust in government, concern for election outcomes, and evaluations of the electoral process, where we did find effects for total exposure in Chapter 7, these effects could not be explained by the tone of the ad.

Third, as in Chapter 8, we found ads had little direct impact on mobilizing voters, but we also found no evidence that ads were demobilizers. In the turnout model using the 2000 ANES data, we showed that exposure to negative/contrast ads led to a higher probability of turning out to vote; using the 2004 DDB Needham "Life Style" data, we showed that negative/contrast exposure led citizens to encourage others to vote. But beyond these important effects, tone did little. We concluded from these results, as we did in the previous chapter, that to the extent that ads increased citizens' store of knowledge—as well as interest, trust, and evaluations of politics and campaigns—exposure (and, in this case, negative, contrast, and positive ad exposure) may not have encouraged, but it certainly did little to discourage citizens from casting a ballot.

Finally, we disaggregated further still, looking for evidence that policy-based negative/contrast ads had different effects from "mudslinging" personality-focused negative/contrast ads. We concluded from that analysis that this most definitely was the case. Citizens exposed to higher levels of policy negative/contrast ads had more information and higher levels of interest. They also were more likely to turn out to vote. In no case did exposure to personality-based negative/contrast ads inform or pique interest. Indeed, in one case—Bush-Gore issue placement—higher exposure reduced the store of accurate knowledge.

One thing we did not do in this chapter was look for differential effects (by levels of political information and partisanship) of exposure tone. In previous chapters, we failed to find an authoritative story to the question of whether exposure to political ads matters for different types of voters. It is certainly possible, however, that when disaggregating ads into different types, voters of varying backgrounds will respond in divergent ways. Indeed, there is exciting new research into such questions (Stevens, Sullivan, Allen, and Alger 2007), and we encourage additional work in this area. We believe that such questions represent the next stage of the scholarly search for advertising effects.

This chapter, however, concludes our own rigorous investigation of advertising exposure effects. The journey began with an analysis of total exposure on measures of political knowledge, and we finish in this chapter with a lengthy analysis of exposure tone. We conclude the book in the next chapter with a brief discussion of the implications of this research.

CHAPTER TEN

Campaign Advertising and American Democracy

ACCORDING TO THE conventional wisdom put forth by many pundits and some scholars, campaign advertising (and negative advertising in particular) serves to corrupt and debase democratic discourse, mislead and confuse citizens, shrink and polarize the electorate, and constrain elected representatives in their efforts to promote good public policy. Collectively, according to this popular and unfortunately robust view, campaign advertising serves to undermine the integrity of our political system. It is something we should try to restrain, limit, or even eliminate here at home, and it decidedly is not something we should wish upon the citizens of an emerging democracy.

We began this project with a different view. We thought there were good theoretical and normative reasons to believe that campaign advertising—even ads that were strikingly negative—might inform, engage, and stimulate voters. We were skeptical about arguments that blamed advertising for some of our country's most significant political failings. Still, while we had some admittedly strong priors and clearly were more partial to the arguments of Geer (2006) than to those of Ansolabehere and Iyengar (1995), it was obvious that the question of advertising's effects on political knowledge, turnout, and other measures of democratic engagement demanded more thorough empirical investigation. In the face of myriad conflicting hypotheses in the existing scholarly literature and a surfeit of arguments and assumptions saturating cable news and coursing through the blogosphere, good empirical tests were needed, and good empirical tests required good measures of exposure to advertising.

Summary of Findings

In Chapter 3, we summarized and critiqued the various ways that scholars have measured ad exposure and gauged advertising effects. We argued that each of these methods—aggregate campaign spending data, archival collections of television commercials, logs from the public files of television stations, experiments, self-reports by survey respondents, and proxy measures of exposure—had weaknesses that made it difficult at best for scholars to characterize accurately the advertising environment, to measure exposure, and ultimately to infer how campaign messages influenced the attitudes, knowledge, and behavior of citizens.

Instead, in Chapter 4, we argued for a method that combined information on what was aired (using Wisconsin Advertising Project data on the content, timing, volume, and targeting of campaign advertising) with information on the viewing patterns of respondents to various surveys, including the American National Election Studies. The Wisconsin Advertising Project data gave us the ability to provide a uniquely detailed, accurate portrait of campaign advertising at the level of the media market. By combining these data with standard demographic, political, and social psychological instrumentation and questions on television-viewing habits from academic surveys, we were able to construct a new and more valid individual-level measure of exposure to campaign advertising.

Using this combined method of measuring exposure, we set out to examine empirically the use of advertising and its effects on a variety of dependent variables. The results did not come from a single year or from a single study. Rather, we drew on data from four different surveys over two election years, and we investigated the aggregate effects of advertising as well as effects in House, Senate, and presidential races across the two election years. We tailored the data we used appropriately for each analysis: When we examined the effect of advertising on knowledge of presidential candidates' positions, it made sense to look only at advertising in the presidential race. When we looked at citizen familiarity with House candidates, we looked at advertising in House races. When the question revolved around turnout, we examined the complete advertising environment. We included ads aired by interest groups and parties as well as candidate advertising. Given the diversity of datasets and electoral contexts, and given the convergent validity of our findings, we have a good deal of confidence in our results.

In addition, we found strong evidence for the discriminant validity of our exposure measure. Comparing findings from the same surveys in the same years, we were reassured that measures specific to one race had no impact on attitudes and behavior in another race (except when we were looking specifically at combined or cumulative effects), and that our measures of exposure to ads did not predict people's knowledge of facts that were not contained within the advertising. And, of course, in every model we controlled for a range of rival hypotheses in an effort to rule out alternative explanations for our findings. Even taking into account such factors as demographic characteristics, partisanship, preexisting political information, campaign contact, and news consumption, it is clear that advertising matters for political attitudes and political participation. To be sure, these effects, while discernable, often are relatively modest. Advertising matters at the margin, but, as we have noted, in politics the margin is what matters.

Some have claimed that the relationship between competitiveness and advertising levels creates an endogeneity problem in which strategic decisions on when and where to advertise are tied to expectations about turnout. However, as we described in Chapters 4 and 5, candidates do not target markets based on predictions about aggregate turnout. The problem is not endogeneity, but instead a need for electoral competitiveness to be controlled for properly.

As we demonstrated in Chapter 5, a competitive race in a given media market not only leads to more advertising (and more negative advertising), but to increased media coverage, greater get-out-the-vote efforts, and increased discussion about the campaign, all of which make voter turnout more likely. Additionally, competitive races increase the perception among potential voters that their vote is more likely to make a difference. It is, therefore, essential to control for electoral competitiveness if one wants to make accurate inferences about the impact of campaign advertising.

Employing our exposure measure across different years, different elections, and a number of different datasets, we found that campaign ads play a role in informing and mobilizing Americans. We did not find large and significant positive effects in every case, but, having examined a large collection of attitudes and behaviors, we found only a single instance in which campaign ads have what could be seen as a negative effect on democratic citizenship: As we showed in Chapter 8, all else equal, exposure to campaign advertising is associated with a slightly lower probability of displaying a bumper sticker or yard sign.

Beyond this somewhat puzzling anomaly, we found that campaign ads have the potential to bring about a more attentive, more informed, and more participatory citizenry. Specifically, we found that exposure to campaign advertising in general, and negative advertising in particular, produces citizens who are more interested in the election, have more to say about the candidates, are more familiar with who's running, and ultimately are more likely to vote. In short, people can and do learn from television ads, and campaign advertising thereby fulfills a vital democratic function. And importantly, at least some of these beneficial effects are concentrated among those who need them most: the least informed and least engaged members of the electorate.

Multivitamins and the Health of American Democracy

To be sure, there is much to be concerned about when it comes to the health of American democracy. At a time when even the fundamental act of counting votes is heatedly contested; when, more than forty years after the Voting Rights Act, serious concerns about voter disenfranchisement emerge anew every election; and when our elected representatives seem to be under constant fire for improprieties of every sort, it is certainly reasonable to ask where we have gone wrong. There is little wrong with American democracy, however, that reasonably can be laid at the feet of campaign advertising.

For example, many observers worry about the decline in the number of competitive Congressional districts, which they argue contributes to congressional polarization and parochialism. However, while declining competitiveness may contribute to polarization, it's doubtful that campaign ads are a primary cause of diminished competition; strategic politicians using sophisticated gerrymandering techniques to protect their own positions and their party's fortunes are much more likely suspects.

Similarly, while many campaign ads may include passionate rhetoric, it is surely no worse than what is conveyed through speeches, interviews, and direct mail. Furthermore, when it comes to polarization in Congress, the priorities and influence of campaign contributors, homogenous congressional districts, and unrepresentative primary-election voters no doubt do much more to influence congressional voting behavior than do the appeals contained in campaign ads. In other words, the causal arrow is more likely to run from polarization (which creates differences one can point to in advertising) to the nature of advertising than from advertising to polarization.

Observers also have bemoaned what they see as a lack of political courage from our political leaders and the inability of our representatives to have serious debate about long-term problems like Social Security, energy consumption, or global warming. Could our leaders show more political courage? Absolutely. Would it be better if we could have reasoned debates about the long-term health of the Social Security system and a rational, forward-thinking energy program? For certain. Is political advertising to blame for skittish legislators and the lack of serious discussion of pressing public policy issues? We do not believe so.

The logic of policy-making described by such scholars of Congress and public policy-making as Douglas Arnold (1992), along with a multitude of empirical cases, convincingly has demonstrated that there is little incentive for representatives to support legislation that imposes direct early-term costs on intense minorities, even if there will be broad benefits down the line. This is a function of representative government and the short terms of members of Congress. It has little to do with how candidates represent themselves and their opponents in television advertising; instead, it has much more to do with the basic structure of representative democracy and a system of district-based elections.

Moreover, as we noted in Chapter 1, negative advertising is not something unique to modern politics or to the medium of television. In his recent book *Mudslingers*, Kerwin Swint (2006) chronicled the "top 25 negative campaigns" in American history. Although these assessments represented the judgment of one particular researcher, it is interesting to note that four out of the five most negative campaigns in the book occurred before 1890, long before the advent of television. Furthermore, the most negative campaign in the book, the 1970 Alabama Democratic gubernatorial primary runoff between George Wallace and Albert Brewer, had few television ads and did not need them to achieve the campaign's high levels of vitriol. Negative campaigns were in abundance long before television advertising came on the scene.

Geer (2006) has made this very argument in much greater detail. He cited the work of historians of the eighteenth century (McGerr 1987; Silbey 1999; Altschuler and Blumin 2000) to make the point that "No historian paints a picture of that period as anything but highly negative, especially by today's standards." Geer also noted that the great majority (70 percent) of the comments in the Declaration of Independence were negative, and he conducted a study of newspaper advertising in the first half of the twentieth century that showed levels of negativity virtually identical to what we see in modern advertising campaigns.

Candidates and campaigns must raise and spend large sums of money on political advertising—over $1.5 billion in 2004 alone. Are such sums immense, obscene, and inefficient, as conventional wisdom seems to hold? To put this figure into context, consider that almost $54 billion was spent on television advertising as a whole in 2004, and across all media (print, radio, television, internet) advertisers spent more than *$139 billion.* Political television advertising thus comprised less than 3 percent of all television advertising spending in 2004. Automobile manufacturers and local car dealerships alone spent more than four times as much on television advertisements than political campaigns spent on election advertisements; Proctor and Gamble alone spent more than twice as much.[1] When compared to how much advertisers spend on cars and soap, are campaigns spending too much on election advertising, or too little?

What about efficiency when it comes to such a massive investment? Frankly, campaigns care little about efficiency and care intensely about winning elections. They are willing to spend as much as they can—and waste a great deal of it—in their quest for electoral victory. There is no prize for the campaign that was most efficient. Nevertheless, one can compare the "information" and "turnout" returns on all this spending to other sorts of campaign contact, like telephone or in-person grassroots mobilization. In our models, we consistently showed positive effects for mobilization contacts, usually in the 2 to 4 percentage point range. These results were consistent with many previous observational and experimental studies (Blydenburgh 1971; Gerber and Greene 2001; Rosenstone and Hansen 1993; Verba, Schlozman, and Brady 1995) and were greater and more consistent than the effects we saw from television ads. This is not surprising, because increasing voter turnout is the express objective of such efforts. As we have argued, it is largely a spillover effect from campaign advertising.

Yet, findings in the literature have been contradictory. In a field experiment, Vavreck (2006) showed that the cost per voter mobilized for television advertising was less than the per-voter cost for individual contacts. And, in a recent article about television advertising and turnout in the 2000 presidential election, Krasno and Green argued that individual mobilization efforts were more efficient than television advertising (2008). To be sure, political advertisements can be expensive, but they have the potential to be seen by many people, thereby amortizing the marginal cost of an ad over many more citizens than is the case for individual voter contacts. Furthermore, while individual mobilizing contacts may have a greater effect on voters than television ads do, the way grassroots efforts are pursued also makes it likely that the net impact of advertising will be higher.

Why? While field experiments with a random sample of potential voters get around issues of external validity and can identify causal connections by randomly assigning who is contacted and who is not, they are unlikely to be able to gauge correctly the magnitude of effects or the net impact in an actual campaign. Unlike in experiments, in real life, campaigns do not randomly assign people to mobilization treatments. Instead, they aggressively try to get their most likely voters to the polls. In 2004, the Republican Party put in place an extensive program to mobilize base supporters (Bai 2004). Their targets, who may have received scores of telephone and in-person contacts, often were likely voters in the first place who were being targeted because they were members of church groups, were gun owners, or sent their children to private schools.

These "rifle shot" targeted mobilization efforts were excellent strategy, but they were less likely to hit or reach casual or mildly informed potential voters— the ones most in need of information and a spur to vote. These voters were much more likely to get hit by ads with the shotgun method of television advertising. Put another way, experiments get around the thorny statistical problem of endogeneity by randomly assigning subjects to treatment and control groups. In actual campaigns, endogeneity is reality when it comes to targeting. Field experiments thus will provide excellent estimates of individual mobilization's potential, but they will, in most cases, systematically overstate the actual efficacy of the approach. And the effect of contacts on overall turnout and knowledge is likely to be mitigated because campaigns are striving for turnout (as well as increased knowledge) among their most likely supporters.

Final Thoughts

As should be obvious by now, we are not alarmed about the role of television advertising in American politics; indeed, we are encouraged by the positive, demonstrable spillover effects that accrue from exposure to campaign ads. We are not, however, completely sanguine about the role of television advertising in American politics. While we have shown that there are positive effects from political advertising in general and negative advertising in particular, there may be other ways in which the content and sheer volume of political advertising may adversely affect the political process. Three caveats should serve to temper irrational exuberance regarding the salutary effects of campaign advertising.

First, even in this post-BCRA era, campaign advertising obviously costs money, and a lot of it. The resources expended to raise the money to fund an effective advertising campaign are considerable and cause elected officials to pay close attention to citizens with the requisite disposable income. Although instances of flat-out vote buying are difficult to document in contemporary elections, money can buy access to members of congress and their staffs, and can mobilize legislators to be more active on particular pieces of legislation. And even in the absence of clear quid-pro-quo behavior, critics have raised concerns that the appearance of substantial impropriety undermines the integrity of the democratic system. Additionally, potentially strong leaders may be deterred from running for office because of the burden of raising large amounts of money to pay for advertising and other campaign activities. In recruiting candidates, parties clearly have an affinity for wealthy individuals who can finance their own campaigns. But even putting aside considerations about distortions in the candidate recruitment process, the time that it takes any candidate to raise the money necessary to mount an effective media campaign clearly detracts from other duties.

Second, at their worst, campaign ads can be every bit as disingenuous, manipulative, and misleading as their critics charge. But one certainly does not need to watch campaign ads to find examples of political disingenuousness. Debates, speeches, interviews, mailings, blogs, and opinion pieces provide ample opportunities for candidates and their partisans to mislead and manipulate, equivocate and obfuscate. To be sure, ads do not keep candidates honest. But they represent clear, simple statements that are hard to take out of context and for which candidates—especially when required to "stand by their ads"—readily are held accountable. A thirty-second ad is a public, highly visible statement. In an era of ad watches and endless cable-news loops, it is hard for candidates to get away with campaign ads that factually are untrue, or that even stretch the truth very far.

Of course, advertising provides a visible and relatively effective way to respond to attacks. One can be concerned about the "Swift-Boating" of American politics, and many were deeply angered by the ads aired by Swift Boat Veterans for Truth that maligned the war record of 2004 Democratic presidential nominee John Kerry, unfairly in the eyes of his supporters and many commentators. Still, the Kerry campaign had ample opportunity to rebut the ad and to counterattack. They failed to do so until a good deal of damage had been done. In fact, some have argued that Senator Kerry offered his first coherent response almost two years after the spot aired (Zernike 2006). One lesson of the Swift Boat ads is that in the face of such attacks, one must respond, well, swiftly.

Fortunately, campaign ads provide the ability, when necessary, to fight fire with fire. For every thirty-second distortion, there can be a thirty-second clarification; every accusation can be met, every charge responded to in an effective, efficient way. Notwithstanding Kerry's silence in the face of the Swift Boat ads, most national elections constitute relatively evenly matched, two-sided flows of information. Competitive candidates usually are well funded, and there are fewer examples of completely partisan news organizations than there were in this country in the nineteenth century. Even if one believes a network such as CNN or FOX News is biased, candidates and their supporters have plenty of other venues in which to appear.

Are we advocating some kind of advertising arms race, with an inevitable escalation of charges and countercharges, reducing election campaigns to an endless series of attacks? To the contrary. We believe that the sorts of campaign tactics most critics decry actually are less likely when players know that their opponents can respond in kind.

Our final caveat involves the larger informational diet of American citizens. We have called campaign advertisements political multivitamins, adding to the store of information that voters have at their disposal and helping them access additional information. But like all vitamins, political advertisements are most effective when they are supplementing, rather than supplanting, more substantial sources of nutrition. Just as people require a balanced diet and cannot survive on vitamins alone, citizens cannot and should not rely on campaign advertising as their only source of political information. Ideally, campaign ads simply would serve as accompaniments to a more substantial informational diet. However, with declining network news coverage of politics, diminishing newspaper readership, and a din of heated opinions dominating the news media, campaign ads may be playing a larger and more important role than might otherwise be the case. And as with any new nutritional supplement, the long-term effects of ad exposure are unknown.

In the short-term, however, campaign advertising can help contribute to a healthy democracy. And, going back to the emergence of democracy in new quarters around the globe, we can only hope for a world in which Iraqis and others have the luxury of worrying about television campaign advertising. Then, democracy will have arrived.

Assessing the Validity of the
CMAG Tracking Data

TO ASSESS THE VALIDITY of the 2000 CMAG data, we visited eight television stations in 2001 in five different markets: WJRT in Flint, Michigan; WISN in Milwaukee, Wisconsin; WTAE and KDKA in Pittsburgh, Pennsylvania; WRIC in Richmond, Virginia; and WJLA, WRC, and WUSA in Washington, D.C. At each station, we obtained photocopies of a sample of billing invoices prepared for various political advertising buyers. Each invoice included the name of the advertiser (e.g., Gore/Lieberman, Inc.; the Virginia Democratic Party) and a list of the dates on and times at which spots aired. Next, we matched the spots listed on the invoices with those listed in the CMAG dataset.

With one exception, we found the tracking data to be highly accurate (see Table A.1). At WJRT in Flint, for example, we collected a total of forty-one invoices representing 618 individual ad airings. Six spots listed on the invoices were not found in the CMAG dataset; the remaining 612 were listed accurately to within one minute. As for the six discrepancies, it is important to note that these spots may, in fact, never have been aired, in which case the error would be one of inadequate record-keeping on the part of the station, not an error in the CMAG data. At WISN in Milwaukee, the error rate was slightly higher. On the thirty-nine

TABLE A.1 Assessments of Tracking Data Accuracy

Television station	Percentage correct within 1 minute	Percentage off by more than 1 minute	Percentage not located	Total spots
WJRT Flint	99	0	1	618
WISN Milwaukee	97	<1	2.3	977
KDKA Pittsburgh	80	0	20	308
WTAE Pittsburgh	97	0	3	773
WRIC Richmond	96	2	2	161
WJLA Washington, D.C.	98	1	1	698
WRC Washington, D.C.	99	<1	0	363
WUSA Washington, D.C.	97	0	3	1433

invoices collected, 977 airings were documented. For five of those, the time stamp given by CMAG differed from the television station records by more than one minute, and we were unable to locate twenty-two of the airings recorded on the invoices. Still, more than 97 percent of the time, the CMAG data and the station invoices agreed within one minute as to when a spot aired. At WTAE, WRIC, and the three Washington, D.C., stations, accuracy was similarly high.

The one trouble spot was KDKA in Pittsburgh. For reasons unknown to us, we were unable to locate in the CMAG tracking data 62 of the 308 spots listed on the invoices obtained from the television station. The missing spots, however, were not related to any candidate or any period of time in particular, suggesting that in even this one outlier case, the error was essentially random.

In all, we were able to locate 96 percent of the airings listed in the station invoices, and more than 95 percent of cases were accurate to within one minute. In sum, there seems to be little need for researchers to invest the time and resources into traveling to television stations to collect advertising data; advertising tracking data provide an accurate and reliable substitute.

Assessing the Reliability of the CMAG Storyboard Coding

I N THIS APPENDIX, we explore the accuracy of the human coding. Many of the categories in our coding scheme were relatively "objective," requiring little in the way of subjective judgment (e.g., did the ad feature a candidate?). Other categories entailed a greater level of judgment and therefore raised concerns about intercoder reliability. In particular, it was important to establish the reliability of the coding of ad tone.

To examine this question, we randomly selected 150 unique advertisements from the over 4,000 advertisements airing in 2000.[1] As part of a larger project, we asked five undergraduate students to code the ads using our coding sheet, thus allowing us to compare our original coding with five independent assessments. We then compared each coder's results with those of the CMAG database. In general, we found intercoder reliability to be high.

Below, we report the results for four questions of interest:

1. Is the ad positive, negative, or contrasting in tone?
2. Is the primary focus of this ad the personal characteristics of either candidate, policy matters, or both?
3. Does the ad direct the viewer to take any action?
4. Does the favored candidate appear on screen narrating his or her ad?

Most assessments of intercoder reliability report the percentage of cases in which coders were in agreement. We did this in addition to providing correlation coefficients, specifically Kendall's tau-b statistic.[2] For our tests relating to the advertisements' tone, we reported both the correlation coefficient and the percentage agreement with the original coding (reported in Table B.1). The numbers in parentheses in the first column are the number of ads each individual coded. (These are fewer than 150 due to nonpolitical spots, issue ads not fully coded in the original data, and missing data for some coders.) Finally, the numbers in parentheses in the other three columns are the number of ads in each tone category. Thus, percentage agreement expresses the percentage of those ads for which the coder and the original data were in agreement.

In all five cases, the two-tailed correlation test was significant, and there was overwhelming agreement among the five coders on positive ads. There was less agreement, however, for

TABLE B.1   Accuracy of Advertising Tone

		Percentage agreement		
	Kendall's tau-b	Positive	Contrast	Negative
Coder 1	.822 (127)**	95.6 (68)	72.4 (29)	90.0 (30)
Coder 2	.740 (124)**	97.0 (67)	74.1 (27)	70.0 (30)
Coder 3	.677 (129)**	98.5 (68)	54.8 (31)	70.0 (30)
Coder 4	.683 (129)**	98.5 (68)	80.6 (31)	53.3 (30)
Coder 5	.820 (120)**	94.0 (67)	83.3 (24)	86.2 (29)

Numbers in parentheses indicate number of relevant ads. Coefficient indicates correlation with original Wisconsin Advertising Project coding. Percentage agreement indicates number of cases in which coder agreed with original coding.
**$p < .01$ (two-tailed test)

contrast and negative advertisements; this finding was not unexpected, given that by definition contrast spots are negative in tone. Despite this lesser degree of reliability, however, on average our re-coders agreed with the initial coding in more than 73 percent of the cases for contrast and negative spots, and more than 96 percent of the cases for positive spots.

We next report results for ads that dealt with policy issues or candidate characteristics (Table B.2). The interpretation of the numbers in parentheses is the same as above. The number of ads reported in the first column is lower because this test only considered election-related ads that originally were coded as dealing with policy or personal issues.

While the reliability indicators were less robust, they were still encouraging. The tau-b coefficients, while considerably lower than in the case of tone, were still statistically significant. When we examined the percentage agreement, we could assess the source of the problem. Coders readily were able to determine ads that dealt with both policy issues and personal characteristics, but they had a much harder time differentiating between ads that were strictly policy or strictly personal. Our experience with coding hundreds of campaign ads tells us that, although the categories are conceptually clear, in practice strictly personal ads often implicate policy issues, while policy ads can be interpreted as having a personal dimension. For example, consider an ad highlighting a candidate's policy commitment to Social Security. The candidate may say something such as, "I have cared about this issue for over twenty years, especially as I get older." While this would be coded as a policy ad, it brings up a personal dimension that

TABLE B.2   Accuracy of Advertising Focus (Policy or Personal Issues)

		Percentage agreement		
	Kendall's tau-b	Policy	Personal	Both
Coder 1	.413 (115)**	60.0 (10)	40.0 (40)	84.6 (65)
Coder 2	.438 (115)**	40.0 (10)	45.0 (40)	87.7 (65)
Coder 3	.457 (115)**	40.0 (10)	45.0 (40)	78.5 (65)
Coder 4	.454 (115)**	70.0 (10)	45.0 (40)	73.8 (65)
Coder 5	.329 (115)**	50.0 (10)	52.5 (40)	70.8 (65)

Numbers in parentheses indicate number of relevant ads. Coefficient indicates correlation with original Wisconsin Advertising Project coding. Percentage agreement indicates number of cases in which coder agreed with original coding.
**$p < .01$ (two-tailed test)

TABLE B.3   Kendall's Tau-B Correlation for Two "Objective" Measures

	Does the ad direct the viewer to take action?	Does the candidate narrate his or her ad?
Coder 1	.719 (136)**	.796 (127)**
Coder 2	.690 (139)**	.832 (124)**
Coder 3	.759 (139)**	.903 (129)**
Coder 4	.705 (139)**	.856 (129)**
Coder 5	.557 (137)**	.895 (120)**

Numbers in parentheses indicate number of relevant ads. Coefficient indicates correlation with original Wisconsin Advertising Project coding.
**$p < .01$ (two-tailed test)

could blur the lines for some coders. It is not surprising, therefore, that we saw a lower level of intercoder reliability in this category.

In many ways, such ambiguity is inherent in the process of coding more subjective questions. We should expect this to be less so for relatively objective measures, in which less judgment and interpretation are required. We report reliability results for two such questions in Table B.3. When it came to coding whether an ad "directs the viewer to take action" and whether a candidate narrated his or her own ad, as one would expect, the correlations were higher (and statistically significant) than for the more subjective questions.

In the end, the results reported here were encouraging. Note that, if anything, these reliability measures were conservative for a rather mundane reason: When using a storyboard to code an ad, visual frames can be difficult to read; and with each successive photocopy of the storyboard, words in the visual frames become less and less legible. Thus, accurate coding is hampered with this format; in particular, our efforts to ascertain reliability likely were biased downward, because the original coders used fresh storyboards. And while we did not have unanimity across coders, there was every indication that the coding of the CMAG data produced results that were reliable. Additionally, on such subjective measures as an advertisement's tone—a question of extreme importance—we saw that reliability was very high.

Datasets and Variables

2000 American National Election Study

The sample size of the 2000 ANES is 1,807 respondents.

Turnout: v001241: "In talking to people about elections, we often find that a lot of people were not able to vote because they weren't registered, they were sick, or they just didn't have time. Which of the following statements best describes you: One, 'I did not vote' (in the election this November); Two, 'I thought about voting this time—but didn't'; Three, 'I usually vote, but didn't this time'; or Four, 'I am sure I voted'?" 0 = did not vote, 1 = voted.

Presidential Candidate Likes: How many pro-Gore and pro-Bush mentions, total:
   v000306–v000310: "Is there anything in particular about Vice President Al Gore that might make you want to vote for him? (What is that?)" UP TO FIVE MENTIONS.
   v000318–v000322: "Is there anything in particular about Texas Governor George W. Bush that might make you want to vote for him? (What is that?)" UP TO FIVE MENTIONS.

Presidential Candidate Dislikes: How many anti-Gore and anti-Bush mentions, total:
   v000312–v000316: "Is there anything in particular about Vice President Al Gore that might make you want to vote against him? (What is that?)" UP TO FIVE MENTIONS.
   v000324–v000328: "Is there anything in particular about Texas Governor George W. Bush that might make you want to vote against him? (What is that?)" UP TO FIVE MENTIONS.

Preelection Interest in Campaign: v000301: "Some people don't pay much attention to political campaigns. How about you? Would you say that you have been very much interested, somewhat interested, or not much interested in the political campaigns so far this year?" 1 = not much interested, 2 = somewhat interested, 3 = very much interested.

Postelection Interest in Campaign: v001201: "Some people don't pay much attention to political campaigns. How about you? Would you say that you have been very much interested, somewhat interested, or not much interested in the political campaigns so far this year?" 1 = not much interested, 2 = somewhat interested, 3 = very much interested.

Recall of House Candidates: v000343: "Do you happen to remember the names of the candidates for Congress—that is, for the House of Representatives in Washington—who are running in the November election from this district?" 0 = no, 1 = yes.

Recall-Accuracy of House Candidates: v000347: If "yes" to v000343, "Who are they?" 0 = incorrect candidate name given, 1 = correct candidate name given.

Presidential Candidate Issue Knowledge:
   Abortion: v000696, v000698.
   Gun Control: v000735, v000739.
   Environment versus Jobs: v000718, v000723.
   Environmental Regulation: v000783, v000790.
   Government Spending and Services: v000562, v000568.
   Defense Spending: v000592, v000597.
   Aid to African Americans: v000655, v000660.
   Jobs: v000625, v000630.
   Summary: Summed Gore/Bush issue dummy variables (0–8).

Trust in Government: v001534: "How much of the time do you think you can trust the government in Washington to do what is right—just about always, most of the time, only some of the time, or never?" 0 = never . . . 3 = just about always.

Care about Presidential Election: v000302: "Generally speaking, would you say that you personally care a good deal who wins the presidential election this fall, or that you don't care very much who wins?" 0 = don't care, 1 = care a great deal.

Attend Rally: v001227: "Did you go to any political meetings, rallies, speeches, dinners, or things like that in support of a particular candidate?" 0 = no, 1 = yes

Display Sticker: v001226: "Did you wear a campaign button, put a campaign sticker on your car, or place a sign in your window or in front of your house?" 0 = no, 1 = yes

Contact Official: v001492: "During the past twelve months, have you telephoned, written a letter to, or visited a government official to express your views on a public issue?" 0 = no, 1 = yes

Local-News Viewing: v000332: "How many days in the past week did you watch the local TV news shows in the late evening?" Coded 0–7.

Newspaper Reading: v000335: "How many days in the past week did you read a daily newspaper?" Coded 0–7.

Mobilized: v001219: "As you know, the political parties try to talk to as many people as they can to get them to vote for their candidate. Did anyone from one of the political parties call you up or come around and talk to you about the campaign this year?" 0 = no, 1 = yes.

External Efficacy: v001527, v001528: Sum of two five-point scales expressing agreement with the following statements. 'Please tell me how much you agree or disagree with these statements. 'Public officials don't care much what people like me think.' 'People like me don't have any say about what the government does.'" 1 = agree strongly, 2 = agree somewhat, 3 = neither agree nor disagree, 4 = disagree somewhat, 5 = disagree strongly.

Age: v000908: Age of respondent in years.

Black: v001006: "What racial or ethnic group or groups best describes you?" 0 = other, 1 = black.

Sex: v001029: 0 = male, 1 = female.

Income: v000994: Household income at category midpoints and with missing values given $53,488 (variable mean).

Education: v000913: 1 = eight grades or less, 2 = nine to eleven grades, 3 = high school diploma or equivalency, 4 = more than twelve years of schooling, 5 = junior or community college level, 6 = bachelor-level degree, 7 = advanced degree.

Partisanship: v000523: A zero-to-six scale, ranging from strong Democrat to strong Republican.

General Political Information: Number of times (out of six) the respondent answered the following questions correctly:
> v001446–v001457: "Now we have a set of questions concerning various public figures. We want to see how much information about them gets out to the public from television, newspapers, and the like.
>> "The first name is TRENT LOTT. What job or political office does he NOW hold?"
>> "WILLIAM REHNQUIST. What job or political office does he NOW hold?"
>> "TONY BLAIR. What job or political office does he NOW hold?"
>> "JANET RENO. What job or political office does she NOW hold?"
> v001356–v001357: "Do you happen to know which party had the most members in the House of Representatives [U.S. Senate] in Washington BEFORE the election (this/last) month?"

Partisan Strength: v000523: "Generally speaking, do you think of yourself as a Republican, a Democrat, an Independent, or what? Would you call yourself a strong Democrat/Republican or a not-very-strong Democrat/Republican? Do you think of yourself as closer to the Republican Party or to the Democratic party?" 0 = Independent-Independent, .33 = Independent-Democrat/Republican, .67 = Weak Democrat/Republican, 1 = Strong Democrat/Republican

Media Consumption (to create individual-level exposure measures): v001424–v001427, v000331– v000332: "How many days a week do you watch . . . " (scaled zero to one):
> *Jeopardy!*
> *Wheel of Fortune*
> Morning news (i.e., the *Today Show*)
> Daytime talk show (i.e., the *Oprah Winfrey Show*)
> Early local news
> Late local news

Total TV watching (composite of the above six, re-scaled zero to one).

2000 DDB Needham "Life Style Study"

Baseline data were collected in February 1999 as part of an annual mail survey—the "Life Style Study"—conducted by Market Facts on behalf of DDB-Chicago. The following waves were collected in collaboration with researchers from the University of Wisconsin, Ohio State University, and University of Michigan (see Eveland, Shah, and Kwak 2003). The initial wave of the survey had 3,388 respondents, a response rate of 67.8 percent. Wave 2, conducted in June 2000, resulted in 1,902 respondents, and in Wave 3, conducted in November 2000,

1,315 respondents remained. The final wave of the survey (Wave 4) was completed by 971 respondents in July 2001.

Efficacy: Sum of three six-point scales tapping agreement with the following statements: "People like me don't have a say in government decisions," "People like me can solve community problems," and "No matter whom I vote for, it won't make any difference." 1 = definitely disagree, 2 = generally disagree, 3 = moderately disagree, 4 = moderately agree, 5 = generally agree, 6 = definitely agree. Coding was reversed on the first and third statements so that larger scores represented more efficacious answers.

Interest: Six-point scale tapping agreement with the following statement: "I was very interested in the presidential campaign this year." 1 = definitely disagree, 2 = generally disagree, 3 = moderately disagree, 4 = moderately agree, 5 = generally agree, and 6 = definitely agree.

Attend Rally: Reported frequency with which the respondent had "Attended a political meeting, rally, or speech" in the previous three months. 0 = none in last three months, 1 = one time, 2 = two times, 3 = three times, 4 = four to six times, 5 = seven to twelve times, 6 = thirteen to twenty-four times, 7 = twenty-five or more times.

Display Sticker: Reported frequency with which the respondent had "Displayed a campaign button, sticker, or sign" in the previous three months. 0 = none in last three months, 1 = one time, 2 = two times, 3 = three times, 4 = four to six times, 5 = seven to twelve times, 6 = thirteen to twenty-four times, 7 = twenty-five or more times.

Circulate Petition: Reported frequency with which the respondent had "Circulated a petition for a candidate or issue" in the previous three months. 0 = none in last three months, 1 = one time, 2 = two times, 3 = three times, 4 = four to six times, 5 = seven to twelve times, 6 = thirteen to twenty-four times, 7 = twenty-five or more times.

Contact Official: Reported frequency with which the respondent had "Contacted a local public official" in the previous three months. 0 = none in last three months, 1 = one time, 2 = two times, 3 = three times, 4 = four to six times, 5 = seven to twelve times, 6 = thirteen to twenty-four times, 7 = twenty-five or more times.

Knowledge of Facts in Ads: Number of correct responses to the following four questions (0 to 4 correct): "Which candidate, Bush or Gore, favors allowing young people to devote up to 1/6 of their Social Security taxes to individually controlled investment accounts?" "Favors providing targeted tax cuts to a particular group?" "Favors drilling for oil in Alaska's Arctic National Wildlife Refuge?" "Served as a journalist in Vietnam?"

Knowledge of Facts Not in Ads: Number of correct responses to the following four questions (0–4 correct): "Which candidate, Bush or Gore, has a brother who is currently a state governor?" "Gave a dramatic kiss to his wife at the national nominating convention?" "Used to be partial owner of a major league baseball team?" "Favors a seventy-two-hour waiting period for gun purchases at gun shows?"

Turnout: "In talking to people about this year's presidential election, we often find that a lot of people were not able to vote because they weren't registered, they were sick, they did not like their choices, or they just didn't have time. How about you—did you vote for a presidential candidate in this year's election?" 0 = did not vote, 1 = voted.

Talk with Friends: Reported frequency with which the respondent had "Talked about politics with friends" in the previous three months. 0 = none in last three months, 1 = one time, 2 = two times, 3 = three times, 4 = four to six times, 5 = seven to twelve times, 6 = thirteen to twenty-four times, 7 = twenty-five or more times.

Talk with Family: Reported frequency with which the respondent had "Talked about politics with family" in the previous three months. 0 = none in last three months, 1 = one time, 2 = two times, 3 = three times, 4 = four to six times, 5 = seven to twelve times, 6 = thirteen to twenty-four times, 7 = twenty-five or more times.

Local News Use: Reported time respondent spent with "local TV news" on "the average day." 0 = don't use, 1 = less than thirty minutes, 2 = thirty minutes to one hour, 3 = one to two hours, 4 = two to three hours, 5 = three to four hours, 6 = four to five hours, 7 = five to six hours, 8 = six to seven hours, 9 = seven or more hours.

Newspaper Use: Reported time respondent spent with "a newspaper" on "the average day." 0 = don't use, 1 = less than thirty minutes, 2 = thirty minutes to one hour, 3 = one to two hours, 4 = two to three hours, 5 = three to four hours, 6 = four to five hours, 7 = five to six hours, 8 = six to seven hours, 9 = seven or more hours.

Age: Age of respondent in years.

Black: 0 = other race, 1 = black.

Sex: 0 = male, 1 = female.

Income: "Into which of the following categories does your annual household income fall?" 1 = under $10,000; 2 = $10,000–$14,999; 3 = $15,000–$19,999; 4 = $20,000–$24,999; 5 = $25,000–$29,999; 6 = $30,000–$34,999; 7 = $35,000–$39,999; 8 = $40,000–$44,999; 9 = $45,000–$49,999; 10 = $50,000–$59,999; 11 = $60,000–$69,999; 12 = $70,000–$79,999; 13 = $80,000–$89,999; 14 = $90,000–$99,999; 15 = $100,000 or more.

Education: Educational attainment of respondent. 1 = attended elementary school, 2 = graduated from elementary school, 3 = attended high school, 4 = graduated from high/trade school, 5 = attended college, 6 = graduated from college, 7 = postgraduate school.

General Political Information: Eight-point scale, 0–7 indicating how many of the following questions respondents answered correctly: "Which political party is more liberal?" "Which political party holds a majority in the U.S. Senate?" "Which political party holds a majority in the U.S. House?" "To which political party does Trent Lott belong?" "To which political party does Tom Daschle belong?" "Which political party opposes a seventy-two-hour waiting period for handgun purchases?" "Which political party voted in higher numbers for the recently passed tax cut?"

Strength of Partisanship: "Which one of the following best describes your political affiliation?" 1 = very strong Republican, 2 = not-so-strong Republican, 3 = Republican-leaning Independent, 4 = Independent, 5 = Democratic-leaning Independent, 6 = not-so-strong Democrat, 7 = very strong Democrat. Recoded so that 0 = Independent, 1 = partisan-leaning Independent, 2 = not-so-strong partisan, 3 = strong partisan.

Contact: 0–1 variable indicating whether the respondent "Was contacted by a political party or candidate representative."

Media Consumption (to create individual-level exposure measures): "Listed below are different television programs. Please 'X' each television show you watch because you really like it":

Local News
Daytime serials/soap operas
Morning network news shows (the *Today Show, Good Morning America,* the *Early Show*)
Game shows
National talk shows (the *Rosie O'Donnell Show,* the *Oprah Winfrey Show,* etc.)

Total TV watching: "How much time do you spend on the following on an average day? TV" 1 = don't use, 2 = less than thirty minutes, 3 = thirty minutes to one hour, 4 = one to two hours, 5 = three to four hours, 6 = five or more hours.

2004 DDB Needham "Life Style Study"

The first wave of data was collected in February 2000 by Synovate, a commercial survey research firm, for DDB-Chicago's annual mail survey, the "Life Style Study." This study used stratified quota sampling in recruiting respondents. The initial wave of 5,000 mail surveys sent resulted in 3,580 responses, a response rate of 76.1 percent. A second wave of the panel study was conducted in November 2004. Because of panel attrition, only 2,450 questionnaires were sent out, of which 1,484 were returned. This resulted in a response rate of 60.1 percent against the mail-out, and a panel retention rate of 41.4 percent.

Turnout: "In talking to people about this year's presidential election, we find that a lot of people were not able to vote because they weren't registered, they were sick, they did not like their choices, or they just didn't have time. How about you—did you vote for a presidential candidate in this year's election?" 0 = did not vote, 1 = voted.

Efficacy: Sum of two six-point scales tapping agreement with the following statements: "People like me don't have a say in government decisions" and "No matter whom I vote for, it won't make any difference." 1 = definitely disagree, 2 = generally disagree, 3 = moderately disagree, 4 = moderately agree, 5 = generally agree, and 6 = definitely agree. Coding was reversed on both statements so that larger scores represented more efficacious answers.

Attend Rally: Reported frequency with which the respondent had "Attended a political meeting, rally, or speech" in the previous three months. 0 = none in last three months, 1 = one time, 2 = two times, 3 = three times, 4 = four to six times, 5 = seven to twelve times, 6 = thirteen to twenty-four times, 7 = twenty-five or more times.

Display Sticker: Reported frequency with which the respondent had "Displayed a campaign button, sticker, or sign" in the previous three months. 0 = none in last three months, 1 = one time, 2 = two times, 3 = three times, 4 = four to six times, 5 = seven to twelve times, 6 = thirteen to twenty-hour times, 7 = twenty-five or more times.

Circulate Petition: Reported frequency with which the respondent had "Circulated a petition for a candidate or issue" in the previous three months. 0 = none in last three months, 1 = one time, 2 = two times, 3 = three times, 4 = four to six times, 5 = seven to twelve times, 6 = thirteen to twenty-four times, 7 = twenty-five or more times.

Talk with Friends: Reported frequency with which the respondent had "Talked about politics with friends" in the previous three months. 0 = none in last three months, 1 = one time,

2 = two times, 3 = three times, 4 = four to six times, 5 = seven to twelve times, 6 = thirteen to twenty-four times, 7 = twenty-five or more times.

Talk with Family: Reported frequency with which the respondent had "Talked about politics with family" in the previous three months. 0 = none in last three months, 1 = one time, 2 = two times, 3 = three times, 4 = four to six times, 5 = seven to twelve times, 6 = thirteen to twenty-four times, 7 = twenty-five or more times.

Talk with Opponents: Reported frequency with which the respondent had "Talked about politics with people who disagree with me" in the previous three months. 0 = none in last three months, 1 = one time, 2 = two times, 3 = three times, 4 = four to six times, 5 = seven to twelve times, 6 = thirteen to twenty-four times, 7 = twenty-five or more times.

Encourage to Vote: Reported frequency with which the respondent had "Encouraged someone to register to vote" in the previous three months. 0 = none in last three months, 1 = one time, 2 = two times, 3 = three times, 4 = four to six times, 5 = seven to twelve times, 6 = thirteen to twenty-four times, 7 = twenty-five or more times.

Election Fairness: Six-point scale tapping agreement with the statement "I think the election process is fair." 1 = definitely disagree, 2 = generally disagree, 3 = moderately disagree, 4 = moderately agree, 5 = generally agree, and 6 = definitely agree.

Election Reform: Six-point scale tapping agreement with the statement "We need some serious changes in the electoral process." 1 = definitely disagree, 2 = generally disagree, 3 = moderately disagree, 4 = moderately agree, 5 = generally agree, and 6 = definitely agree.

Money Decides Elections: Six-point scale tapping agreement with the statement "Money determines who wins elections." 1 = definitely disagree, 2 = generally disagree, 3 = moderately disagree, 4 = moderately agree, 5 = generally agree, and 6 = definitely agree.

Local News: Reported time respondent spent with "local TV news" on "the average day." 0 = don't use, 1 = less than thirty minutes, 2 = thirty minutes to one hour, 3 = one to two hours, 4 = two to three hours, 5 = three to four hours, 6 = four to five hours, 7 = five to six hours, 8 = six to seven hours, 9 = seven or more hours.

Newspaper: Reported time respondent spent with "a newspaper" on "the average day." 0 = don't use, 1 = less than thirty minutes, 2 = thirty minutes to one hour, 3 = one to two hours, 4 = two to three hours, 5 = three to four hours, 6 = four to five hours, 7 = five to six hours, 8 = six to seven hours, 9 = seven or more hours.

Education: Educational attainment of respondent. 1 = attended elementary school, 2 = graduated from elementary school, 3 = attended high school, 4 = graduated from high/trade school, 5 = attended college, 6 = graduated from college, 7 = postgraduate school.

Age: Age of respondent in years.

Black: 0 = other race, 1 = black.

Sex: 0 = male, 1 = female.

Income: "Into which of the following categories does your annual household income fall?" 1 = under $10,000; 2 = $10,000–$14,999; 3 = $15,000–$19,999; 4 = $20,000–$24,999,

5 = \$25,000–\$29,999; 6 = \$30,000–\$34,999; 7 = \$35,000–\$39,999; 8 = \$40,000–\$44,999;
9 = \$45,000–\$49,999; 10 = \$50,000–\$59,999; 11 = \$60,000–\$74,999; 12 = \$75,000–\$99,999;
13=\$100,000 or over.

Contact: 0–1 variable indicating whether the respondent "was visited by a candidate representative" or "received a call or email from a candidate representative."

Media Consumption (to create individual-level exposure measures): "I have listed below a variety of media that you, yourself, may or may not use. For each of the following, please place an 'X' in the appropriate box to indicate how much time you spend with each medium on the average day." 1 = don't use in average day, 2 = less than thirty minutes, 3 = thirty minutes to one hour, 4 = one to two hours, 5 = two to three hours, 6 = three to four hours, 7 = four to five hours, 8 = five to six hours, 9 = six to seven hours, 10 = seven or more hours.

Game shows
Daytime talk shows
Local television news
Morning news shows

Total TV watching (composite of the amount of television watching during different periods of the day).

2004 UW–BYU Election Panel Study

The three-wave 2004 UW–BYU panel study was sponsored by the Center for the Study of Elections and Democracy (CSED) at Brigham Young University and the Center for the Study of Politics at the University of Wisconsin–Madison. The first wave (N = 2,782) was conducted in June 2004. The second wave (N = 1,523) was conducted in September 2004, and the final, postelection wave (N = 1,438) was conducted in November 2004. Respondents were sampled from the U.S. voting-age population, with oversampling potential voters in battleground Senate and presidential states.

Senate Candidate Recall (Wave 3 questions: w3sengop, w3sendem): "Is your opinion of [Senate candidate] very favorable . . . very unfavorable, or haven't heard enough yet to make a decision?" 0 = haven't heard enough yet, 1 = some listed opinion.
Incumbent recall (above question for Senate incumbent candidate in respondent's state)
Challenger recall (for challenger in respondent's state, if seat was not open)
Open-seat recall (for both candidates in respondent's state, if seat was open)
Coded zero to two.

Campaign Truthfulness (Wave 3 question: w3prestr): "Has the campaign for president made you feel more confident that campaigns are truthful?" –1 = less confident, 0 = no effect, 1 = more confident.

Turnout (Wave 3 question: w3didrvo): "Did you vote in the November election?" 0 = no, 1 = yes.

Education (Wave 1 only: w1educat): "What is the highest level of education you completed?" 1 = elementary school only; 2 = some high school, did not finish; 3 = completed high school; 4 = some college, did not finish; 5 = 2-year college degree/AA/AS; 6 = 4-year college degree/BA/BS; 7 = some graduate work; 8 = completed Master's or professional degree; 9 = advanced graduate work or PhD.

Age (Wave 1: w1age): Age of respondent in years.

Black (Wave 1 only: w1race): "Would you describe yourself as white, black, Asian, Hispanic, American Indian, or other?" 0 = all else, 1 = black.

Sex (Wave 1 question: w1gender): 0 = male, 1 = female.

Party (Wave 3 branching questions: w3pidste): A zero-to-six scale, ranging from strong Democrat to strong Republican.

Local-News Viewing (Wave 3 questions: w3earlyn, w3latene, w3noonne): Additive scale of three composite questions ("how many days in past week did you watch noon/early/late local news?"), coded zero to twenty-one.

Newspaper Reading (Wave 3 question: w3readpa): "How many days in the past week did you read the newspaper?" Coded zero to seven.

Mobilized (Wave 3 question: w3f2ftal): "Have you had a face-to-face conversation with someone from a campaign?" 0 = no, 1 = yes.

General Political Information (Wave 1 only: w1knowfr, w1knowre, w1knowbl, w1knowas): Number of times (out of four) the respondent answered the following questions correctly:
    What job or political office does Bill Frist now hold?
    What job or political office does William Rehnquist now hold?
    What job or political office does Tony Blair now hold?
    What job or political office does John Ashcroft now hold?

Media Consumption (first four only asked in Wave 1; last two asked in all three waves): "How many days a week do you watch . . .":
    Jeopardy!
    Wheel of Fortune
    Morning news (i.e., the *Today Show*)
    Daytime talk show (i.e., the *Oprah Winfrey Show*)
    Early local news
    Late local news

    Total TV watching (Wave 1; composite of total television watching during different periods of the day).

Competitiveness Data

House Competitiveness (2000): Did the respondent live in a competitive House district? Competitiveness identified from *Cook Political Report*: AR04, CA15, CA20, CA27, CA36, CA49, CT02, CT05, FL03, FL08, FL12, FL22, IL10, IL17, IN08, KS03, KY01, KY03, KY06, MI08, MN06, MO06, MS04, MT01, NC08, NC11, NH02, NJ07, NJ12, NM01, NV01, NY02, OH12, OK02, PA04, PA10, PA13, UT02, VA02, WA01, WA02, WA05, WV02.

House Competitiveness (2004) (used only in Chapter 5): Was the race competitive? Competitiveness identified from *Cook Political Report*: AZ01, CO03, CO07, CT02, IL08, IN08, IN09, IA03, KS03, KY03, KY04, LA03, ME02, NV03, NM01, NY27, NC11, OR01, OR05, PA13, PA15, TX02, TX17, TX32, UT02, WA05, WA08.

Senate Competitiveness (2000): Did the respondent live in a competitive Senate state? Competitiveness identified from *Cook Political Report*: FL, MI, MN, MT, NV, NJ, NY, PA, VA, WA.

Senate Competitiveness (2004): Did the respondent live in a competitive Senate state? Competitiveness included in UW–BYU survey: CA, CO, FL, GA, IL, KY, LA, MO, NC, NV, OK, PA, SC, SD, WA, WI.

Presidential Competitiveness (2000): Did the respondent live in a competitive presidential state? Competitiveness identified from *Cook Political Report*: AZ, ME, OH, MI, NM, OR, MO, WA, WI.

Presidential Competitiveness (2004): Did the respondent live in a competitive presidential state? Competitiveness included in UW–BYU survey: AR, AZ, CO, FL, IA, LA, ME, MI, MN, MO, NH, NM, NV, OH, OR, PA, WA, WI, WV.

Wisconsin Advertising Project
Coding Sheet for 2000 Ads

SPONSOR

Presidential

1. Bush
2. Gore
3. Republican Party
4. Democratic Party
5. Interest Group (pro-Bush)
6. Interest Group (pro-Gore)
7. Bush/Republican Party coordinated
8. Gore/Democratic Party coordinated
9. Buchanan
10. Browne (Libertarian)
11. Nader
12. Other candidate
13. Republican-unclear
14. Democrat—unclear

Presidential Primary

15. Republican primary
16. Democratic primary
17. Interest Group (pro-Republican primary)
18. Interest Group (pro-Democratic primary)

Senate

21. Republican candidate
22. Democratic candidate
23. Republican Party
24. Democratic Party
25. Interest Group (pro-Republican)

26. Interest Group (pro-Democrat)
27. Independent/third-party candidate
28. Republican—unclear
29. Democrat—unclear

Senate Primary

30. Republican primary
31. Democratic primary
32. Interest Group (pro-Republican primary)
33. Interest Group (pro-Democratic primary)

House

41. Republican candidate
42. Democratic candidate
43. Republican Party
44. Democratic Party
45. Interest Group (pro-Republican)
46. Interest Group (pro-Democrat)
47. Independent/third-party candidate
48. Republican—unclear
49. Democrat—unclear

House Primary

50. Republican primary
51. Democratic primary
52. Interest Group (pro-Republican primary)
53. Interest Group (pro-Democratic primary)

Governors

61. Republican candidate
62. Democratic candidate
63. Republican Party
64. Democratic Party
65. Interest Group (pro-Republican)
66. Interest Group (pro-Democrat)
67. Independent/third-party candi-
    date
68. Republican—unclear
69. Democrat—unclear

Gubernatorial Primary

70. Republican primary

71. Democratic primary
72. Interest Group (pro-Republican
    primary)
73. Interest Group (pro-Democratic
    primary)

Other

80. Issue Advocacy
81. Regarding a proposition/other
82. Other primary candidacy
83. Vote Republican
84. Vote Democratic
99. Other type of candidacy

Race Number

1-55. House District
60. Senate
70. Governor
80. Issue Advocacy
95. Presidential
99. Other

Is the ad aired for a general election or a primary election?

1. Primary
2. General

What is the party of the favored candidate?

1. Democrat
2. Republican
3. Other

What is the seat's incumbent status?

1. Open seat
2. Republican seat
3. Democratic seat
4. Other (Independent seat)

Does the ad direct the viewer to take any action (as opposed to merely providing information)?

0. No
1. Yes

(If yes to previous question) What is that action?

0. Not applicable
1. Other
2. To vote for someone
3. To support someone
4. To elect or re-elect someone
5. To write, call, or tell someone to do something
6. To reject someone
7. To urge action or attention to a particular matter

8. To defeat someone
9. To send a message or call someone to express yourself
10. To vote against someone
11. Other magic word

(If an ad asks people to contact a public official) Does it provide a specific bill number to discuss or urge action on?

0. No
1. Yes
2. Unclear/Unsure

(If an ad asks people to contact a public official) Does it provide a phone number or address to help them do so?

1. Toll number listed
2. No
3. Toll-free telephone number listed
4. Address listed

In your opinion, is the purpose of the ad to provide information about or urge action on a bill or issue, or is it to generate support or opposition for a particular candidate?

1. Generate support or opposition for candidate
2. Provide information or urge action
3. Unsure/unclear

Is the favored candidate ...

0. Not applicable
1. Mentioned
2. Pictured in the ad
3. Not identified at all
4. Both mentioned and pictured in the ad

Is the favored candidate's opponent ...

0. Not applicable
1. Not identified at all
2. Both mentioned and pictured in the ad
3. Pictured in the ad
4. Mentioned by name in the text of an ad

In your judgment, is the primary purpose of the ad to promote a specific candidate ("In his distinguished career, Senator Jones has brought millions of dollars home. We need Senator Jones."), to attack a candidate ("In his long years in Washington, Senator Jones has raised your taxes over and over. We can't afford six more years of Jones."), or to contrast the candidates ("While Senator Jones has been raising your taxes, Representative Smith has been cutting them.")?

0. Not applicable
1. Attack
2. Contrast
3. Promote
4. Unsure/Unclear

Does the favored candidate appear on screen narrating his or her ad?

   0. No
   1. Yes
   2. Not applicable

Is the office at stake mentioned in the ad?

   0. Not applicable
   1. Yes, referred to in text of the ad
   2. No
   3. Yes, written in one of the visual frames of the ad
   4. Yes, referred to in both the text and visuals of the ad

Is an opponent's commercial mentioned or shown on screen?

   0. Not applicable
   1. Yes, opponent's commercial is shown on screen
   2. Yes, opponent's commercial is referred to in text and on screen
   3. No
   4. Yes, opponent's commercial is referred to in text

Does the ad use any of the following adjectives to characterize the favored candidate? (up to two mentions)

   0. Not applicable
   1. Common-sense leadership
   2. Independent
   3. Innovative
   4. Self-made
   5. Caring or compassionate
   6. Bold
   7. Principled
   8. Tough or a fighter
   9. Proven, tested, experienced
  10. Values (shares them, has American ones . . .)
  11. No adjectives or descriptions of candidates
  12. Protector
  13. Moderate, middle of the road, mainstream
  14. Conservative
  15. Fiscally conservative
  16. Hard-working
  17. Friend of Clinton
  18. Committed
  19. Visionary
  20. Reformer
  21. Competent and knows how to get things done
  22. Honest
  23. Family man
  30. Other

Does the ad use any of the following adjectives to characterize the opposing candidate? (up to two mentions)

   0. Not applicable
   1. Dishonest, corrupt

2. Dangerous
3. Friend of Pat Robertson, religious right
4. Reckless
5. Too risky
6. Turncoat
7. Incompetent
8. Taxing (or some version of liking taxes)
9. Hypocrite
10. Extremist or radical
11. Career politician
12. Heartless (may be used in reference to Social Security)
13. Friend of Newt Gingrich
14. Negative
15. Liberal
16. Reactionary or right-wing
17. Friend of special interests
18. No adjectives or description
19. Friend of Clinton
30. Other

Does the ad mention the party label of the favored candidate or the opponent?

0. Not applicable
1. No
2. Yes, opposing candidate's party
3. Yes, both candidates' party affiliations are mentioned
4. Yes, favored candidate's party

Does the ad use technology to distort (i.e., morph) the opposing candidate's face?

0. No
1. Yes
2. Not applicable

Is the ad funny or is it intended to be humorous?

0. No
1. Yes

Does the ad refer to newspaper stories or editorials?

1. Yes, in both the text and visuals
2. No
3. Yes, in the visuals of the ad
4. Yes, in the text of the ad

Does the ad cite supporting sources (including in footnotes) to bolster various claims?

1. Yes, in the visuals of the ad
2. No
3. Yes, in the text of the ad

In your judgment, is the primary focus of this ad on the personal characteristics of either candidate or on policy matters?

1. Policy matters
2. Personal characteristics

3. Both
4. Neither

Does the ad feature a celebrity or a politician endorsing the candidate?

1. Celebrity
2. Politician
3. Neither

Is the ad in Spanish?

0. No
1. Yes

Is the ad directly targeted to appeal to a racial minority?

0. No
1. Yes

Are the people in the ad racially diverse?

0. No
1. Yes

Campaign themes (up to three mentions)

1. Background
2. Political record
3. Attendance record
4. Ideology
5. Personal values
6. Honesty/integrity
7. Special Interests
10. Taxes
11. Deficit/surplus/budget/debt
12. Government spending
13. Minimum wage
14. Farming (e.g., friend of)
15. Business (e.g., friend of)
16. Employment/jobs
17. Poverty
18. Trade/NAFTA
19. Other economic reference
20. Abortion
21. Homosexuality
22. Moral values
23. Tobacco
24. Affirmative action
25. Gambling
26. Assisted suicide
27. Gun control
28. Other reference to social issues
30. Crime
31. Drugs
32. Death penalty
33. Other reference to law and order
40. Education
41. Lottery for education
42. Child care
43. Other child-related issues
50. Defense
51. Missile defense/Star Wars
52. Veterans
53. Foreign policy
54. Bosnia
55. China
59. Other defense/foreign policy issues
60. Clinton
61. Ken Starr
62. Whitewater
63. Impeachment
64. Sexual harassment/Paula Jones
70. Environment
71. Immigration
72. Health care
73. Social Security
74. Medicare
75. Welfare
76. Civil rights/race relations
77. Campaign finance reform
78. Government ethics
95. Other
99. None

Wisconsin Advertising Project
Coding Sheet for 2004 Ads

Does the ad say who paid for it?

    0. No
    1. Yes
    2. Yes, undecipherable from the storyboard but discovered by other means
    98. Possibly, but undecipherable

Specifically what is the wording of the acknowledgement of sponsorship?
Does not need to include "Paid for by," just "PFB" in the wording you type.

Does the ad direct the viewer to take any action (as opposed to merely providing information)?

    0. No
    1. Yes
    99. Not applicable

What is the action?

    1. To vote for someone
    2. To elect or reelect someone
    3. To support someone
    4. To vote against someone
    5. To defeat someone
    6. To reject someone
    7. To write, call, or tell someone instructing them to do something (e.g., to vote for or against a bill)
    8. To urge action or attention to a particular matter
    9. To send a message or call someone to express yourself on a particular subject
    10. To join an organization
    11. To contribute money
    90. Other
    98. No action
    99. Not applicable

Does the ad mention any of the following specific words or phrases: "vote for," "elect," "support," "cast your ballot," "[Smith] for Congress," "vote against," "defeat," or "reject"?

    0. No
    1. Yes

2. Yes, but only in the "Paid for by" (PFB)
99. Not applicable

(Specify any other variation or synonym of the above words or phrases.)

Does it provide a phone number?

0. No
1. Yes, toll number listed
2. Yes, toll-free telephone number listed
98. Don't know
99. Not applicable

Does it provide a mailing address?

0. No
1. Yes
98. Don't know
99. Not applicable

Does it provide a website address?

0. No
1. Yes
98. Don't know
99. Not applicable

Is the favored candidate mentioned in the ad?

0. Not identified at all
1. Mentioned by name in the text of the ad
2. Pictured in the ad
3. Both mentioned and pictured in the ad
4. Mentioned only in the "PFB" of the ad
98. Don't know
99. Not applicable

Small picture graphics in the logo or "Paid for by" message do not count as being pictured in the ad.

Does the favored candidate appear on screen narrating his or her ad?

0. No
1. Yes
98. Don't know
99. Not applicable

If the BCRA statement (where the candidate endorses the message) is extended to include a substantive message as well, choose the "Yes" option.

Is the favored candidate's opponent mentioned in the ad?

0. Not identified at all
1. Mentioned by name in the text of an ad
2. Pictured in the ad
3. Both mentioned and pictured in the ad
98. Don't know
99. Not applicable

In your judgment, is the primary purpose of the ad to promote a specific candidate ("In his distinguished career, Senator Jones has brought millions of dollars home.

We need Senator Jones."), to attack a candidate ("In his long years in Washington, Senator Jones has raised your taxes over and over. We can't afford six more years of Jones."), or to contrast the candidates ("While Senator Jones has been raising your taxes, Representative Smith has been cutting them.")?

  1. Attack
  2. Contrast
  3. Promote
  98. Don't know
  99. Not applicable

The BCRA statement alone does not change the overall tone of the ad. The ad is still an attack ad if the BCRA statement is the only positive part.

If the ad is a contrast ad, what proportion of the ad promotes (as opposed to attacks) a candidate?
  1. More promote than attack
  2. About equal promote and attack
  3. More attack than promote
  99. Not a contrast ad
  99. Not applicable

If the ad is a contrast ad, does it finish by promoting a candidate or attacking a candidate?
  1. Finishes promoting
  2. Finishes attacking
  3. Unsure/Unclear
  99. Not applicable (not a contrast ad)

If the ad is a negative or contrast ad, who is being attacked or who is the favored candidate being contrasted with?
  0. Not a negative or contrast ad
  1. Primary opponent(s)
  2. General election opponent(s)
  3. Both primary and general election opponents
  4. Unsure of primary or general election opponents

These only refer to attacks on specific candidates. If the ad attacks a party or incumbent not running for re-election, choose "Unsure."

Is the office at stake mentioned in the ad?
  0. No
  1. Yes, referred to in transcript of the ad
  2. Yes, written in one (or more) of the visual frames of the ad
  3. Yes, referred to in both the transcript and in the visuals of the ad
  98. Don't know
  99. Not applicable

If the candidate's logo includes the name of the office, count this as being written on a visual frame if the logo is large enough to decipher the name of the office.

Are any of the listed characterizations used to describe the favored candidate?
(Space is available for three different characterizations of the candidate.)

0. No adjectives or descriptions of candidates
1. Bipartisan
2. Bold
3. Caring
4. Committed
5. Common-sense leadership
6. Compassionate
7. Competent/knows how to get things done
8. Conservative
9. Family man/family woman
10. Father/fatherly
11. Fiscally conservative
12. Friend of Bush
13. Hard-working
14. Honest
15. Independent
16. Innovative
17. Liberal
18. Leader
19. Moderate/middle of the road/mainstream
20. Mother/motherly
21. Patriotic/American values
22. Progressive
23. Protector
24. Principled
25. Proven/tested/experienced
26. Reformer
27. Religious/spiritual/moral values
28. Self-made
29. Tough/a fighter
30. Visionary
90. Other, specify in box below
99. Not applicable

If more than three adjectives appear, choose those most prominent in the ad. If they have equal prominence, choose the first three.

Are any of the listed characterizations used to describe the opposing candidate?
(Space is available for three different characterizations of the opponent.)

0. No adjectives or descriptions of candidates
1. Career politician
2. Dishonest/corrupt
3. Dangerous
4. Extremist/radical
5. Failure
6. Friend (puppet) of National Rifle Association
7. Friend (puppet) of religious right
8. Friend (puppet) of special interests
9. Friend (puppet) of Bush
10. Heartless (may be used in reference to Social Security)
11. Hypocrite
12. Incompetent
13. Liberal
14. Negative
15. Partisan/uncompromising
16. Reckless
17. Right-wing/reactionary
18. Risky
19. Soft/weak
20. Taxing (or some version of liking taxes)
21. Turncoat
22. Unpatriotic
23. Washington insider
90. Other
99. Not applicable

If more than three adjectives appear, choose those most prominent in the ad. If they have equal prominence, choose the first three.

Does the ad mention the party label (i.e., Democrat or Republican) of the favored candidate or the opponent?

0. No
1. Yes, favored candidate's party
2. Yes, opposing candidate's party

3. Yes, both candidates' party affiliations are mentioned
4. Yes, favored candidate's party affiliations are mentioned but only in the "PFB" of the ad
98. Don't know
99. Not applicable

The parties do not have to be attributed to any particular candidate. Any mention of the political parties should be counted in this question.

Is the ad funny or intended to be humorous?

0. No
1. Yes
98. Don't know
99. Not applicable

Does the ad cite supporting sources (including footnotes) to bolster various claims?

0. No
1. Yes, a newspaper article
2. Yes, a newspaper editorial
3. Yes, an opponent's campaign advertising
90. Yes, other
98. Don't know
99. Not applicable

Is an opponent's commercial mentioned or shown on screen?

0. No
1. Yes, opponent's commercial is referred to in text of the ad
2. Yes, opponent's commercial is shown on screen
3. Yes, opponent's commercial is referred to in text and on screen
98. Don't know
99. Not applicable

Does the ad refute any specific claims made about the favored candidate by an opponent?

0. No
1. Yes
98. Don't know
99. Not applicable

Does the ad mention "negative" or "dirty" campaigning by opponents?

0. No
1. Yes
98. Don't know
99. Not applicable

In your judgment, is the primary focus of this ad the personal characteristics of either candidate or on policy matters?

0. Neither
1. Personal characteristics
2. Policy matters
3. Both personal characteristics and policy matters
98. Don't know
99. Not applicable

Does the ad make reference to religion or faith?

    0. No
    1. Yes
    98. Don't know
    99. Not applicable

This includes any religious reference. The word "faith" is not necessarily religious. "I have faith that the citizens of this state . . . " is different from "Because of my faith, I am the right leader for this state." "Faith-based" should be coded "Yes."

What is the primary language of the ad?

    1. English
    2. Spanish
    98. Don't know
    99. Not applicable

Does an American flag appear in the ad?

    1. No
    2. Yes
    99. Not applicable

Is there an explicit mention of September 11th or the attack on the World Trade Center?

    0. No
    1. Yes
    98. Don't know
    99. Not applicable

Do not include vague "terror"/"terrorism" references.

Is George W. Bush mentioned or pictured in the ad?

    0. No
    1. Yes, in a way to show support/approval of G.W.B. or associate a favored candidate with G.W.B.
    2. Yes, in a way to show opposition/disapproval of G.W.B. or associate opposing candidate with G.W.B.
    3. Yes, unclear whether in support/approval or opposition/disapproval
    98. Don't know
    99. Not applicable

Is there a central figure, a person that would receive "top billing" if the actors were credited, in the ad?

    0. No
    1. Yes
    98. Don't know
    99. Not applicable

If yes, who is it?

(Central figure is the person who appears most often in the ad, who the ad is about, or who is giving information.)

    1. Favored Candidate
    2. Opponent

3. Male noncandidate
4. Female noncandidate
5. Newspaper—disembodied person
90. Don't know
98. No central figure
99. Not applicable

The central figure may be the narrator who is never shown, if that person is a candidate. Any inanimate object (buildings, hospitals) or animal should be coded as a disembodied person if they are the central character.

Does the favored candidate appear with this person?

0. No
1. Yes
60. Central figure is favored candidate
70. Central figure is opponent
80. Central figure is disembodied person
00. Don't know
98. No central figure
99. Not applicable

In terms of life cycle, how old is the central figure?

1. Infant (0–2)
2. Child (3–11)
3. Adolescent (12–17)
4. Young adult (18–40)
5. Middle age (40–65)
6. Elderly (65+)
60. Central figure is favored candidate
70. Central figure is opponent
80. Central figure is disembodied person
90. Don't know
98. No central figure
99. Not applicable

What is the race/ethnicity of this person?

1. White/Caucasian
2. African American
3. Asian American
4. Hispanic
80. Other
90. Don't know
98. No central figure
99. Not applicable

What is the main basis of credibility of the central figure in the ad?

0. No main source of credibility
1. Candidate—general
2. Personal relationship with candidate
3. Worker
4. Teacher
5. Parent/family

    6. Law enforcement
    7. Politician, other than candidate
    8. Senior citizen
    9. Woman
  10. Doctor/Medical personnel/pharmacist
  11. Celebrity
  12. Citizen
  13. Veteran/Military Personnel
  14. Farmer
  80. Other, specify
  90. Don't know
  98. No central figure
  99. Not applicable

Only when the candidate stresses a particular aspect of his or her life, should you mark something other than "1." For example, when the candidate says "As a mother, I know . . . " or "As a former teacher, I understand," the category of parent and educator should be used because the candidates are intentionally emphasizing a different part of their lives.

If the spouse of a candidate emphasizes his or her background as a teacher/veteran/politician, etc., the main connection is still their marriage. Those should be coded "2."

Aside from the central figure (or, if there is no central figure) who else figures prominently in the ad?

    0. None
    1. Children
    2. Adolescents
    3. Elderly
    4. Citizens
    5. Workers
    6. Teachers
    7. Parents/families
    8. Law enforcement
    9. Politicians, other than candidate
  10. Women

  11. Doctors/medical personnel/pharmacist
  12. Celebrities
  13. Opponent
  14. Favored candidate
  15. Friends or family of candidate
  16. Veteran/military personnel
  17. Farmer
  90. Other
  98. Don't know
  99. Not applicable

If candidate appears only for BCRA statement, he or she is still a supporting actor.

If family of candidate, which member(s) in particular?
(Space is available for up to five different family members to be listed.)

    1. Mother
    2. Father
    3. Spouse
    4. Daughter
    5. Son
  98. Don't know
  99. Not applicable/no other family members

If a candidate is pictured with his or her family (and the sex of the children is not determinable either in the ad or on their campaign website) mark spouse, daughter, and son.

Does the favored candidate appear with supporting actors?

0. No
1. Yes
98. Don't know
99. Not applicable

If yes, are the supporting actors (if more than one actor, choose the main) ...

1. Props: seen but not heard from
2. Delivering a message
98. Don't know
99. Favored candidate not appearing with supporting actors
99. Not applicable

Location: Where does the ad take place? If there is a central figure, answer only for this person.

(Space is available for the three most prominent locations.)

0. No location
1. School
2. Hospital/Pharmacy/Healthcare
3. Old age home
4. Blue-collar worksite (factory, construction site, etc.)
5. White-collar office
6. Streets
7. Court/justice system/prison
8. Domestic uniformed protection (police or firefighters)
9. Military setting
10. Natural (forest, river, lakes, streams, etc.)
11. Political setting (office, legislature, rally, political meeting)
12. Home, neighborhood
13. Farm/ranch
90. Other, specify
98. Don't know
99. Not applicable

An office is a political setting when it can be determined to be a specifically political office—flag or seal in the background, name plate (i.e., U.S. Senator X) in the foreground. If the office is "generic"—without any political signs—mark "white collar office."

Community parks (not national or state parks, which would be "natural") should be marked "12. Home, neighborhood." These might include park benches or play areas that are obviously not at school.

If favored candidate is NOT the central figure, but appears in the ad, where does he or she appear?

0. No location
1. School
2. Hospital/pharmacy/health care
3. Old-age home

4. Blue-collar worksite (factory, construction site, etc.)
5. White-collar office
6. Streets
7. Court/justice system/prison
8. Domestic uniformed protection (police or firefighters)
9. Military setting
10. Natural (forest, river, lakes, streams, etc.)
11. Political setting (office, legislature, rally, political meeting)
12. Home, neighborhood
13. Farm/ranch
80. Other, specify
90. Don't know
98. Favored candidate is the central figure
99. Not applicable

Narration: Who speaks to the audience in the ad?

(Space is available to allow for both primary and secondary narrators.)

1. Central figure
2. Supporting actors
3. Voiceover/announcer
4. Supporting actor only in BCRA message
90. Other
98. Don't know
99. Not applicable

If "I approved of this message" is the only statement, choose the BCRA option. If the BCRA statement is extended to include a substantive message as well, choose the appropriate option (central figure or supporting actor).

Endorsements: Does the ad include endorsements?

(An endorsement is support from politicians, law enforcement, or other political leaders, but not celebrities, which are addressed separately. Endorsement ads include: written or oral phrases such as "California prosecutors endorse candidate X" as well as a politician who does an ad for candidate X.)

0. No
1. Yes
98. Don't know
99. Not applicable

If yes to endorsements, by whom?

(Space is available for five different endorsers or groups of endorsers.)

1. Newspaper(s)
2. Law enforcement (police and prosecutors)
3. Politicians
4. Unions
5. Interest groups
6. Teacher groups
90. Other, specify

98. Don't know
99. Not applicable/no other endorsements/no endorsement

Is a political figure or celebrity featured in the ad supporting the candidate?

0. No
1. Yes
98. Don't know
99. Not applicable

If yes, specify who.

(Fill in the blank.)

Is a political figure or celebrity featured in the ad in a way that associates them with the OPPONENT?

0. No
1. Yes
98. Don't know
99. Not applicable

If yes, specify who.

(Fill in the blank.)

Do any of the following campaign themes appear in the ad? If so, which ones?

(Space is available for up to five themes to be mentioned.)

0. None
1. WOMEN'S HEALTH CONCERNS: breast cancer, reproduction (NOT ABORTION)
2. EDUCATION: financial assistance for schools/colleges/students, quality of education/the learning environment/teaching
3. AGED/ELDERLY: Social Security benefits, administration of Social Security, medical care for the aged, Medicare benefits, insuring against catastrophic illness, prescription drug program for elderly
4. HEALTH PROBLEMS/COST OF MEDICAL CARE: quality of medical care, medical research/training of doctors and other health personnel, hospitals, national health insurance program
5. POVERTY: aid to the poor/underprivileged people, help for the (truly) needy, welfare programs (such as ADC), general reference to antipoverty programs, hunger/help for hungry people in the United States
6. CRIME/VIOLENCE: too much crime, streets aren't safe, mugging, murder, shoplifting, drug-related crime, NOT guns or "law and order" issues like death penalty or prisons
7. General mention of MORAL/RELIGIOUS DECAY (of nation): sex, bad language, adult themes on TV
8. Against (increased) government spending, balancing of the (national) budget, against government stimulation of the economy, the size of the budget deficit, NOT taxes or tax reform
9. NARCOTICS: availability of drugs, extent of drug/alcohol addiction in the United States, interdiction of drugs coming to the United States from foreign countries, alcohol- or drug-related crime, drug laws
10. RECESSION, DEPRESSION: prosperity of the nation, economic growth, GNP

CAMPAIGN ISSUES

(Up to four coded)

Personal Characteristics of the Candidate

1. Background
2. Political record
3. Attendance record
4. Ideology
5. Personal values
6. Honesty/integrity
7. Special interests
8. Constituent service/casework

Policy Issues

Economy

10. Taxes
11. Deficit/surplus/budget/debt
12. Government spending
13. Minimum wage
14. Farming (e.g., friend of)
15. Business (e.g., friend of)
16. Employment/jobs
17. Poverty
18. International trade/globalization/NAFTA
19. Union (e.g., friend of)

Social Issues

20. Abortion
21. Homosexuality/gay and lesbian rights
22. Moral/family/religious values
23. Tobacco
24. Affirmative action
25. Gambling
26. Assisted suicide/euthanasia
27. Gun control
28. Civil liberties/privacy
29. Other reference to social issues

Law and Order

30. Crime
31. Narcotics/illegal drugs
32. Death penalty/capital punishment

Education

40. Education/schools
41. Lottery for education
42. Child care
43. Other child-related issues

44. Prescription drugs
45. Women's health

Foreign Policy/Defense

50. Defense/military
51. Missile defense/Star Wars
52. Veterans
53. Foreign policy
54. Bosnia
55. China
56. Foreign aid
57. Terrorism
58. Middle East
59. Afghanistan

Presidential

60. Clinton
61. Ken Starr
62. Whitewater
63. Impeachment
64. Sexual harassment/Paula Jones
65. Bush
66. Supreme Court/Florida/ballot reform
67. Karl Rove/Bush staff
68. Competence

Other/Assorted

70. Environment
71. Immigration
72. Health care
73. Social Security
74. Medicare
75. Welfare
76. Civil rights/race relations
77. Campaign finance reform
78. Government ethics
79. Energy
80. Local issues
81. Term limits
82. Enron/corporate fraud
83. September 11th
84. Pledge of Allegiance (restrictions on the use of)
90. Other (please specify)
99. None/No other issues

NOTES

Chapter One: Campaign Advertising

1. These data provided by Nielsen Monitor-Plus, which tracks political television advertising in all 210 media markets across the nation.

2. See Geer (2006), especially chapter one, for an extensive summary of the many criticisms of negative advertising in particular.

3. BCRA (PL 107–155) section 311.

4. Brunelle, Jim. 2005. If the public rates Congress poorly, there's a good reason: Congress. *Portland Press Herald*, January 16, A9.

5. Ralph Nader, however, was characteristically less charitable: "Let's examine these two candidates briefly," Nader said on the stump. "George W. Bush's motto is 'Leave no child behind,' which is about all he's done in Texas... Al Gore is a more interesting character. On any given day I can't figure out whether he's the great impostor or the great pretender. You look at all his promises and insights in his book, *Earth in the Balance,* you'll never meet a politician who's broken more of them or turned his back on more of them" (http://www.pbs.org/newshour/bb/politics/july-dec00/stump_10-26.html).

6. http://www.americanpresident.org/history/johnquincyadams/biography/printable.html (accessed May 24, 2006)

7. http://www.americanpresident.org/history/johnquincyadams/biography/printable.html (accessed May 24, 2006)

8. http://price.house.gov/News/DocumentSingle.aspx?DocumentID=4931 (accessed Dec 12, 2004)

Chapter Two: Campaign Ads as Information Supplements

1. For additional evidence that citizens learn from campaign ads, see Ansolabehere and Iyengar 1995; Atkin and Heald 1976; Brians and Wattenberg 1996; Dalager 1996; Faber and Storey 1984; Hitchon and Chang 1995; Kahn and Kenney 2000; Pfau et al 2002; Valentino, Hutchings, and Williams 2002; Zukin and Snyder 1984.

2. Ansolabehere and Iyengar (1995) were so concerned about this potential that they suggested ways in which the government might discourage the use of negative advertising.

These ideas included requiring television stations to charge their lowest rate for positive advertising and guaranteeing that candidates who were the targets of attacks would have equal time to respond.

3. An important distinction must be made between Lau and Pomper's focus on negative campaigning in general and claims in the literature about negative advertising. Their findings relate to their analysis of campaigns as a whole, of which advertising is, of course, an important component.

4. Patterson and McClure (1976), for example, find the greatest learning among the least politically informed, and Iyengar and Kinder (1987) find greater effects from television news among those who have fewer resources and are less politically involved. However, Ansolabehere and Iyengar (1995) and Valentino, Hutchings, and Williams (2002), who take experimental approaches to the question of informational effects from advertising, find evidence of equal or greater learning among subjects with relatively higher levels of information.

5. This is a serious liability. Just as it is a mistake to use self-reported exposure as a measure of reception (Price and Zaller 1993), it can be equally misguided to infer exposure from measures of reception. Doing so tells us little about individuals who were exposed to but failed to receive particular messages.

6. When it comes to questions of persuasion, there is an expected curvilinear relationship. This expectation is grounded in the assumption that citizens with intermediate levels of political sophistication and engagement will be more likely than their less-informed compatriots to encounter political messages through the media, but that they will be less likely than their more-informed counterparts to resist information that is inconsistent with their predispositions (Zaller 1992).

Chapter Three: Measuring Exposure to Campaign Ads

1. Television stations are required by law to give their lowest rates to campaigns buying political ads, but these rates do not guarantee that an ad will be run. Thus, many candidates will purchase un-preemptable time at a higher rate.

2. One other approach that deserves a brief mention is the coding of newspapers. Scholars such as Lau and Pomper (2004) have used this approach to tap the overall campaign, not just advertising (which is one component of the total campaign environment). There are a number of downsides to this approach. First, a newspaper-based measure is not an individual-level measure—something desirable if one's research question has to do with the effects of ad exposure on individuals. Second, newspaper accounts offer filtered reports of the reality of the campaign and thus do not necessarily correspond with the messages citizens receive. To the extent that people's exposure to the campaign comes from the news media, that is not a problem. To the extent that their exposure comes from candidate advertising, a newspaper-based measure could be misleading.

3. Two final points about the Ansolabehere, Iyengar, and Simon instrument: Using date of interview as a proxy for exposure is a dangerous strategy. Advertising is not evenly distributed across all markets. Two states could have identical GRP totals but drastically different patterns in the timing of the advertisements. Moreover, there is no justification for using the day of the week a respondent was interviewed as part of the exposure instrument.

Chapter Four: Tracking the Volume and Content of Political Advertising

1. In 2004, the Project also collected ad data on all 210 U.S. media markets from Nielsen Monitor Plus. We do not employ these data, however, because only presidential ads were tracked.

2. Scholars have begun to put these data to fruitful use: In addition to the work of the current authors, see Krasno and Green (2008) and Stevens (forthcoming),

3. DDB Needham is one of the biggest advertising agencies in the world. It conducts a yearly survey on media habits, consumer habits, and other attitudes for marketing and targeting purposes. Dhavan Shah has added content to the survey during the last two election cycles. This survey was extensively used by Putnam (2000) in *Bowling Alone* to track a range of different behaviors.

4. These relationships hold up across our surveys in 2000 and 2004. For example, in the 2004 UW–BYU survey, the correlations between talk shows/game shows and general political information are all negative (the largest being –0.117 for *Wheel of Fortune*), and the correlation between local news and political knowledge is near 0.

Chapter Five: What, When, and Where: Making Sense of Campaign Advertising

1. This analysis is restricted to the top seventy-five media markets in each year, for ease of comparison across election cycles.

2. We use the September *Cook Political Report* to identify competitive races. Although competitiveness ratings are available from a number of sources, there is virtually no difference in the preelection competitive assessments of various pundits. See Appendix C on variable coding for the list of Senate and House races coded as competitive. Although some markets cover multiple states, we assign competitiveness for House, Senate, and the presidential markets based on the state in which the market principally lies.

3. We code the number of electoral votes in each market based on the state in which the market principally lies. As for margin of victory, we assigned each county a media market and aggregated Clinton (in 1996) or Gore (in 2000) votes minus Dole (in 1996) or Bush (in 2000) votes by market, taking the average of the absolute value from covered counties.

4. We estimate these three models using ordinary least squares (OLS) regression. Because the dependent variable is left censored at 0 (a market with 0 negative ads) and right censored at 1 (a market with only negative ads), the correct specification should be a beta-binomial model. We re-estimated these models under that specification, and the substantive results are identical to the OLS framework. We report the latter set of results for ease of interpretation.

5. Those magic words were: "vote for," "elect," "support," "cast your ballot for," "Smith for Congress," "vote against," "defeat," or "reject." These come from a footnote in the landmark Supreme Court case *Buckley v. Valeo* (1976), which held that these words were clear examples of communications meant to influence voters' decisions in the ballot box.

6. Candidates also avoided the use of "magic words" during this time. For example, of the nearly 1,000,000 federal campaign ads in 2000, less than 8 percent of all candidate-sponsored ads, only 2 percent of party-sponsored ads, and 2 percent of interest-group ads used them.

7. See also Franz, Rivlin, and Goldstein (2006) for a longer discussion of the BCRA effect on federal campaign advertising.

8. The MoveOn.org ad total includes about 12,000 ads aired by the group's hard money PAC.

Chapter Six: What Did They Know and When Did They Know It?

1. In later chapters, we also make use of a fourth survey, the 2004 DDB Needham "Life Style" study. We do not utilize it in this chapter because the survey did not contain instruments of campaign knowledge.

2. We chose June 1, 2000, as the start date of the general election, because by then both parties had selected their de facto presidential nominees. This cutoff means we lose some

exposure to a very small number of advertisements (approximately 2,000) that, although aired during the primary season, were actually intended to affect the general election outcome.

3. It should be noted, though, that our "start date" for general election advertising in 2004 was a bit more complex. For example, the March 3 cut-off was for presidential advertising. For general election Senate ads, we identified the date of the primary for all Senate races and included only exposure to Senate ads after those dates; for Senators running unopposed in the primary, all of their ads were included as general election ads.

4. The DDB "Life Style" data contain no identifier of the House district in which respondents lived, and thus we cannot control for the competitiveness of the House race when using this dataset.

5. The other variables in the model (see Appendix C for coding) work much as one might expect, with both likes and dislikes increasing with education and general political information. Strong partisans are somewhat more likely to mention something that they like (but not dislike) about the presidential candidates, and women tend to mention more likes (but not dislikes) than men.

6. We report only exposure effects because of space constraints. In this chapter alone, we estimated thirty multivariate models, each with at least a dozen independent variables.

7. Note that this effect is significant at the .10 level, using a two-tailed test. Because our hypothesis is clearly directional, we could have used a one-tailed test, which would have provided a much higher level of significance. Other variables positively (and significantly) associated with knowledge of facts in the ads were newspaper readership, income, general political knowledge, having been contacted by a political party or campaign, and the competitiveness of the presidential race.

8. This is admittedly a crude measure of campaign information. Conceivably, candidates could take positions inconsistent with their party and general ideology. More likely, they may move toward the center or seek to blur distinctions with their opponent. However, in the context of the 2000 election, and given the issues at hand, such a crude approach seems to be a reasonable one. It is also similar to approaches others have taken, e.g. Alvarez (1997). Our measure of relative-issue position placement is correlated with education ($r = 0.36$) as well as general political information ($r = 0.55$).

9. Other factors positively associated with the number of correct issue placements were the respondent's level of education, strength of partisanship, level of general political knowledge, having been contacted by a party or campaign, and being male. Age was negatively associated with the number of correct issue placements.

10. In both models, newspaper readership, level of education, the competitiveness of the House race, age, general political knowledge, and having been contacted were all positively associated with the dependent variable.

11. We counted undecideds as holding opinions for the purposes of this analysis because respondents were given the distinct option of registering a nonopinion, and because it was entirely possible that one could be undecided even in the face of considerable information. Doing so, however, means we likely overstated opinion-holding somewhat. Our multivariate results are largely intact if we coded "undecideds" as not holding opinions.

12. In addition, newspaper readership, party or campaign contacts, the competitiveness of the Senate race, and general political information were all positively related to expressing an opinion of a challenger. Generalized political information was positively related to expressing an opinion of both candidates in an open-seat race.

13. In the 2000 ANES, those scoring two or lower on the six-point scale were coded low-information; in the 2000 DDB Needham "Life Style" study, those scoring three or lower on the seven-point scale were coded low-information; in the 2004 UW–BYU panel study, those scoring one or lower on the four-point scale were coded low-information.

14. At the same time, both insignificant coefficients in the presidential candidate likes model are indicative of limited exposure effects. But because the overall effect for low-information respondents depends on both coefficients (as described in the text), the combined effect signifies that low-information respondents actually did learn from presidential ad exposure (in fact, p <.01).

15. We also combined pure independents with independent leaners, but the results were unchanged.

Chapter Seven: Campaign Advertising and Voter Attitudes toward the Political Process

1. As such, we feel we are advancing the study of videomalaise in ways Mutz and Reeves might endorse. First, by studying campaign ads, we help the investigation into which television effects might influence attitudes. Second, with our measure of exposure, we improve on methodological challenges in finding media effects.

2. We have discussed the concept of videomalaise. The dependent variable most commonly associated with this concept is trust in government (or political institutions). We are expanding the focus here to include a number of additional attitudinal variables (as do Brooks and Geer [2007]).

3. For those respondents in the middle category during the preelection phase, 31 percent moved into the highest category by the postelection. On the other hand, 171 total respondents expressed lower levels of interest in the postelection interview (moving from either the middle or highest category).

4. The control variables in this model work in much the same way as in the interest models, except for both media consumption questions, which are not significant predictors.

5. In the campaign truthfulness model, women, more-educated, and older respondents evaluated campaigns as less than truthful. By contrast, stronger partisans and consumers of local news were more confident that campaigns were honest.

6. As for control variables, higher levels of trust were associated with age and strength of partisanship, while African Americans were significantly distrustful of government. In a more direct test of the videomalaise hypotheses, we found no relationship between media consumption and trust. Finally, external efficacy rose with education, strength of partisanship, and party mobilization. The impact of general political information on trust and efficacy will be discussed further below.

7. We also investigated whether high exposure had any relationship to internal efficacy, beliefs individuals may hold about their own capabilities to influence the political process. We found no such effects.

8. As with Chapter 6, we dichotomized low information—those scoring below the mean of the full-range generalized political information scale were coded 1. Note, also, because the 2000 DDB Needham "Life Style" survey carried no measure of generalized political information, we cannot report results for the interest and efficacy measures from that survey.

9. Recall, the main effect for these heterogeneity tests signify the coefficient for political sophisticates; the interactive coefficient tests whether the politically uninformed are affected to a greater or lesser extent than their high-information counterparts.

10. Despite an insignificant interactive effect for independents in the trust model (Table 7.6), the total effect for independents (the positive main effect plus the negative interactive coefficient) is statistically insignificant. As such, only partisans in this test respond to exposure relative to trust in government.

Chapter Eight: Campaign Advertising and Citizen Participation

1. Estimates come from the 2004 American National Election Studies (ANES).
2. http://www.census.gov/population/socdemo/voting/tabA-1.xls
3. http://www.census.gov/population/socdemo/voting/tabA-1.xls
4. We experimented with several different models, including ones that contained several different demographic characteristics of the county, but we opted for the briefer models given that results were consistent across specifications. Recently, Krasno and Green (2008) have argued that aggregate models of turnout must include fixed effects for states. They examine 128 "media zones" in 2000 and find no significant relationship between presidential ad volume and turnout, especially after fixed effects are included in the specification. We take issue with their measurement of the ad environment and when re-estimating their models using a different measure (all ads in the media zone instead of presidential ads), we find a significant effect of ad volume in 6 of 12 model specifications, including two with fixed effects (see Franz, Freedman, Goldstein, and Ridout 2008).
5. In the individual-level model, newspaper readership, educational level, age, being black, strength of partisanship, level of general political knowledge, and having been contacted by a party or campaign were all positively associated with voter turnout. In the county-level models, all four independent variables were positive and significant predictors of turnout.
6. We defined a hypothetical, "average" person here in the same way we did in previous chapters: a 30-year old non-black female living in an area without a competitive presidential, U.S. Senate or U.S. House of Representative campaign. She has not been contacted by a party asking her to vote, and her local news viewing and newspaper reading are average for the sample of respondents. Her level of education, income, generalized political knowledge and partisanship are also the mean of the sample.
7. We should also note that the turnout effects for respondents in the UW-BYU survey were weakly suggestive of a demobilizing effect for low-information respondents. The main and interactive effect were insignificant, but the combined effect was marginally significant ($p = .10$). We interpret this very cautiously, however, since so many respondents (over 90 percent, as described earlier in the chapter) report having turned out.
8. Because the 2000 DDB Needham "Life Style" survey carried no measure of generalized political information, we did not report results for the political chatter variables in that year.

Chapter Nine: Advertising Tone and Political Engagement

1. Consider again the results from Chapter 5, where the distribution of political ads was the dependent variable. After controlling for other factors, including competitiveness, we found that although negativity went down in congressional races between 2000 and 2004 (all else equal), it went slightly up in the presidential race.
2. Despite the occasional tendency for personal ads to mention policy issues and policy ads to mention personal themes, any ads coded as referencing both policy and personal characteristics were only those ads where each was the principal theme.
3. In addition to this theoretical reason for combining negative and contrast ads into a single category, we had a statistical reason as well. Including three exposure measures in our models (exposure to positive ads, exposure to contrast ads, and exposure to negative ads) tended to induce multicollinearity, which made it difficult to estimate precise errors around the model coefficients.
4. As in Chapters 6 through 8, we reported coefficients only for the exposure variables. Once again, other variables in the models included controls for respondents' media habits, their demographics, and the competitiveness of various political races in the locale in which they

lived. Relevant effects for some of these control variables were discussed in each substantive chapter. Because the effect of the variables was nearly unchanged by disaggregating exposure by tone, we did not include discussion of those variables here.

5. We did so for a "typical" respondent, operationalized here in the same manner as throughout the book.

6. Although the negative coefficient on exposure to positive ads was somewhat surprising—particularly when estimating reported candidate likes—it may in part have reflected the fact that, as noted earlier, negative and contrast ads were more likely to contain issue-based messages. As a result, they may have been more likely to be considered relevant, and therefore to yield something worth mentioning about the candidates. Positive ads, on the other hand, seemed not only to add little but actually to detract from what voters remembered about the candidates.

7. Because the number of respondents was only 111 in these reduced models, we also interacted House competitiveness with exposure, so as to leverage the full set of data on this question. The interaction of competitiveness with positive and negative/contrast exposure produced insignificant coefficients, but in the same direction as reported in the constrained model.

8. Brooks and Geer (2007) present evidence from experimental manipulations that uncivil negative ads have little influence on democratic attitudes. Their larger substantive conclusions are in line with ours—little evidence that ads harm the electoral process, but modest evidence that it can enhance political evaluations and participation.

9. It is worth noting that we also examined differences in positive ads by dichotomizing them in the same manner—into positive ads with some policy content versus positive ads only focused on the candidate's personal characteristics. In only one of the models with this specification did positive policy ads give a unique boost to respondents (exposure to positive policy ads was responsible for higher levels of external efficacy). As such, we concluded confidently that the results witnessed in Table 9.5 were the consequence of the combination of a negative spin on policy topics, as opposed to the policy discussion alone.

Chapter Ten: Campaign Advertising and American Democracy

1. http://www.tns-mi.com/news/02282006.htm

Appendix B: Assessing the Reliability of the CMAG Storyboard Coding

1. These 150 randomly selected ads initially included spots that were never coded in the original dataset. This is because these ads were not political (i.e., public service announcements), but were nonetheless included in the data provided by CMAG. We dropped these ads from the intercoder reliability tests but did not replace them with additional random advertisements.

2. Weisberg (1974) reviewed models of statistical relationships, noting the different assumptions underlying alternative measures of correlation. Kendall's tau-b (like Pearson's R) is appropriate when testing for independence (as in a chi-square test) and "strong monotonicity." Essentially, it is a strict test of correlation, where a perfect relationship between two (identical) variables exists only when all observations match up on the diagonal of a cross-tabulation.

REFERENCES

Adatto, Kiku. 1990. Sound bite democracy: Network evening news presidential campaign coverage, 1968 and 1988. Research Paper R-2, Joan Shorenstein Barone Center for Press, Politics, and Public Policy.

Althaus, Scott L. 1998. Information effects in collective preferences. *American Political Science Review* 92(3): 545–58.

Altschuler, Glenn, and Stuart Blumin. 2001. *Rude republic: Americans and their politics in the nineteenth century*. Princeton: Princeton University Press.

Alvarez, R. Michael. 1997. *Information and elections*. Ann Arbor: University of Michigan Press.

Ansolabehere, Stephen, and Alan Gerber. 1994. The mismeasure of campaign spending: Evidence from the 1990 U.S. House elections. *Journal of Politics* 56(4): 1106–18.

Ansolabehere, Stephen, Shanto Iyengar, Adam Simon, and Nicholas Valentino. 1994. Does attack advertising demobilize the electorate? *American Political Science Review* 88(4): 829–38.

Ansolabehere, Stephen, and Shanto Iyengar. 1995. *Going negative: How political ads shrink and polarize the electorate*. New York: The Free Press.

Ansolabehere, Stephen, Shanto Iyengar, Adam Simon. 1999. Replicating experiments using aggregate and survey data: The case of negative advertising and turnout. *American Political Science Review* 93(4): 901–9.

Arnold, R. Douglas. 1992. *The logic of congressional action*. New Haven, CT: Yale University Press.

Ashworth, Scott, and Joshua D. Clinton. 2005. Does advertising exposure affect turnout? Working Paper, Princeton University.

Atkin, Charles, and Gary Heald. 1976. Effects of political advertising. *Public Opinion Quarterly* 40(2): 216–28.

Bai, Matt. 2004. Who Lost Ohio? *New York Times*. Accessed April 16, 2007. Online http://www.nytimes.com/2004/11/21/magazine/21OHIO.html?ex=1258779600&en=2a9da5f1ef7580c&ei=5090&partner=rssuserland.

Bartels, Larry M. 1986. Issue voting under uncertainty: An empirical test. *American Journal of Political Science* 30(4): 709–28.

———. 1996. Uninformed votes: Information effects in presidential elections. *American Journal of Political Science* 40(1): 194–230.

Benoit, William L. 1999. *Seeing spots: A functional analysis of presidential television advertisements, 1952–1996*. Westport, CT: Praeger.

Berelson, Bernard R., Paul F. Lazarsfeld, and William N. McPhee. 1954. *Voting: A study of opinion formation in a presidential campaign*. Chicago: University of Chicago Press.

Berke, Richard. 1992. The media: What is scarier than Halloween? Tune in to candidates' ads and see. *New York Times*, October 31, Late Edition-Final, Section 1: 7.

Blydenburgh, John. 1971. A contolled experiment to measure the effect of personal contact campaigning. *Midwest Journal of Political Science*. 15: 365–81.

Brader, Ted. 2005a. *Campaigning for hearts and minds: How emotional appeals in political ads work*. Chicago: University of Chicago Press.

———. 2005b. Striking a responsive chord: How political ads motivate and persuade voters by appealing to emotions. *American Journal of Political Science* 49(2): 388–405.

Brady, Henry E., and Paul M. Sniderman. 1985. Attitude attribution: A group basis for political reasoning. *American Political Science Review* 79(4): 1061–78.

Brians, Craig Leonard, and Martin P. Wattenberg. 1996. Campaign issue knowledge and salience: Comparing reception from TV commercials, TV news and newspapers. *American Journal of Political Science* 40(1): 172–93.

Broder, David S. 2002. Death by negative ads. *Washington Post*, November 3, Final Edition: B07.

Brooks, Deborah Jordan. 2006. The resilient voter: Moving toward closure in the debate over negative campaigning and turnout. *Journal of Politics* 68(3): 684–96.

Brooks, Deborah, and John Geer. 2007. Beyond negativity: The effects of incivility on the electorate. *American Journal of Political Science*. 51(1): 1–16.

Campbell, Angus, Phillip Converse, Warren Miller, and Donald Stokes. 1960. *The American voter*. New York: Wiley.

Capella, Joseph N., and Kathleen Hall Jamieson. 1997. *Spiral of cynicism: The press and the public good*. New York: Oxford University Press.

Chaiken, Shelley. 1980. Heuristic versus systematic information processing and the use of source versus message cues in persuasion. *Journal of Personality and Social Psychology* 39: 752–66.

Clinton, Joshua, and John Lapinski. 2004. 'Targeted' advertising and voter turnout: An experimental study of the 2000 presidential election. *Journal of Politics*. 66: 69–96.

Clymer, Adam. 1980. Voters grow weary of negative campaign tactics. *New York Times*, October 13, Final Edition, Section 2: 5.

Coleman, John J. 2001. The distribution of campaign spending benefits across groups. *Journal of Politics* 63(3): 916–34.

Coleman, John J., and Paul F. Manna. 2000. Congressional campaign spending and the quality of democracy. *Journal of Politics* 62(3): 757–89.

Condorcet, Jean-Antoine-Nicolas de Caritat. 1785 [1976]. *Selected works*. Indianapolis: Bobbs-Merrill.

Converse, Philip E. 1964. The nature of belief systems in mass publics. In *Ideology and discontent*, ed. David Apter. New York: Free Press.

———. 1990. Popular representation and the distribution of information. In *Information and democratic processes*, ed. John A. Ferejohn and James H. Kuklinski. Urbana: University of Illinois Press.

Corrado, Anthony. 2005. Money and politics: A history of federal campaign finance law. In *The new campaign finance sourcebook*, ed. Anthony Corrado, Thomas Mann, Daniel Ortiz, and Trevor Potter. Washington, D.C.: Brookings Institution Press.

Dalager, Jon K. 1996. Voters, issues, and elections: Are the candidates' messages getting through? *Journal of Politics* 58(2): 486–515.

Delli Carpini, Michael X., and Scott Keeter. 1996. *What Americans know about politics and why it matters*. New Haven: Yale University Press.

Djupe Paul A., and David A.M. Peterson. 2002. The impact of negative campaigning: evidence from the 1998 senatorial primaries. *Political Research Quarterly* 55: 845–60.

Downs, Anthony. 1957. *An economic theory of democracy*. New York: Harper.

Eveland, William P., Jr., Dhavan V. Shah, and Nojin Kwak. 2003. Assessing causality: A panel study of motivations, information processing and learning during campaign 2000. *Communication Research* 30: 359–86.

Faber, Ronald J., and M. Claire Storey. 1984. Recall of information from political advertising. *Journal of Advertising* 13(3): 39–44.

Farnsworth, Stephen J., and S. Robert Lichter. 2003. *Nightly news nightmare: Network television's coverage of U.S. presidential elections, 1988–2000*. Lanham: Rowman and Littlefield.

Finkel, Steven E. 1993. Reexamining the "minimal effects" model in recent presidential campaigns. *Journal of Politics* 55(1): 1–21.

Finkel, Steven E., and John G. Geer. 1998. A spot check: Casting doubt on the demobilizing effect of attack advertising. *American Journal of Political Science* 42(2): 573–95.

Fiske, Susan T., and Shelley E. Taylor. 1991. *Social cognition*, 2nd ed. New York: McGraw-Hill.

Franz, Michael M., Paul Freedman, Kenneth M. Goldstein, and Travis N. Ridout. 2008. Understanding the effect of political advertising on voter turnout: A response to Krasno and Green. *Journal of Politics*. Forthcoming.

Franz, Michael, Joel Rivlin, and Kenneth Goldstein. 2006. Much more of the same: Television advertising pre- and post-BCRA. In *The election after reform: Money, politics, and the bipartisan campaign reform act*, ed. Michael J. Malbin. Lanham, Md.: Rowman and Littlefield.

Freedman, Paul, and Ken Goldstein. 1999. Measuring media exposure and the effects of negative campaign ads. *American Journal of Political Science* 43(4): 1189–1208.

Fritz, Sara, and Dwight Morris. 1992. *Gold-plated politics: Running for Congress in the 1990s*. Washington, D.C.: Congressional Quarterly Press.

Garramone, Gina M., Charles K. Atkin, Bruce E. Pinkleton, and Richard T. Cole. 1990. Effects of negative political advertising on the political process. *Journal of Broadcasting and Electronic Media* 34: 299–311.

Geer, John G. 2006. *In defense of negativity: Attack ads in presidential campaigns*. Chicago: University of Chicago Press.

Gelman, Andrew, and Gary King. 1993. Why are American presidential election polls so variable when votes are so predictable. *British Journal of Political Science* 23(1): 409–51.

Gerber, Alan. 1998. Estimating the effect of campaign spending on Senate election outcomes using instrumental variables. *American Political Science Review* 92(2): 401–11.

Gerber, Alan, and Donald P. Green. 2000. The effect of canvassing, telephone calls, and direct mail on voter turnout: a field experiment. *American Political Science Review*. 94: 653–62.

Goldstein, Ken, and Paul Freedman. 2002a. Campaign advertising and voter turnout: New evidence for a stimulation effect. *Journal of Politics* 64(3):721–40.

———. 2002b. Lessons learned: Campaign advertising in the 2000 elections *Political Communication* 19(1): 5–28.

Goodman, Walter. 1989. Despite good intentions, political ads on TV still accentuate the negative. *New York Times*, October 27, Final Edition: B02.

Graber, Doris A. 2002. *Mass media and American politics*, 6th ed. Washington, D.C.: Congressional Quarterly Press.

———. 2004. Mediated politics and citizenship in the twenty-first century. *Annual Review of Psychology* 55: 545–71.

Green, Donald Philip, and Jonathan S. Krasno. 1990. Rebuttal to Jacobson's "New evidence for old arguments." *American Journal of Political Science* 34(2): 363–72.

Herrnson, Paul. 2001. Political party and interest group issue advocacy advertising in the 2000 congressional elections. Paper presented at a conference on televised campaign advertising, in Chicago. April.

Hitchon, Jacqueline C., and Chingching Chang. 1995. Effects of gender schematic processing on the reception of political commercials for men and women candidates. *Communication Research* 22(4): 430–58.

Holbrook, Allyson L., Jon A. Krosnick, Penny S. Visser, Wendi L. Gardner, and John T. Cacioppo. 2001. Attitudes toward presidential candidates and political parties: Initial optimism, inertial first impressions, and a focus on flaws. *American Journal of Political Science* 45(4): 930–50.

Hovland, Carl I., Irving Janis, and Harold H. Kelley. 1953. *Communication and persuasion*. New Haven: Yale University Press.

Ito, Tiffany A., Jeff T. Larsen, N. Kyle Smith, and John T. Cacioppo. 1998. Negative information weighs more heavily on the brain: The negativity bias in evaluative categorizations. *Journal of Personality and Social Psychology* 75(4): 887–900.

Iyengar, Shanto. 1991. *Is anyone responsible? How television frames political issues*. Chicago: University of Chicago Press.

Iyengar, Shanto, and Donald R. Kinder. 1987. *News that matters: Television and American opinion*. Chicago: University of Chicago Press.

Jacobson, Gary C. 1992. *The politics of congressional elections*, 3rd ed. New York: Addison-Wesley.

———. 1997. *The politics of congressional elections*, 4th ed. New York: Longman.

Jamieson, Kathleen Hall. 1996. *Packaging the presidency: A history and criticism of presidential campaign advertising*. Oxford: Oxford University Press.

Jamieson, Kathleen Hall, Paul Waldman, and Susan Sherr. 2000. Eliminate the negative? Categories of analysis for political advertisements. In *Crowded airwaves: Campaign advertising in elections*, eds. James A. Thurber, Candice J. Nelson, and David A. Dulio. Washington, D.C.: Brookings Institution Press.

Just, Marion R., Ann N. Crigler, Dean E. Alger, Timothy E. Cook, Montague Kern, and Darrell M. West. 1996. *Crosstalk: Citizens, candidates, and the media in a presidential campaign*. Chicago: University of Chicago Press.

Just, Marion R., Ann N. Crigler, and Lori Wallach. 1990. Thirty seconds or thirty minutes: What viewers learn from spot advertisements and candidate debates. *Journal of Communication* 40(3): 120–33.

Kahn, Kim Fridkin, and John G. Geer. 1994. Creating impressions: An experimental investigation of political advertising on television. *Political Behavior* 16(1): 93–116.

Kahn, Kim, and Patrick Kenney. 1999. *The spectacle of U.S. Senate campaigns*. Princeton, N.J.: Princeton University Press.

———. 2000. How negative campaigning enhances knowledge of Senate elections. In *Crowded airwaves: Campaign advertising in elections*, eds. James A. Thurber, Candice J. Nelson, and David A. Dulio. Washington, D.C.: Brookings Institution Press.

Kahneman, Daniel, Paul Slovic, and Amos Tversky. 1982. *Judgment under uncertainty: Heuristics and biases*. Cambridge: Cambridge University Press.

Kahneman, Daniel, and Amos Tversky. 1984. Choices, values, and frames. *American Psychologist* 39: 341–50.

Kaid, Lynda Lee, and Ann Johnston. 1991. Negative versus positive television advertising in U.S. presidential campaigns, 1960–1988. *Journal of Communication* 41: 53–64.

Kelley, Stanley. 1983. *Interpreting elections*. Princeton: Princeton University Press.

Kinder, Donald. 1983. Diversity and complexity in American public opinion. In *Political science: The state of the discipline II*, ed. Ada Finifter. Washington, D.C.: American Political Science Association.

Kinder, Donald R., and Thomas R. Palfrey. 1993. On behalf of an experimental political science. In *Experimental foundations of political science*, eds. Donald R. Kinder and Thomas Palfrey. Ann Arbor: University of Michigan Press.

Krasno, Jonathan, and Donald Green. 2008. Do televised presidential ads increase voter turnout? Evidence from a natural experiment. *Journal of Politics*. Forthcoming.

Lau, Richard R. 1982. Negativity in political perception. *Political Behavior* 4(4): 353–77.

———. 1985. Two explanations for negativity effects in political behavior. *American Journal of Political Science* 29(1): 119–38.

Lau, Richard R., and Gerald M. Pomper. 2001. Effects of negative campaigning on turnout in U.S. Senate elections, 1988–1998. *Journal of Politics* 63(3): 804–19.

———. 2004. *Negative campaigning: An analysis of U.S. Senate elections.* Lanham, Md.: Rowman and Littlefield.

Lau, Richard R., and David P. Redlawsk. 2001. Advantages and disadvantages of cognitive heuristics in political decision marking. *American Journal of Political Science* 45(4): 951–71.

Lazarsfeld Paul F., Bernard Berelson, and Hazel Gaudet. 1948. *The people's choice: How the voter makes up his mind in a presidential campaign.* New York: Columbia University Press.

Lodge, Milton, Kathleen M. McGraw, and Patrick Stroh. 1989. An impression-driven model of candidate evaluation. *American Political Science Review* 83(2): 399–419.

Lupia, Arthur. 1994. Shortcuts versus encyclopedias: Information and voting behavior in California insurance reform elections. *American Political Science Review* 88(1): 63–76.

Macek, Steve. 2004. A deluge of political advertising threatens our democracy. *Naperville Sun*, March 15.

Magleby, David, and J. Quin Monson (eds). 2004. *The last hurrah? Soft money and issue advocacy in the 2002 congressional elections.* Washington, D.C.: Brookings Institution Press.

Marcus, George E., and Michael B. Mackuen. 1993. Anxiety, enthusiasm, and the vote: The emotional underpinnings of learning and involvement during presidential campaigns. *American Political Science Review* 87(3): 672–85.

Marcus, George E., W. Russell Neuman, and Michael MacKuen. 2000. *Affective intelligence and political judgment.* Chicago: University of Chicago Press.

McFadden, Kay. 2004. Political ads: Pox or vital part of political process? *Seattle Times*, August 13: E1.

McGerr, Michael. 1987. *Decline of popular politics.* New York: Oxford.

McGuire, William J. 1969. Attitudes and attitude change. In *Handbook of social psychology*, vol. 2, eds. G. Lindzey and E. Aronson. Reading, MA: Addison-Wesley.

Milbank, Dana. 2000. Is negativity good for politics? Positively. *Washington Post*, April 2, Final Edition: B01.

Mutz, Diana C., and Byron Reeves. 2005. The new videomalaise: Effects of televised incivility on political trust. *American Political Science Review* 99(1): 1–15.

Nagourney, Adam. 2006. New campaign ads have a theme: Don't be nice. *New York Times*, September 27: A1.

Niemi, Richard G., Richard S. Katz, and David Newman. 1980. Reconstructing past partisanship: The failure of the party identification recall questions. *American Journal of Political Science* 24(4): 633–51.

Noggle, Gary, and Lynda Lee Kaid. 2000. The effects of visual images in political ads: Experimental testing of distortions and visual literacy. *Social Science Quarterly* 81(4): 913–27.

Norris, Pippa A. 2000. *A virtuous circle: Political communications in postindustrial societies*. Cambridge: Cambridge University Press.

Page, Benjamin I., and Robert Y. Shapiro. 1992. *The rational public*. Chicago: University of Chicago Press.

Patterson, Thomas E. 1994. *Out of order*. New York: Vintage Books.

Patterson, Thomas E., and Robert D. McClure. 1976. *The unseeing eye: The myth of television power in national elections*. New York: Putnam.

Pfau, Michael, R. Lance Holbert, Erin A. Szabo, and Kelly Kaminski. 2002. Issue-advocacy versus candidate advertising: Effects on candidate preferences and democratic process. *Journal of Communication* 52(2): 301–15.

Pinkleton, Bruce. 1998. Effects of print comparative political advertising on political decision-making and participation. *Journal of Communication* 48(Autumn): 24–36.

Popkin, Samuel L. 1991. *The reasoning voter: Communication and persuasion in presidential campaigns*. Chicago: University of Chicago Press.

Price, Vincent, and John Zaller. 1993. Who gets the news? Alternative measures of news reception and their implications for research. *Public Opinion Quarterly* 57(2):133–64.

Prior, Markus. 2001. Weighted content analysis of political advertisements. *Political Communication* 18(3): 335–45.

Putnam, Robert D. 2000. *Bowling alone: The collapse and revival of American community*. New York: Simon and Schuster.

Rahn, Wendy M. 2000. Affect as information: The role of public mood in political reasoning. In *Elements of reason: Cognition, choice, and the bounds of rationality*, eds. Arthur Lupia, Mathew D. McCubbins, and Samuel L. Popkin. Cambridge: Cambridge University Press.

Ridout, Travis, and Michael M. Franz. Forthcoming. Evaluating measures of campaign tone, *Political Communication* 24 (4):

Ridout, Travis N., Dhavan V. Shah, Kenneth M. Goldstein, and Michael M. Franz. 2004. Evaluating measures of campaign advertising exposure on political learning. *Political Behavior* 26(3): 201–25.

Robinson, Michael J. 1975. American political legitimacy in an era of electronic journalism: Reflections on the evening news. In *Television as a social force: New approaches to TV criticism*, eds. Douglass Cater and Richard Adler. New York: Praeger.

Rosenstone, Steven, and John Mark Hansen. 1993. *Mobilization, participation, and democracy in America*. New York: Macmillan Press.

Seelye, Katherine Q. 2004. Kerry pulls ads from some states as spending is limited. *New York Times*, September 19, Section A: 21.

Shaw, Daron R. 1999. The effect of TV ads and candidate appearances on statewide presidential votes, 1988–96. *American Political Science Review* 93(2): 345–62.

———. 2006. *The race to 270: The electoral college and the campaign strategies of 2000 and 2004*. Chicago: University of Chicago Press.

Silbey, Joel. 1999. *The American party battle*. Cambridge: Harvard University Press.

Simon, Adam F. 2002. *The winning message: Candidate behavior, campaign discourse, and democracy*. New York: Cambridge University Press.

Sniderman, Paul M., Richard A. Brody, and Philip E. Tetlock. 1991. *Reasoning and choice: Explorations in political psychology*. Cambridge: Cambridge University Press.

Stevens, Daniel, John Sullivan, Barbara Allen, and Dean Alger. 2007. What's good for the goose is bad for the gander. *Journal of Politics*. Forthcoming.

Swint, Kerwin. 2006. *Mudslingers: The top 25 negative political campaigns of all time*. Westport, CT: Praeger.

Taylor, Paul. 1988. Negative campaign draws to end; Balloting may bring continuation of divided federal government. *Washington Post*, November 8, Final Edition: A1.

Taylor, Paul, and David S. Broder. 1988. Evolution of the TV era's nastiest presidential race; Bush team testmarketed negative themes. *Washington Post*, October 28:A1.

Teixeira, Ruy. 1992. *The disappearing American voter*. Washington, D.C.: Brookings Institution.

Tversky, Amos, and Daniel Kahneman. 1974. Judgment under uncertainty: Heuristics and biases. *Science* 185(Sept. 27): 1124–31.

Valentino, Nicholas A., Vincent L. Hutchings, and Dmitri Williams. 2004. The impact of political advertising on knowledge, internet information seeking and candidate preference. *Journal of Communication* 54(2): 337–54.

Vavreck, Lynn. 2006. "High Fidelity? Campaign Content, the Lack of Media Accountability, and Voters' Evaluations." Unpublished manuscript.

Verba, Sidney, Kay Lehman Schlozman, and Henry R. Brady. 1995. *Voice and equality: Civic voluntarism in American politics*. Cambridge, MA: Harvard University Press.

Wattenberg, Martin P., and Craig L. Brians. 1999. Negative campaign advertising: Demobilizer or mobilizer? *American Political Science Review* 93(4): 891–99.

Weisberg, Herbert. 1974. Models of statistical relationship. *American Political Science Review* 68(4): 1638–55.

Weissman, Steve, and Ruth Hassan. 2005. BCRA and the 527 groups. In *The election after reform: money, politics and the bipartisan campaign reform act*, ed. Michael J. Malbin. Lanham, MD: Rowman and Littlefield.

West, Darrell M. 2001. *Air wars: Television advertising in election campaigns, 1952–2000*, 3rd ed. Washington, D.C.: Congressional Quarterly Press.

———. 2005. *Air wars: Television advertising in election campaigns, 1952–2004*, 4th edition. Washington, D.C.: Congressional Quarterly Press.

Zaller, John. 1992. *The nature and origins of mass opinion*. New York: Cambridge University Press.

———. 1996. The myth of massive media impact revisited. In *Political persuasion and attitude change*, eds. Diana C. Mutz, Paul M. Sniderman, and Richard A. Brody. Ann Arbor: University of Michigan Press.

Zernike, Kate. 2006. Kerry pressing swift boat case long after loss. *New York Times*, May 28: A1.

Zhao, Xinshu, and Steven H. Chaffee. 1995. Campaign advertisements versus television news as sources of political issue information. *Public Opinion Quarterly* 59(1): 41–65.

Zukin, Cliff, and Robin Snyder. 1984. Passive learning: When the media environment is the message. *Public Opinion Quarterly* 48(3): 629–38.

INDEX

Michael M. Franz is Assistant Professor of Government and Legal Studies at Bowdoin College.

Paul B. Freedman is Associate Professor in the Department of Politics at the University of Virginia. Since 2000, he has been an election analyst for ABC News in New York.

Kenneth M. Goldstein is Professor of Political Science at the University of Wisconsin-Madison and director of the University of Wisconsin Advertising Project. He has appeared on numerous network and cable news broadcasts as well as being quoted extensively in *The New York Times*, *The Washington Post*, and *The Wall Street Journal*. He is currently a member of the ABC News Election Night Decision team.

Travis N. Ridout is Assistant Professor of Political Science at Washington State University in Pullman. He also has served as an election night consultant for CBS News.